ON THE EDGE

ON
THE
EDGE

POLITICAL CULTS
RIGHT AND LEFT

DENNIS TOURISH
TIM WOHLFORTH

M.E. Sharpe
Armonk, New York
London, England

Library of Congress Cataloging-in-Publication Data

Tourish, Dennis.
    On the edge : political cults right and left / Dennis Tourish and Tim Wohlforth.
      p. cm.
    Includes bibliographical references and index.
    ISBN 0-7656-0639-9 (alk. paper)
    1. Radicalism. 2. Social movements. 3. Politics and culture. 4. Cults. I. Wohlforth,
Tim. II. Title.

HN17.T69 2000
303.48′4—dc21   00-024818

Printed in the United States of America

The paper used in this publication meets the minimum requirements of
American National Standard for Information Sciences
Permanence of Paper for Printed Library Materials,
ANSI Z 39.48-1984.

∞

BM (c) 10   9   8   7   6   5   4   3   2   1

For Gemma Tourish and Joyce Gibrick,
whose love and encouragement make everything possible.

Contents

Acknowledgments

We are grateful to many people who helped us with the production of this text. Janja Lalich played a critical role in the early stages of this project. She brought to it a broad knowledge of all varieties of cults as well as her own experience with Marlene Dixon's Democratic Workers Party. Alex Stein read portions of the manuscript at various stages and made invaluable suggestions. Scott McLemee was very encouraging as we began our research and, in addition, supplied important documents on the history of the Newman/Fulani cult. Rick Ross maintains an excellent Internet archive on cultic and hate groups. It provided a much appreciated starting point to several of our investigations. Jeff Witnack and Irene Davison supplied considerable information and documents on the NATLFED cult.

Many people spoke to us informally and off the record about the groups profiled in the following pages. In many cases, they gave us access to documents not normally in the public domain, but which greatly enriched our understanding of political cults from the inside. We are grateful to them all for sharing with us their views, their experiences and, in many cases, their anguish.

Other people have provided us with intellectual and moral stimulation over the years, as we struggled in our own lives to make sense of the world around us and of the necessity but seeming impossibility of engaging in effective political action. They therefore contributed to this book in one way or another. These include Willie Breslin, John Throne, and Hilda McGrann. Robin Blick, Mark Jenkins, and the late Adam Westoby were among the first to point out the cultic nature of the Healy group and to encourage a look at the political cult phenomenon as a whole. Dave Hollis brought the two authors together via the internet and therefore made the final product possible. Their input, when both agreeing and, more important, disagreeing with us has always been educational.

We are also grateful to Peter Coveney, Esther Clarke, and Eileen Maass at

M.E. Sharpe, and Georgia Kornbluth, the copyeditor, for their incisive editorial contribution in bringing this book to press.

None of the above necessarily share all or any of our conclusions and can in no way be held responsible for errors of fact or interpretation in the book that follows.

Dennis Tourish and Tim Wohlforth
June 2000

Introduction

We believe that the practice of politics is vital to the health of a free society. Without a widespread commitment to participation in political life, democratic action would be impossible. However, across the world, people are more disillusioned with politics than ever before. Fewer and fewer can be bothered to vote, and fewer still to join established political parties. President Clinton was elected in 1992 with only 43 percent of the vote. Given that a mere 44 percent of the electorate voted, he assumed office with the support of only 23 percent of those eligible to vote.[1] A bumper sticker, popular at the time, read: "If God had meant us to vote, He would have given us candidates."

Such quiescence is unhealthy for democracy, but there is another consequence, so far largely unexplored. It is that dysfunctional, damaging, and dangerous organizations have entered the political arena in search of money, recruits, and influence. We define such organizations as cults. They hurt those whom they recruit and inject the venom of hatred into the injured body of political discourse. Our book is an analysis of this phenomenon, a warning of its effects, and an argument for a renewed commitment to a balanced form of political activity on the part of many more people.

The Impact of Disillusionment

Most of us want to believe in something bigger than ourselves and to create a better world for our children: in short, to make a difference. We still have a need to believe in politics. Yet the mainstream parties are losing their appeal. In part, this is due to the rise of "centrist" politics, personified in the 1990s ascendancy of Bill Clinton and Tony Blair. Both have rushed to capture the "middle" ground, by moving their respective parties further to the right and away from their more radical traditions. One important effect has been to blend political differences into a succession of unappetizing soufflés, in which every new dish tastes as bland as the last. The dividing line between left and right has been, at least temporarily, erased. Everyone now stands on the right, and all debate is conducted within ideological paradigms that reflect the priorities, beliefs, and prejudices of the right. More and more often, voters struggle to detect genuine differences between the choices presented to them in elections. The less substantial such differences are, the more politicians resort to ballyhoo, in order to camouflage the emptiness of what is offered. Official politics has been dumbed down to a mud wrestling match, complete with skimpy costumes, fake grunts, and simulated grudge matches. In the United States, party conventions now have more balloons than ideas.

Furthermore, the blurring of difference has coincided with the reemergence of desperate social and economic problems in every area of the globe. These conditions are a radical departure from those most people were brought up to expect. The conviction that one's children would be better off than you were has long defined the "American dream." In Western Europe, Australia, and New Zealand, welfare states were established in the postwar period, promising care from the cradle to the grave. People believed in a better future. Today, these hopes are fragile husks. The gap between rich and poor is wider than ever, job security has been vanquished, and unquestioning faith in society and its institutions has crumbled. These conditions create a fertile soil for the doomsday messages of totalitarian cults. Though cults are commonly assumed to exist only in terms of some well-known "religious" organizations, we argue that cultic forms of organization and belief have now begun to infect the realm of politics.

The despairing mood that is gaining ground in society, and that facilitates the growth of political cults, was illustrated by the *State of Disunion Survey* conducted by Gallup in 1996.[2] This involved face-to-face interviews with some two thousand American adults. Three out of five respondents feared for their families, the ethical condition of society, and the state of the economy. Twenty-one percent said they were "angry" or "resentful" about the criminal justice system. Only 10 percent thought the United States was improving, and half felt the United States was in decline. Seventy-seven percent believed that government is usually run by "a few big interests" looking out for themselves. One in five described the elite in Washington as being "involved in conspiracy" against the interests of the American people. Only 5 percent of Americans had "a great deal of confidence" in members of Congress. By contrast, in 1966 the comparable figure was 42 percent.

Such findings testify to a widespread sense of unfairness, exclusion, and impotence in the face of what are seen as powerful vested interests. This is fueled by the awareness that a privileged elite continues to share in the good times. The average pay of a corporate chief executive in the United States, by 1990, was 135 times greater than that of the average worker. In 1960, it was "only" thirty times greater. Chief executives in 1990 enjoyed a median salary plus cash bonuses of more than $2 million a year.[3]

A similar situation exists in Britain. Sir Clive Thompson was appointed president of the main employers' organization, the Confederation of British Industry, in 1998. As the chief executive of Rentokill, he enjoyed a fourfold increase in pay and share options during the previous year, from £2.8 million to £11.5 million. When appointed, he warned Tony Blair's Labour government against interfering with executive pay. He also opposed fair employment rights and trade union recognition and condemned Labour's plans for a modest minimum wage, arguing that it would wipe £10 million (2.4 percent!) off the £417 million profit made by Rentokill. He has described trade unions as "clutter" and compared dealing with them to "pest control"—a remark he later described as "a joke."[4]

"Downsizing" has also become a global trend. For decades Australians prided themselves on the sobriquet "the lucky country." Yet it was estimated in 1997 that almost one-third of Australian households had experienced job retrenchment during the previous five years.[5] Not accidentally, racism in this continent is also on the rise, with the anti-immigration party One Nation dominating the media, beginning to score important victories in elections, and claiming up to 13 percent in some national opinion polls. In an echo of other cult practices, the three hundred branches that One Nation claims to have are banned from communicating with one another, ensuring that all information is controlled by the top leadership.[6]

In a climate that provides greater rewards for a few and restricts opportunity for the rest, notions of upward mobility perish. People may believe that they can climb a short social ladder. However, most recognize that butlers rarely end up running their own stately homes. Aspiration is replaced by desperation. In a society driven by consumerism, the conviction that there is no way up the social hierarchy threatens social cohesion and renders people vulnerable to the quick-fix "solutions" of political extremists. By 1993, it was estimated that three-quarters of Americans no longer trusted the federal government to do the right thing when taking decisions. Back in the far-off 1950s public opinion held a directly opposite view: three-quarters of Americans then trusted the government to behave ethically and appropriately.[7] Uncertainty has bred disillusionment, and, for many, opened the door to the unthinkable.

Yet, in the face of such problems, most mainstream parties are anxious to avoid taking a definite position, in case they offend some important section of the electorate or alienate those movers and shakers in the boardrooms who also just happen to be party financiers. They explain their inability to offer solutions by invoking the specter of "globalization," or other nebulous forces outside their control. Increasingly, they proclaim what they cannot do, rather than what they can. Politicians, these days, resemble eunuchs who have commandeered the airwaves to boast of their impotence. Faced with declarations of irrelevance from most of the political establishment, what can people do? Where can they turn?

The Cultic Alternative

If established politics has been practically emptied of its content, passion, and commitment to social justice, there are plenty of others prepared to fill the vacuum left behind with a poison of their own concoction. Accordingly, politics at the edge has been colonized by extremist sects of the left and right. These prey upon our uncertainties about the future and create what are, in effect, miniature totalitarian societies organized around a few simplistic but compelling myths. They pose a danger to society and lay waste the talents and commitment of their own members.

In these groups, doubt is replaced by total and all-consuming belief. The one-dimensional nature of the message becomes its main selling point. Comprehensive but paper-thin solutions for all the world's problems are proposed, invariably involving changes on a revolutionary scale. Such revolutions might involve (on the left) a reenactment of the 1917 October Revolution, or (on the right) race attacks against whichever group the cult designates as the prime enemy—blacks, Jews, whites, Hispanics, or gays. The common defining characteristic is the need for enemies. Their annihilation is perceived as the only route to global salvation.

The world is portrayed as a perilous place, in which all mainstream solutions have either failed or are simply a cover for a vast conspiracy against the people. Democracy is veiled dictatorship; all politicians are crooks; business is inherently criminal; Armageddon is imminent. Examples of ongoing normality are discounted. Each and every social problem is exaggerated and is taken as proof that the cult's doomsday scenario is about to be played out in full. Only the extreme ideology of the group offers any hope, but redemption is possible only if there are enough true believers prepared to embrace the group's inflexible theology, strict organizational practices, and often strange public rituals.

In the industrial nations, the growth of political cults in the recent period has been almost entirely on the right. However, the strip-tease routine by which mainstream parties are unveiling the full extent of their ideological weakness is still in its early stages. We are on the right side of midnight— just. As their nakedness becomes more fully exposed, it is likely that left-wing cults will also face opportunities for growth. Politics is entering a period of unprecedented volatility, in which a frenzied public opinion, desperate for reassurance and solutions, is capable of swinging from one extreme to the other. The more shallow the programs offered by established parties and the more cynical the conduct of their representatives, the more likely it is that such swings will occur. The effects are likely to be severe.

What Lies Ahead

This book argues that many extremist organizations, on both the left and right, can best be understood as cults on a par with the Unification Church (the Moonies), Scientologists, and other bizarre groupings who regularly capture media headlines. In chapter 1, we explore this notion in more depth, and offer definitions of cults in general and political cults in particular. The opening chapters of this book are concerned with establishing the psychological processes that render us vulnerable to the simplistic messages of cults, and the persuasive devices they employ to ensnare people in their activities.

To date, cults in politics have attracted relatively little attention. There has been a reluctance on the left to acknowledge that the underlying ideology of Marxism-Leninism creates thought-starved organizations, who severely limit the freedom of their own members and seek to impose a vision of regimented dreariness on everyone else. There has been a similar refusal to define the racism and fundamentalist Christian theology of the far right as innately subversive of those democratic norms that distinguish the society it is supposedly attempting to preserve. We challenge what we see as the complacency of those on the left and right of politics on these issues. In separate chapters, we explore the real ideological legacy of Marxism-Leninism for today and how the passions of prejudice impose blinkers on the thinking of many on the far right of politics. A curious hybrid formation also exists in the form of psychotherapy cults that see themselves as political movements and pursue an increasingly open political agenda. The personal has married the political.

The groups we discuss in this book are a threat that needs to be taken seriously. There are many historical episodes where organizations that can be defined as cults have taken state power—for example, in Russia, Germany, and Cambodia. In each case, the consequences have been calamitous. The fact that political cults are at present little more than flaccid sects does not guarantee that they will maintain a low-risk profile in the future. If disenchantment with normal politics continues to grow at its present rate, more people will prove vulnerable to the simplistic sloganeering of the far left and right.

In particular, we argue that a commitment to political action on the part of many people is a necessary feature of a normal democratic society. However, cults sidetrack political commitment into an environment dominated by a guru bent on self-promotion. Such groups are characterized by intense levels of destructive activity and extreme conformity around a handful of basic ideas. The eventual outcome is usually burnout and disillusionment on the part of most people who become involved. In addition, since the central concern of all cults is to recruit other members and raise money, they prioritize this agenda in their dealings with others. This distracts political activists from whatever their primary purpose is supposed to be. In this way, political cults inflict damage out of all proportion to their numerical strength.

Thus, this book analyzes the extent to which a variety of well-known movements fall within the spectrum of what could be defined as cultic organizations. We examine the organizational measures they employ to suppress dissent, achieve intense conformity, and extract extraordinary levels of commitment from their members. In the process, we discuss how political activists and organizations can avoid falling into the trap of cultism. We encourage a critical attitude of inquiry toward the core ideology of all groups to which people belong, while ensuring that their organizational practices facilitate the expression rather than the suppression of dissent.

Healthy political organizations and movements are characterized by dissent, disagreement, and conflict rather than by stultifying conformity. People need to abandon the widely held view that political organizations that permit frequent important disagreements among their members are unsuitable to exercise political power. We defend the principles of political involvement and political action. However, such involvement needs to be kept within a framework that permits healthy debate and maintains the independence of each individual concerned.

The tendency of political cults to destroy people's commitment to political activity over time is one of the most pernicious consequences of their destructive activities in modern society. But politics in general is currently in an enfeebled condition and in need of intensive care. Under unsanitary conditions, a scratch can develop into gangrene. It is our hope that the present text will help alert a wider public to the risk of cultic infection and stimulate discussion about how to maintain healthy political activity capable of revitalizing our wounded political process.

Part One

The Nature of Cults

Chapter 1

Cults in Politics

Nothing . . . can disturb the convert's inner peace and
serenity—except the occasional fear of losing faith again,
losing thereby what alone makes life worth living, and
falling back into the outer darkness
—Arthur Koestler, 1950

What Are Cults?

Destructive cults have been defined as organizations that remold individuality to conform to the codes and needs of the cult, institute taboos that preclude doubt and criticism, and generate an elitist mentality whereby members see themselves as lone evangelists struggling to bring enlightenment to the hostile forces surrounding them.[1] There is only one truth—that espoused by the cult. Competing explanations are not merely inaccurate but degenerate. Cults do not have opponents. They have enemies and frequently dream about their ultimate destruction.

In *political cults,* people are encouraged to fantasize about what society will be like when they have seized state power. Members are hailed as inspired founders (sometimes called "cadres"), who will be guaranteed a particularly powerful position in the new world order. Simultaneously, they are denounced in the present day for their weak grasp of the founders' inspired ideals. Their inability to work even harder is blamed for the slow rate at which the cult's dream is being realized. The cult's achievements are credited to the wisdom of the leader. Whatever goes wrong is attributed to the slovenly behavior of the members. Thus, grandiosity of vision is combined with a punitive internal atmosphere, aimed at suppressing all dissent. There is a pathological fear of anything that calls even peripheral aspects of the group's ideology into question.

Cults embrace the fields of psychotherapy, religion, New Age, self-help, business training—and politics.[2] Michael Langone,[3] one of the leading authorities on the subject, has calculated that as many as 4 million Americans may have been involved with cult groups. It has been estimated that there are around 500 cults active in Britain today[4] and between 3 and 5 thousand in the United States.[5] These figures are almost certainly an underestimate. Larger cults are full of "wannabe" gurus, who frequently split off to create their own private little empires. Cults can consist of as few as two people, in which one person dominates the other and claims a position of privileged insight for himself or herself.

Political cults form the principal focus of this book. An important reason for the lack of attention they have so far received may be that political life is often characterized by frantic activity and intense feelings of party loyalty. This makes it difficult to differentiate between "normal" political parties and groups that have reached such a point of obsession that they can be regarded as cults. In cults, the passion, enthusiasm, and commitment of members is ruthlessly exploited to achieve ever-higher levels of activity. Members often feel like athletes competing in permanent Olympic games. When they are injured or become too downhearted to carry on, their usefulness is over and they are discarded in favor of the latest enthusiastic recruit.

Broad agreement exists in the research literature on general characteristics that define cult groupings. The American Family Foundation defined cults as

> [a] group or movement exhibiting great or excessive devotion or dedication to some person, idea, or thing, and employing unethical manipulative or coercive techniques of persuasion and control (e.g. isolation from former friends and family, debilitation, use of special methods to heighten suggestibility and subservience, powerful group pressures, information management, suspension of individuality or critical judgement, promotion of total dependency on the group and fear of leaving it), designed to advance the goals of the group's leaders, to the actual or possible detriment of members, their families or the community.[6]

Such groups strive to achieve extreme conformity, an outcome that Lifton[7] characterizes as "ideological totalism," and that we discuss in detail later in this chapter. The roller-coaster highs and lows of cult recruitment mean that people are constantly switched between disorientating and mutually opposed emotional states. Feelings and ideas lose subtlety, shade, and color. Paltry insights are sold as having cosmic implications. Ideas that may be held by many people are presented as the sole moral property of the group. This further inflates that group's already magnificent sense of intellectual superiority.

Under these conditions, members develop a sense of splendid isolation. Cherished beliefs that predate cult membership are derided as ancient baggage, to be lightly discarded. A new you is in prospect, in which every waking moment will be imbued with more meaning than you have ever dreamed possible. The potential recruit is hurtled along at a constantly increased speed, and faces the prospect of retreating "into doctrinal and organizational exclusiveness, and into all or nothing emotional patterns more characteristic . . . of the child than of the individuated adult."[8] Paradoxically, they may on journey's end feel endowed with superhuman insight into themselves and the surrounding world, rather as some drunks seem to imagine that they are constantly on the verge of achieving startling new insights into the human condition. The reality of what is on offer is invariably rather different.

Throughout, the cult attempts to represent its vision as a series of noble insights capable of transforming the present miserable condition of humanity into something far grander and more noble than anything it has so far been able to achieve. A moral imperative is created, in which the cult members are encouraged to believe that only their actions can redeem the world. The alternative, it is alleged, is some form of barbarism, in which all humanity will most probably perish.

A spin on this idea, common in right-wing cults, is the notion that a sizable proportion of the world's population (blacks, gays, or other allegedly degenerate elements) must be annihilated in any event, to save the rest. There is no apparent sense of contradiction between the glowing future, which the group assures its members is its main objective, and the means (civil war, insurrection, racial genocide, an authoritarian inner-party regime) that are assumed to be necessary for its realization.

Intense activism prevents members from having a personal life outside their role as party members. Rival social networks atrophy through neglect, ensuring that members soon come to devote all their spare time to the cult. The unrelenting pace induces exhaustion and depression, making it harder to "think your way out"—too many commitments have been made, all bridges back to sanity are long dynamited, and too little time is left over from party activity for reflection. In a paradox far from unique to political cults, the more ensnared people become in the perfumed trap of activism, the harder it is to escape. Members tend not to leave as the result of rational reflection and conscious decision, but to drop out in despair, exhaustion, and crisis.

Underlying these practices are the cardinal assumptions that social, economic, and political catastrophe lies on the immediate horizon, that a special organization in the shape of the cult is necessary to avert this, and that the nucleus of such a party is to band in the form of the cult. This assumed specialness encourages illusions of correctness, unanimity, and total political prescience. Armed with such conviction, cult members embark on a frantic quest to save the world by recruiting as many other members as possible. It might be thought that such a quest is doomed to failure. Who in their right mind would *join a cult?* Yet, as the figures cited above suggest, many of us are in fact vulnerable to the attractions of cult membership.

How Cults Recruit and Hold Members

Two leading social psychologists specializing in persuasion, Pratkanis and Aronson,[9] summarize the research on this issue by humorously suggesting that anyone can create a cult by following a series of simple guidelines derived from what cults actually do. These are:

1. *Create your own social reality.* What we think we know about the world is in large part derived from our interactions with others, and from the way in which we contrast and compare perspectives derived from different individuals, groups, and media. Cults short-circuit this process by eliminating all sources of information other than that provided by the cult. Members work so hard that they interact only with other cult members, or with people they are in the process of recruiting. They read mostly cult literature. In time, their vocabulary shifts, so that cult-sanctioned words and expressions predominate. It becomes even harder to communicate with nonmembers, since both sides lack a common vocabulary with which to exchange ideas. This leaves cult followers more disposed than ever to the uncritical acceptance of their organization's propaganda.

2. *Create a grandfalloon.* The term "grandfalloon" is derived from a Kurt Vonnegut novel (*Cat's Cradle*, 1963), while the process referred to is known in social psychology as the *minimal group paradigm.* It reflects the research finding that when people are assigned to spurious groups, on the basis of random or minimal criteria, they still identify strongly with those groups and disparage those outside its ranks.[10] A "grandfalloon" describes an out-group of some kind, which can be regarded as unredeemed. Who constitutes the out-group is immaterial—the point is to have one, thereby enhancing the in-group loyalty of cult members. In the case of left-wing cults, the most obvious out-group is the "bourgeoisie." This is supplemented by an assortment of other equally heinous grandfalloons—liquidationists, revisionists, opportunists, ultraleftists, or running dogs of imperialism. On the right, typically, racial minorities, gays, and other races outside the chosen nation are assumed to be much more different from white Anglo-Saxon Protestant males than they actually are. Differences are stressed, while similarities are ignored. Humanity is divided into the chosen and the not chosen, with only those in the former camp worthy or capable of being saved.

3. *Create commitment through dissonance reduction.* When a contradiction arises between our behavior, on the one hand, and our feelings and attitudes on the other, we feel uneasy. For example, we may possess a strong

commitment to the values of democracy. If we engage in some action contrary to such values (such as signing a petition demanding that communists be suppressed), we experience an unease which Festinger[11] describes as "dissonance." The only way to resolve this conflict is by changing either our attitudes or our behavior, to bring them more in line with each other. Research suggests that most of us have a desire to feel and appear consistent, both to ourselves and others.[12] Accordingly, once we have embarked on a particular course of action, we are more likely to adopt further behavior in that general direction, to create an impression of consistency. We may even help ourselves along this road, by displaying ever more extreme behaviors at odds with our previous convictions. The outcome of this process is called *conversion*.

Cults manipulate it by establishing *a spiral of escalating commitment*.[13] Prospective members adopt what are at first small behaviors in line with the group's belief system, and which do not require the formal endorsement of its ideology. An example would be the act of attending a group meeting. In the first instance, the new behaviors are not perceived as challenging the prospective recruit's preexisting belief systems. However, the new behaviors are slowly escalated. Attendance at a meeting might be followed by a forceful "request" to participate in a weekend conference, followed by voting for the group's proposals at other public forums, leading to asking others to do likewise, resulting in the selling of group literature on the streets and climaxing in a public identification with the group's goals.

The gradual nature of what is involved enables the recruit's belief system to slowly adjust to the new behaviors they have adopted. By the time the full impact of the changes is apparent, they have become for all practical purposes a new and permanent identity.

4. *Establish the leader's credibility and attractiveness*. Most cults promulgate stories and legends concerning the cult leader. Research into the dynamics of persuasion has long established that the credibility and attractiveness of a message's source are vital ingredients in determining its overall impact.[14] Accordingly, cults credit their leaders with superhuman qualities. Lenin on the left and Hitler on the right are viewed in a semidivine light by their followers. They are regarded as possessing uncommon insight into society's problems, and with personal characteristics such as honesty, genius, and compassion which it is assumed will be attractive to prospective recruits. If such founders are dead then the present leaders, in effect, present themselves as the reincarnation of Lenin, Trotsky, Mao, Hitler or whoever. Often, the real problems of the leaders (such as alcoholism and drug dependency) are concealed from both prospective and current members.

5. *Send members out to proselytize the unredeemed*. This ensures that members engage in what is known as *self-generated persuasion*. Recruiting

others means that they are constantly informing other people of all the positive advantages of being in a cult. This relentless (and inaccurate) focus on the positive means that members wind up reconvincing themselves. A feedback loop is created, which is shorn of all interference from the outside world and in which only the liturgy of the cult has any semblance of reality.

6. *Distract members from thinking undesirable thoughts.* The easiest way to accomplish this is through overwork. A recurrent theme in the chapters that follow is the enormous levels of activity required of those involved in political cults. In this, they share much common ground with their better-known religious, New Age, and psychotherapy counterparts. For example, the Workers Revolutionary Party (WRP) in Britain was a small organization (discussed in chapter 10), never capable of mustering more than 1 per cent of the vote when it stood in elections.[15] Nevertheless, it managed to produce a daily newspaper. This would have been a hugely ambitious project for any organization, let alone one that still wore diapers. However, the effort required to write, produce, and distribute a daily paper meant that people were either too busy or too exhausted to question the political direction they were taking.

7. *Fixate members' vision on a phantom.* In particular, cults create an ideal image of a future "promised land," which they contrast with the drab reality of today. This might be a socialist paradise or an ethnically cleansed America. The cult leaders sing its praises, invent past golden ages when the phantom previously walked the earth, and insist on its imminent return. The effect is that true believers are terrified to take a day or an hour off, in case their dereliction of duty proves responsible for a missed opportunity to re-create Utopia.

The primary concerns of all cults are the recruitment of new members and the raising of as much money as possible. To do this the members are kept in permanent war mode. The consequent state of arousal binds them ever more tightly to the group's core belief system. However, aspects of the cult mind set are also given a particular spin in political cults, which generally see themselves as occupying a distinctive position in comparison to their religious, New Age, and psychotherapy rivals. It is to these aspects of cult life that we now turn.

The Nature of Political Cults

All cults have much in common, despite their competing ideologies. Political cults tend to put a particular emphasis on the following:[16]

1. *A rigid belief system.* In the case of left-wing political cults this belief system suggests that all social, natural, scientific, political, economic, historical, and philosophical issues can be analyzed correctly only from within

the group's theoretical paradigm—one that therefore claims a privileged and all-embracing insight. The view that the group's belief system explains everything eliminates the need for fresh or independent thought, prevents a critical reappraisal of past practice or the acknowledgment of mistakes, and removes the need to seek intellectual sustenance outside the group's own ideological fortress.

In right-wing cults, typically, it is assumed that the race question underpins all other social processes. There is a gigantic conspiracy (of Jews, blacks, the United States government, or possibly the United Nations) that explains every twist and turn of events. Whatever happens is interpreted in the light of the governing ideology and is regarded as proof of its correctness.[17]

2. *The group's beliefs are immune to falsification.* No test can be devised or suggested which might have the effect of inducing a reappraisal. The all-embracing quality of the dominant ideology rules out reevaluation, since it implies both omniscience and infallibility. Methods of analysis that set themselves more modest explanatory goals are viewed as intrinsically inferior. Those who question any aspect of the group's analysis are branded as deviationists bending to the "pressures of capitalism" or as traitors colluding with the conspiracy, and are driven from its ranks as heretics.

3. *An authoritarian inner party regime is maintained.* Decision making is concentrated in elite hands, which gradually dismantles or ignores all formal controls on its activities. Members are excluded from participation in determining policy, calling leaders to account, or expressing dissent. This is often combined with persistent assurances about the essentially democratic nature of the organization, and the existence of exemplary democratic controls—on paper. Such a high-control social environment promotes what West and Singer[18] have described as uncertainty, fear, and confusion, with joy and certainty offered as a reward for surrender to the group.

4. *There is a growing tendency for the leaders to act in an arbitrary way, accrue personal power, perhaps engage in wealth accumulation from group members or in the procuring of sexual favors.* Activities that would provoke censure if engaged in by rank-and-file members (e.g., maintaining a reasonable standard of living, enjoying time off, using the organization's funds for personal purposes) are tolerated when they apply to leaders.

5. *Leader figures, alive or dead, are deified.* In the first place, this tends to center on Marx, Hitler, Pol Pot, Stalin, Mao, Trotsky, or another significant historical figure. It also increasingly transfers to existing leaders, who represent themselves as defending the historical continuity of the "great" ideas of the original leaders. In far-right cults this process of identification is accentuated by the wearing of Nazi regalia and the imitation of Nazi salutes. There is a tendency to settle arguments by referring constantly to the sayings

of the wise leaders (past or present), rather than by developing an independent analysis.

6. *There is an intense level of activism, preventing the formation of significant outside interests.* Social life and personal "friendships" revolve exclusively around the group, although such friendships are conditional on the maintenance of uncritical enthusiasm for the party line. Members acquire a specialized vocabulary. For example, they call each other "comrade," or reflexively refer to blacks as the "mud people." This reinforces a sense of distance and difference from those outside their ranks.

Gradually, the cult's all-encompassing vision and global ambitions come to dominate the mind, body, and soul of the recruit. Longstanding interests give way to ceaseless cult activity. Old friends are abandoned, unless they can be viewed as potential recruits. Family ties snap under the strain. Coping with this pressure leads to what Lifton[19] has called "doubling," in which a second self is formed and comes to dominate the earlier, authentic personality. An alternative term proposed is "pseudopersonality."[20] The recruit's real personality is alive and well, but is thoroughly subordinated to the all-embracing demands of the cultic environment. The new language, dress codes, behaviors, and belief systems of the recruit are such that he or she often appears to be a different person.

The formation of such a pseudo-personality is a key to understanding the contradictions that run through life in political cults. In his novel *Nineteen Eighty-Four,* George Orwell coined the expression "doublethink" to describe what happens when two or more conflicting ideas are simultaneously advanced by the same person. He was particularly influenced in this idea by the spectacle of liberty-loving intellectuals insisting that the then–Soviet Union was the most democratic country in the world. Likewise, in political cults, it is still common to find the following contradictory positions held by their members:

1. *Love of liberty alongside support for totalitarianism.* Some left-wing cults continue to promote the myth of a democratic Soviet Union, pre-1989. Others, on the Trotskyist left, visualize the period up to 1923 as a golden age when full democracy existed, until Lenin's legacy was supposedly usurped by a demonic Stalin. Right-wing cults talk of individual liberty but aim to remove democratic rights from everyone they deem socially undesirable—in essence, all those who disagree with them. Democracy is held in platonic esteem. It is an excellent thing—provided no one is ever tempted to consummate it in practice.

2. *A belief in equality, combined with the accumulation of enormous privileges for the cult leaders.* The members spend an inordinate amount of time fundraising on behalf of the group. There are no real controls on how this

money is spent. Leaders lavish funds on pet projects, or a high standard of living for themselves.

3. *The promotion of strict sexual morality, alongside the sexual exploitation of female members, particularly by group leaders.* Several of the case study chapters that follow document the widespread nature of this contradiction. The primary purpose in dictating the sex life of members is to strengthen the leadership's power. When the cult influences even the most intimate area of the members' lives its control is complete. Members who notice that the leaders have a different set of rules for themselves tend to rationalize this as a feature of their higher level of existence, to which ordinary members have not yet ascended.

4. *A demand that society respect the cult's right to free speech, combined with the suppression of all dissent within its own ranks.* The cult zealously defends its right to "free speech," often resorting to the courts. Antidemocratic practices by rival organizations are noted and ridiculed, to convince the membership that higher standards prevail within the cult. In turn, members are told that they are free to raise any criticisms of the group that they wish. However, whichever method they use to do so is lambasted as "inappropriate." The offending critic is first humiliated within the group, and then expelled or otherwise pressured to leave.

Ideological Totalism

"Ideological totalism" is a mood of absolute conviction, which embeds ideas so deeply in people's heads that they grow inoculated against doubt. Ideas cease to be provisional theories about the world and instead become sacred convictions, dependent on the word of hallowed authorities for their validation rather than evidence.

The term "ideological totalism" was introduced by Lifton in 1961, in a book that has become a classic study of the *thought reform process.* This process has been particularly useful in understanding the inner workings of cults, and has been defined as "the coming together of immoderate ideology with equally immoderate individual character traits—an extremist meeting ground between people and ideas."[21] Lifton's original study looked at how Chinese captors reshaped the political convictions of American soldiers captured during the Korean War, so that many of them, at least for a time, publicly extolled the virtues of Chinese communism against the vices of Western capitalism. Given their origins, his ideas are particularly apt in considering the workings of political cults. Lifton made it clear that the potential for the ideological totalism he described is present within everyone, in the sense that extreme conformity exists at one end of a continuum, consisting at the other end of extreme dissent. However, totalistic convictions are "most likely to occur with those ideologies which are most sweeping in their content and most ambitious—or messianic—in their claims, whether religious, political or scientific. And where totalism exists, a religion, a political movement, or even a scientific organization becomes little more than an exclusive cult."[22]

As this chapter suggests, extremist political organizations on both the left and right adhere to what we would describe as such an ambitious and messianic ideology. In consequence, they each possess an extraordinarily exalted view of their role in society. As subsequent chapters will seek to demonstrate, conformity, the banning of dissent, intense activism, and blinkered political thought are the inevitable consequences of such an approach. This analysis is reinforced if we consider the eight main conditions that Lifton identified as indicating the presence of ideological totalism. These are:

1. *Milieu control.* As Lifton postulated it, this is primarily the use of techniques to dominate the person's contact with the outside world but also their communication with themselves. People are "deprived of the combination of external information and inner reflection which anyone requires to test the realities of his environment and to maintain a measure of identity separate from it."[23]

In some political cults blatant measures are employed to achieve such effects. The California-based Democratic Workers Party (DWP), which we discuss in chapter 9, "encouraged" members to share party accommodations, thus ensuring that even sleep brought no respite from the party environment. Members of various right-wing militia movements spend a great deal of time on country "retreats," many of which become semipermanent communities preparing for Armageddon. Still others simply monopolize the membership's time, so that they have no practical opportunity to test the group's ideas against alternatives circulating in the real world.

2. *Mystical manipulation.* Lifton argues that "Included in this mystique is a sense of 'higher purpose,' of 'having directly perceived some imminent law of social development,' of being themselves the vanguard of this development."[24]

Cults, in general, are distinguished from their more rational counterparts by the all-embracing claims which they make for the significance of their ideology. Such claims become a means of achieving higher and higher levels of commitment: at stake is the future of the world. Frantic work rates are intrinsic to vanguard notions of party building and to the one true method of analysis advocated by the group, assumed to be superior to all others. The claim of privileged insight is central to the appeal of cult organizations and is ritually invoked to encourage supporters into binges of party building. Again, we provide many examples of such approaches in the chapters which follow.

3. *The demand for purity.* Here, "the experiential world is sharply divided into the pure and the impure, into the absolutely good and the absolutely evil."[25] Members of the cult are assured that they possess a superior insight to ordinary members of society. At best, nonmembers are considered the dupes, at worst the degenerate accomplices, of a vast conspiracy against the cult's core beliefs. Many groups on the far left characterize those who sympathize with them as the "advanced workers." These are pityingly contrasted with the unredeemed masses, who are as yet too ignorant to appreciate the organization's virtues. Right-wing cults preach racial purity and often argue that blacks are the product of interbreeding between people and animals.

4. *The cult of confession.* In essence, this requires people to confess their inadequacies, their relative unsuitability to act as a vessel for the group's pure ideas, and the many ways in which they have let the organization down. This is usually conducted in group meetings. The central purpose is to break the remaining individuality of members, while intimidating would-be opponents into silence. This is a widely documented phenomenon in all manner of cults.

5. *The "sacred science."* This aspect of ideological totalism is particularly apt to political cults. Lifton describes it as follows:

> The totalistic milieu maintains an aura of sacredness around its basic dogma, holding it out as an ultimate moral vision for the ordering of human existence. This sacredness is evident in the prohibition (whether or not explicit) against the questioning of basic assumptions, and in the reverence which is demanded for the originators of the Word, the present bearers of the Word, and the Word itself . . . the milieu . . . makes an exaggerated claim of airtight logic, of absolute "scientific" precision.[26]

Only the group's ideology offers salvation. The effect is to secure a redoubled effort from the members in party building, presented as a race between the creation of mass parties built in its image and world destruction.

6. *Loading the language.* Lifton has described this as the extensive use of what he termed "the thought-terminating cliché," used as "interpretive shortcuts."[27] Repetitive phrases are regularly invoked to describe all situations, and to prevent further analysis. Expressions such as "bourgeois mentality" or (on the far right) the "mud people" are bandied around as a signifier of something that is an ultimate evil, in contrast to the ultimate goodness of the group's beliefs. Lifton describes the overall effects thus: "For an individual person, the effect of the language of ideological totalism can be summed up in one word: constriction. He is . . . linguistically deprived; and since language is so central to all human experience, his capacities for thinking and feeling are immensely narrowed."[28]

7. *Doctrine over person.* Essentially, Lifton argues that historical myths are engendered by the group as a means of reinforcing its black and white morality. Then, "when the myth becomes fused with the totalist sacred science, the resulting 'logic' can be so compelling and coercive that it simply replaces the realities of individual experience . . . past historical events are retrospectively altered, wholly rewritten, or ignored, to make them consistent with the doctrinal logic."[29]

In subsequent chapters, we outline many major myths advanced on the far left and right to achieve this objective. The most prevalent myth on the left concerns the Russian Revolution of 1917. On the right, a series of myths speak of race pollution in the past, idealize and idolize the Nazi experience in Germany during the 1930s, and often fantasize that whites in North America are the descendants of the lost tribe of Israel.

8. *The dispensing of existence.* Fundamentally, this proposes that only those who adhere to the group's ideology are fully human or fully good. Others are either conscious agents of evil forces or unconscious barriers to historical progress who most probably deserve annihilation. The notion is advanced that outside the ranks of the grouping the member may be corrupted by alien pressures, and can only attain true purity within the cult.

Given that the desire for affiliation is one of the most deeply rooted features of human existence,[30] we have an innate desire to identify with powerful social groups. Developing an identity (on a familial, local, ethnic, and national scale) is an important quest for most people. Thus, if we can be convinced that the core ideas of a particular group represent a set of truths on which rests the fate of humanity, we also find that our sense of identity comes to depend for its vitality on continued group membership. The threat of expulsion, coupled with the implication of damnation, is a powerful tool for keeping members in line and "on message."

Conclusion

This chapter has explored the techniques used by groups on the left and right to maintain high levels of conformity, activism, and intolerance on the part of their members. None of this implies that movements for social change are inherently destined to become obscure cults, or that a sharp critique of modern society is inappropriate. The state of the world is a vitally important issue, and requires a political rather than a psychological analysis. Our planet is beset by real difficulties, crying out for solutions. However, it is important to assess whether those organizations that claim to have embarked on this task are motivated by the quest for genuine understanding. All too many are, instead, intent on building monolithic organizations that threaten individual freedoms and that would replace our present difficulties with ones much worse.

Cults prey upon our aversion to uncertainty. In reality, they only illuminate the darkness with burnt-out candles. The disillusionment they cause becomes an enormous waste of democratic energy. As we argued in the Introduction, participation in political life is a precondition for the effective functioning of democracy. Political cults put all this at risk, and in doing so damage the whole political process.

They also propose totalistic world visions, which suggest that politics embraces everything of importance on the earth and hence justifies their obsessional levels of activity. Paradoxically, it often appears that the more active people are in the service of "The Cause," the less worthwhile become their insights into society. In some cases, their pronouncements degenerate into drivel. Many intelligent, idealistic, and self-sacrificing people belong to political cults. Unfortunately, the damaged social environment they inhabit prevents them from making the powerful contribution to political debate that they intend.

We argue here for a sense of proportion. As Crick expressed it: "Politics is not religion, ethics, law, science, history or economics; it neither solves everything, nor is it present everywhere; and it is not any one political doctrine, such as conservatism, liberalism, socialism, communism, or nationalism, though it can contain elements of most of these things. Politics is politics, to be valued as itself, not because it is 'like' or 'really is' something else more respectable or peculiar."[31]

We have the utmost respect for the practice of politics. In recognizing, with Crick, the limitations of political activity we believe that people will be better placed to genuinely help develop solutions for the world's all too abundant supply of problems.

Chapter 2

Groupthink, Big Brother, and Love Bombing

We dislike arguments of any kind; they are always
vulgar, and often convincing.
—Oscar Wilde

Introduction

Cults exercise an extraordinary influence over the lives of their followers. As we discussed in chapter 1, cult members often break from their families and lose contact with old friends. Cherished belief systems are scrapped. Many cult leaders espouse high-sounding ideals. For all that, their primary goal is obedience. A toxic internal atmosphere is created, in which dissent fights a losing battle against conformity. A cult's idea of teamwork is a thousand people doing what the leader says. Why do their followers tolerate such a lifestyle? Why, as they gasp for air themselves, do they continue to lure others into the stifling environment of cultism?

It is generally assumed that members of political and other cults are different from ordinary people. Since what cults do is "crazy," their members must have been bonkers to join. This view is not supported by the research evidence. A summary of several clinical studies[1] concludes that no more than a third of cult members were psychologically disturbed before their cult experience. Other studies have found that cult members tend to score within a normal range on psychological tests and psychiatric interviews. It does appear that we are more vulnerable to cultic recruitment if we have just lost a job, been divorced, had a severe illness, or experienced other comparable traumas. For some young people about to enter college, the prospect of leaving home for the first time feels like a major personal earthquake. Cult recruiters, accordingly, have been known to target college freshmen for special attention.[2]

If the evidence indicates that cultists are mostly normal before their experience, it also suggests that the intense demands of cult activity create psychological disturbance after they have joined. Ex-cultists often require long periods of counseling before they rebuild a sense of normality. However, this does not mean that those who join cults do so because they have lost their grip on sanity. Psychological damage is a consequence rather than an antecedent of cult membership.

We believe that political cults exercise their influence by manipulating a number of processes that are inherent to the nature and functioning of any group. In particular, most of us have an innate tendency to conform to the emerging norms of the groups to which we belong, or to adopt those pressed on us by our peers. Most groups create balancing mechanisms, which hold such urges in check. Within cults, on the other hand, the breaks on conformity have been disabled. The group races toward disaster, urged on by the frantic demands of the cult leaders for more obedience, greater status for the leader, and higher levels of activity by the members.

In this chapter, we look in detail at those features of group life most open to abuse by cult leaders. These include the issues of how we normally respond to dissent, our basic response to communication with people who have convinced us that they have a greater status than we do, the role of "love bombing" in promoting unhealthy affiliative behaviors, and our tendency to follow bizarre orders on the mere word of authority figures. Unchecked, such social dynamics lead to paranoid group norms. A cult, in essence, is paranoia liberated from its straitjacket. In exploring the dark side of life in groups, we hope that this chapter will assist readers to resist attempts by cultic groups to embroil them in the fantasy worlds of their leaders.

Dissent, Cohesiveness, and "Groupthink"

Our membership in various groups helps us to determine who and what we are, and why. For example, we define ourselves by gender, ethnicity, age range, profession, familial status, and sexual orientation. We also define ourselves by clarifying what we are not. ("I am an atheist, not a Christian"—or vice versa.) Affiliation and disaffiliation are fundamental to the shaping of our self-image.[3]

An intrinsic requirement of group membership is conformity, to one degree or another. Members must broadly agree with each other on such vital issues as what tasks they intend to perform, how decisions will be made, who will perform various leadership functions, and how much freedom group members will have to express dissident viewpoints. The resolution of these issues defines and delineates the norms of the group.

However, and despite the drive toward conformity implicit in resolving these questions, the quality of decision making improves when groups encourage minority dissent. Dissent prevents powerful majorities from erring. It stimulates the detection of correct novel solutions, promotes the deployment of multiple strategies to problem solution, and improves recall of information. Dissent also encourages people to examine an issue from multiple perspectives: precisely what seems to be associated with improved performance and decision making.[4]

Nevertheless, groups have a tendency to be suspicious of disagreement and to punish dissenters, usually through the withdrawal of valued social rewards. Thus, groups often avoid genuine debate and compel members to conform at an early stage to the emerging norms and values of the group. It is difficult to play the role of minority advocate while in the company of strong-minded individuals, already committed to a particular outcome. Few of us relish fending off hecklers, while defending an unpopular position before a hostile audience. It is much more satisfying to align ourselves with the winning team—which usually has superior force on its side.

An important issue here is the extreme conformity that often settles on groups, and that has been termed "groupthink." Janis has described this as "a mode of thinking that people engage in when they are deeply involved in a cohesive in-group, when the members' strivings for unanimity override their motivation to realistically appraise alternative courses of action."[5] Janis, who also popularized the term, investigated a series of defective political and business decisions. He concluded that many poor decisions were the result of a flawed decision-making process within the groups responsible.

Other work has unearthed an interesting consequence of such intense conformity in groups. Most of us imagine that we are "better" than other people at conforming to what we regard as valued group norms. Furthermore, we also believe, quite irrationally, that it is our conformity to group norms that helps us to stand out from the crowd.[6] In reality, the better a soldier is at marching in formation, the harder it is to distinguish him from his colleagues on the parade ground.

A further contradiction is that we are often revolted by the conformist behavior of others. They are described as "crawling to the boss," "becoming two faced," or "are being all things to all men." However, our own conformity is interpreted as evidence of a heightened, and hence positive, awareness of group norms—what has been called the "superior conformity of the self" effect.

What can be done to avert such dangers? In Box 2.1, we list a number of suggestions, derived from the research literature, which members of all groups need to take on board. Groups who obstruct such practices, in our view, have traveled a long distance along the road to becoming a cult.

Box 2.1

Defeating "Groupthink"

- The leader should adopt a more neutral role and avoid stating his or her views at an early stage of group discussion.
- The entire group should encourage the expression of dissident viewpoints.
- It helps if the group assigns the role of "critical evaluator" to at least one, and preferably all, of its members, when it is faced with important decisions.
- After every big decision, ask these questions: What's wrong with this decision? How could it be improved? What alternatives have we overlooked?
- Assign subgroups to develop proposals independently.
- Periodically bring in outside people or experts to review your deliberations.
- Cults are particularly loath to involve outsiders in their affairs. If your suggestions of outside involvement are met with disapproval, reconsider your membership in the group.
- During important discussions, assign one member to play the role of devil's advocate.
- After formulating a plan, hold a "second-chance" meeting. Invite everyone to express residual doubts. Express doubts yourself.
- Always set tasks that involve everyone. Avoid having part of the group wait passively for orders from above.

Decision Making by Groups—A Risk Too Far?

Consider the following dilemma:

"An electrical engineer may stick with his present job at a modest but adequate salary, or may take a new job offering considerably more money but no long-term security."[7]

In the late 1960s, J. Stoner, a leading psychologist, persuaded people to answer this question on their own, and then discuss it in groups with a view to reaching a consensus. Surprisingly, he found that decisions reached by groups were nearly always riskier than the average of the individual members' pregroup discussion sessions. It also emerged that these results were "internalized"—that is, the more extreme opinions advocated by the group were subsequently reproduced by subjects in individual discussions, who argued strongly that they were indeed the best decision which could be reached. This became known as the *risky shift phenomenon*, and at the time created considerable alarm. Many vital decisions are made by groups. If groups make riskier decisions than individuals it would have startling implications for much of human decision making.

Further studies found the process much more complex than at first appeared. Groups do indeed produce different decisions to those which people tend to reach on their own, but these are not always riskier than what individuals decide when by themselves. In fact, in the experiments concerned, they were often much more conservative. More detailed investigation found that riskier outcomes were only obtained when the average score of the decisions people were inclined to reach when on their own was moving that way anyway. In short, groups do not produce riskier decisions than individuals, but they do seem to produce *more extreme versions of the original view which the individuals were beginning to develop prior to a group discussion.*

It seems that, overall, we have an innate tendency to overconform to what we think the emerging norms, values, or decisions of the group are, as a way of gaining influence within it. Remember: dissenters are penalized, often with a loss of influence or a reduction in their perceived levels of credibility. Early dissent from group norms, when the person concerned has yet to build a strong track record of success and hence has limited status, creates the impression of an unreliable maverick. Accordingly, we normally attempt to discover the dominant norms of the group, and align ourselves with them as quickly as possible. Everyone else does likewise, pushing the group's decisions in an ever more extreme direction. Mob justice is always harsher than the sentences imposed by a solitary judge.

Our rush to affiliate leads us to prematurely identify many points of agreement with the views of others. We then adjust our opinions in order to fashion a rapid consensus. It appears that, when we think like this, we often present the group with what has been termed an "empty self,"[8] and invite it to create a personality profile for us. High-activity groups, in particular, offer us regular surges of adrenaline, vistas of unimaginable social change, and an imperative demand for total personal transformation. They also ensure that we have little time left over from cult activity for reflection. Faced with mood swings almost calculated to induce manic depression, recruits grow increasingly reliant on the flawed feedback systems of the group to maintain a sense of balance. Eventually, they are pushed and pulled into a pattern of complete subservience. Their personal identity is stripped of all its individuating markers. Their first response to the unreasonable is no longer "Why?" but "Why not?"

When Some Are More Equal Than Others . . .

Research clearly shows that the quality of decisions made by groups is also deeply influenced by the status of the various people involved. *Who* says something is frequently more influential than *what they have to say.* This process is well illustrated by the work of E. Torrance, a prominent social psychologist in the 1950s. He assembled three-person navy bomber crews consisting of a pilot, a navigator, and a gunner. He then presented them with the following problem:

"A man bought a horse for $60 and sold it for $70. Then he bought the same horse back for $80 and again sold it for $90. How much money did he make in the horse business?"[9]

The correct answer is $20. If you are curious, you can verify this for yourself. Simply add up how much was spent, how much was received, and subtract one from the other. This procedure shows that the difference is $20. However, Torrance found that whether the group would accept this solution depended on who offered it. When the person of highest status, the pilot, put forward the correct answer the group was most likely to accept it, but less so when the navigator advocated it and least of all when the solution was offered by the gunner.

Cultic groups intensify status differentials within their ranks. They encourage us to put blind faith in the opinions of people occupying leadership roles. The ideas of the leaders are embalmed and displayed for veneration in musty mausoleums. This prevents the group from developing sensible solutions to whatever problems it is facing.

It may not be possible to entirely escape the emergence of varied status levels within groups. This is because we all collude in the creation of status differentials, since they satisfy our need for predictability and order.[10] When we identify the degree of status enjoyed by our coaffiliates, we feel better able to predict the kind of behavior they are likely to engage in. This stabilizes the group, and enables it to agree on who does what, when, and where. It also satisfies the attribution urges shared by all of us, which we discuss further in chapter 3. The ability to attribute different levels of status to group members, even if such attributions are mistaken, answers our need to reduce uncertainty.

However, if we cannot eliminate status differentials, then we can at least reduce them, by diminishing the overt emblems of difference and privilege which pervade group life. We would suggest that groups should:

- *Equalize rewards for all members*. Cults allow a few leaders to enjoy sexual, financial, and lifestyle privileges that are explicitly denied to others. They then attempt to control the private lives of their members, as a means of achieving complete domination. Healthy groups will ensure that there is no one set of rules for the leaders, and another for the rank and file.
- *Promote an atmosphere of informality*. For example, it helps if group members are on first-name terms with each other. Healthy groups seek

to eliminate special titles, while unhealthy groups go out of their way to create them. In political cults, terms such as "General Secretary," "Imperial Wizard" and "Grand Dragon" proliferate. Like the designation "Big Brother," they are used to create a false aura of expertise, status, and infallibility around a select few leaders.

• *Respect the ideas of all members, rather than just those at the top.* Cults usually insist that everyone's ideas are ruthlessly criticized—except those of the leader. A healthy group life promotes a critical attitude towards everyone's ideas.

Thus, people whom we perceive to be similar to us exercise a much greater influence over our thinking than do those we consider to be different. Most of us, in any event, exaggerate our similarity to significant others; think that our opinions are more correct than they are; and imagine that our views are more widely endorsed than most other people's.[11] For example, many members of the British public, in the aftermath of Princess Diana's death in 1997, appeared on television to announce that "she was just like me." Politicians frequently claim to be speaking on behalf of the entire nation, although they have no conceivable means of knowing whether they do or not.

If we engage in public statements in favor of a course of action (and all cults encourage this on the part of their members), the false view that what we are commending is widely supported is reinforced all the more. This effect was neatly demonstrated by one important experimental study,[12] which required students to walk around a campus for thirty minutes wearing a board that said simply "Repent." Those who agreed to do this estimated that 63.5 percent of their colleagues would indeed be more likely to repent. Those who refused expected only something in the region of 24 percent to feel this way. The more visible one's group membership is, to oneself and others, the more likely it is that such delusions will develop. It is not surprising that political cults of all hues habitually imagine themselves to be on the verge of significant social influence, and even the seizure of state power.

Obedience to Authority: How Far Would You Go?

In an earlier age, it was openly argued that people should never challenge the decisions of their leaders—under any circumstances. One leader used to such unquestioning obedience was General Douglas Haig. In July 1916 he ordered eleven divisions of English troops to advance on German lines; 110,000 men attacked. Of these, 20,000 were killed and 40,000 wounded. Two years later, when a major battle at the Somme left an unimaginable 300,000 British soldiers dead or wounded, London newspapers printed the following:

How the Civilian May Help in this Crisis.
Be cheerful . . .
Write encouragingly to friends at the front . . .
Don't think you know better than Haig.[13]

Most of us would assume that such attitudes have by now fundamentally changed. In some respects, they have. The edicts of political and military leaders are scrutinized more critically than ever before. Thanks to coverage by the media, the consequences of orders to advance are more obvious to people than was the case in the early days of the twentieth century.

Nevertheless, it remains the case that human behavior is driven by an impulse to *conform to authority*. This impulse means that ordinary people can be compelled, if they believe that they are in the presence of someone with high status, to pursue actions contrary to their deepest value systems and their own best interests. Cults manipulate this process, by (a) depicting their leaders as powerful authority figures; (b) emphasizing the differences in status between such "powerful" leaders and their followers; (c) encouraging their members to engage in activities that further separate them from normal society and so intensify their sense of loyalty to the cult.

It might be assumed that cult leaders achieve these objectives because they possess extraordinary depths of charisma, or employ the services of a paramilitary apparatus that administers painful sanctions to dissidents. Common sense suggests that few of us would willingly engage in blatantly antisocial behaviors, simply because we are asked to do so. However, research into such issues suggests that, in this as in many other respects, common sense would be wrong. Many cults today secure unquestioning obedience from their followers simply by asserting that their leaders deserve an exalted status within the group's ranks. How can this be?

A famous series of studies, known as the Milgram experiments, have helped to illuminate this issue. These were conducted by social psychologist Stanley Milgram, initially in the late 1950s.[14] He placed advertisements in the press and wrote directly to a number of people. In this way he managed to recruit forty subjects, between twenty and fifty years of age. The subjects were informed that they were participants in a study of memory and learning at Yale University. In fact, unknown to them, the real object of the exercise was to measure levels of obedience to authority.

Milgram's recruits were brought to his laboratory one at a time, and introduced to another "participant" who was, in reality, a confederate of the experimenter. They were told that one of them would be required to be a "learner" and the other "a teacher." Slips of paper were picked from a hat to allocate these roles. In reality, each paper bore the word "teacher." This ensured that the genuine subject was always allocated this role. After listening to some general information about human memory, subjects were told:

> But actually, we know *very little* about the effects of punishment on learning, because almost no truly scientific studies have been made of it in human beings. For instance, we don't know how much difference it makes as to who is giving the punishment, whether an adult learns best from a younger person or an older person than himself—or many things of that sort. So in this study we are bringing together a number of adults of different occupations and ages. And we're asking some of them to be teachers and some of them to be learners. We want to find out just what effect different people have on each other as teachers and learners and also what effect punishment will have on learning in this situation. Therefore, I'm going to ask one of you to be the teacher here tonight and one to be the learner.

The so-called learner was then taken into adjacent room and strapped to an electric chair–type apparatus. The straps were excused as a measure to prevent excessive movement while the learner was receiving electric shocks. Electrodes were attached to the learner's wrist, and paste was applied (so the "teacher" was told) to stop blisters and burns. The experimenter explained that he intended asking the learner a series of questions. The subject was instructed to administer electric shocks to the learner each time he or she responded with a wrong answer, and furthermore to move one level higher on a "shock generator," each time that wrong answers were forthcoming. The subject was also told to announce the voltage level before administering the shocks. Thus, there could be no doubt in the subject's mind about the seriousness of what she or he had embarked upon. The "electric shocks" were, of course, bogus: but this was concealed from the person in the role of teacher. What followed was remarkable.

Milgram had primed his learner to emit a series of stock responses to each electric shock. There was no sign of protest or noise from the learner until shock level 300 was reached, but at this point the learner, who was in the next room, pounded on the laboratory wall. This was followed by a silence, during which it could be presumed that the learner was unconscious or worse. If the teacher showed any reluctance to continue the experiment, a series of verbal "prods" was offered. These included "The experiment requires that you continue" and "It is absolutely essential that you continue." The prods were offered in a calm voice by the experimenter, who wore a white coat as a symbol of authority throughout.

As the experiment progressed, many of the genuine subjects showed signs of great nervousness, including sweating, trembling, hysterical laughter, and tears. However, *none* of them stopped short of administering electric shocks at the 300 level. Five out of forty refused to go beyond the 300 level—that is,

beyond the point at which hammering on the wall could be heard. Four more gave one further shock, two stopped at the 330 level, and one each at levels 345, 360, and 376. Thus, a total of fourteen subjects (35 percent) chose to defy the experimenter. This means that fully 65 percent of them carried on with the experiment to the end, despite showing signs of great discomfort.

Milgram repeated his experiment many times, varying the basic procedure to intensify the teacher's awareness of what they were supposedly doing. For example, the learners escalated their levels of protest in subsequent experiments. They made regular requests to "Get me out of here." After 270 volts had been reached, shouting and screaming commenced. At 330 volts there would be an agonized scream, followed by the learner shouting:

"Let me out of here! Let me out of here! My heart's bothering me. Let me out, I tell you! (Hysterically) Let me out of here! Let me out of here! You have no right to hold me here. Let me out! Let me out! Let me out! Let me out of here! Let me out! Let me out!"

These variations made no difference to Milgram's basic results: roughly 65 percent of his subjects continued to follow his instructions, until they thought they had administered the maximum voltage of shocks to the learner. When the experiment has been repeated in other countries and at different times since, similar results have been obtained.

What could have induced normal people to behave in what they must have realized was an extraordinarily antisocial manner? Follow-up interviews showed that the subjects had no doubt they were participating in a real study of memory and learning. Furthermore, they genuinely believed that they had been administering near-lethal electric shocks, for no reason other than that the learner had offered wrong answers. Presumably, this sort of conduct is far from normal practice in civilized societies.

The initial point of interest in Milgram's work arose from the light it shed on the practices of Nazi concentration camp guards. These were wont to cite the "Nuremberg defense" as an excuse for behavior—"I was only following orders." Milgram's work suggested that most of us will inflict harm on others, if placed in a position where someone in authority requests or orders us to do so. We may well experience considerable distress. However, we evidently conclude that this is less painful than the discomfort we would feel if we rebelled against those we perceive as powerful authority figures.

The most important aspect of Milgram's work, in this context, is the fact that the presence of mere authority persuaded people to behave in a very antisocial manner and, presumably, contrary to the norms that would ordinarily be suggested by their belief systems. Authority was nothing more substantial than a white coat, but it was enough. Also, look again at the explanations people received for the experimenter's instructions. These of-

fered them a benign cover for their actions, thereby enabling them to further rationalize their behavior. This suggests that we can be persuaded into all sorts of bizarre activities, if we believe that they are in some way for the common good, and if we are urged to do so by people we regard as credible authority figures.

Members of political cults rarely administer electric shocks to members of the public—or, so far as we know, to their own members. However, they do enter into many activities that violate the values of normal political life—for example, rigging electoral ballots, concealing party affiliations when it suits the cult's overall interests, infiltrating larger organizations to poach their members (while denying that they constitute a separate organization), and defrauding various countries' welfare systems (to pay the salaries of their full-time apparatus). They also create a punishing internal atmosphere, which destroys the quality of life for their own members. In spite of this, the members generally view themselves as morally upright people who are privileged to belong to the cult and on whose actions the future of humanity depends.

In understanding why this should be so, Milgram's experiment suggests that the presence of a *powerful authority figure* is a vital factor in driving human behavior in unfamiliar and self-destructive directions. It encourages us to believe that someone else has taken responsibility for our actions, thereby absolving us of responsibility for what follows. Psychologists refer to this as a state of *diffused responsibility*. Since many people are responsible for what we do, and we therefore feel that relatively little blame will ever be attached to us, it is easy to shrug aside the constraints of conscience. ("I was only following orders.")

When people imagine themselves to be associated with an infallible leader, they are even more willing to suspend their sense of disbelief. Of course, the more outlandish the belief system of the group concerned, the more critical it is that the members be persuaded of the leader's unique genius. Instead of placing faith in their own perceptions, which might suggest that the towering edifice of belief rests on shaky foundations, they are encouraged to place it in the wisdom of the leader. The result is large numbers of people bivouacked on the foothills of insanity and prepared for a fresh march to disaster.

Intergroup Conflict: In-Groups Versus Out-Groups

On June 15, 1990, the Detroit Pistons won the National Basketball Association title for the second time in a row. Fans invaded downtown Detroit to party and celebrate. By the end of the evening, seven people had been killed, twenty others had gunshot wounds, many hundreds more had been hurt in

stabbings and fights, and the city streets were littered with debris from widespread looting.[15] It appears that, when people perceive themselves as belonging to one group and everyone else as being radically different, the potential for aggression and violence is ever present.

Alarming as this prospect is, the research evidence also suggests that people can be divided into warring groups with relative ease (the *minimal group paradigm*). The simple means by which this is accomplished are routinely employed in political cults to heighten group affiliation and suggestibility, and to arouse a sense of embattled opposition to mainstream groupings within society.

Some of the most powerful evidence to support this contention comes from the work of M. Sherif[16] and his colleagues, who conducted an influential series of studies into patterns of friendship formation among young boys in summer camps. The boys were split into two groups. Care was taken to ensure that preexisting friends found themselves in different groups. These were then given separate activities and had minimal contact with each other for a few days. Furthermore, a number of competitions were organized between the groups (for example, tug-of-war contests). This led to intense hostility. Members of different groups showered each other with insults, and a number of physical attacks occurred. Friendships formed with members of the new group rapidly took precedence over the old.

This study offers a number of important lessons for the understanding of group influence within cults. First, it suggests that it is much easier than most people think to create new group affiliations, and to ensure that these replace longstanding loyalties and friendships. Second, group membership promotes powerful feelings of friendship among participants. Third, new ingroup loyalties are often so pronounced, even in the seminormal conditions of Sherif's summer camps, that they encourage the stigmatizing of everyone except the favored few who belong to the group. It seems that strong feelings of group loyalty and the passions of prejudice march hand in hand.

As one writer has expressed it: "Gradually we start classifying people: there are those *in* our group, those *outside* our group and those who *could* be in our group. . . . Before you know it, we're feeling superior and exclusive—better than the unenlightened masses. If only everyone knew what *we* knew."[17]

Cultic influence depends on manipulating these processes. In particular, cults:

- *Ensure that their members spend a great deal of time with fellow members*. For example, both the left- and the right-wing cults reviewed in this book put a huge emphasis on internal meetings, from which nonmembers are excluded. They organize regular "mass" rallies, to create the impression of an enthusiastic following and shore up the belief systems of their members. An inordinate amount of time is devoted to group rituals. Activity within the group is portrayed as a vital investment in the future salvation of humanity.

• *Stress all points of difference between members and nonmembers.* On the right, the wearing of Nazi regalia and the flaunting of Nazi salutes, or the white uniform of the Ku Klux Klan, perform this distancing role. On the left, members are encouraged to believe that Marxism is a complex "science," expressed in the philosophy of dialectical materialism. This is supposed to confer a unique theoretical superiority on adherents of the party line, and to distinguish them from all other trends of thought.

• *Encourage cult members to view themselves as being engaged in a total war against the influence of all other political groups.* Only the party line has the virtue of purity. All other political positions are sullied by their association with the "United Nations conspiracy," or the poisonous tentacles of the bourgeoisie. Political cults see the destruction of competing intellectual currents as central to their mission, and as a vital precondition for the survival of humanity.

Through these means, political cults spend a great deal of time whipping up intense emotions on the part of their members. Aggression is never far below the surface. On the right, Jews, blacks, and gays are pilloried as subhuman. On the left, members are encouraged to feel "class hatred," and to rejoice in the perspective of violent revolution. A small revolutionary group in Britain once ran a regular feature in their newspaper, entitled "Class Traitor of the Month." When the U.S. politician Hubert Humphrey died, a radical sect in America headlined the news: "Humphrey—Dead at Last." The demonstration and counterdemonstration are the favored public arena of the extreme left and the extreme right. Such events create an ideal amphitheater for the dramatization of powerful feelings.

An alternative approach to political activity, aimed at stimulating rationality and a mood of calm reflection, is also suggested by the work of Sherif. It will be recalled that his work involved dividing young people into spurious groups, which proceeded to develop powerful in-group identities and out-group prejudices. The task was then one of reducing the tensions that had been so artificially created. The solution Sherif and his coworkers hit upon, after a number of failures, was the promotion of *positive interdependence*. For example, they arranged for a truck to break down miles from camp. This could not be started by one group on its own, but it could be if two groups cooperated. After a series of such engineered incidents, aggression and prejudice were reduced, while old intergroup friendships were reestablished. This suggests that *positive interdependence* should be regarded as a defining trait of healthy political and group activity. Such interdependence can be promoted if group members ask themselves the following questions:

- Does the group encourage open communication between its members and people who belong to other groups?
- Is such contact rewarded, or is it stigmatized as endangering the purity of the group?
- Is there a willingness to discuss and accept ideas that originate outside the group's own ranks?
- Alternatively, are such ideas viewed with suspicion, precisely because their point of origin is suspect?
- Is most of the group's time spent building alliances with others, or is the recruitment of new members its primary (or, indeed, only) preoccupation?

The Love Bomb—Or the Power of Ingratiation

One of the most commonly cited cult recruitment techniques is generally known as "love bombing."[18] Prospective recruits are showered with attention, which expands to affection and then grows into a plausible simulation of love. Leaders go out of their way to praise the individual's contributions in group meetings. Points of similarity with the group (such as dress codes, positive statements about aspects of the sacred belief system, a concern for the welfare of the underprivileged, attendance at meetings, or participation in demonstrations) are celebrated and encouraged. Dissimilarities and disagreements are ignored. The targets frequently become convinced that they have found truer friends than they have ever known before, and a set of people who bear an uncanny likeness to the person's own ideal self-image. These are, of course, illusions; but by the time prospective members realize this, they may be too deeply submerged in the cult's activities to remember where their own minds begin and where the group mind ends.

A more technical term for the practice of love bombing is *ingratiation*.[19] As one of the pioneer researchers in this area summarized it: "There is little secret or surprise in the contention that we like people who agree with us, who say nice things about us, who seem to possess such positive attributes as warmth, understanding, and compassion, and who would 'go out of their way' to do things for us."[20]

Thus, we generally cling to those who encourage the further expression of our opinions, display approving nonverbals such as smiles and eye contact, express agreement with our beliefs, and shower us with flattery or compliments. Meanwhile, the *law of attraction*[21] holds that the more similar attitudes people have in common, the more they will like each other. As discussed above, cults encourage the notion that all members are more alike than they really are, and are more dissimilar from nonmembers than is actually the case. When this is combined with ingratiation, the consequences are that:

- The persons ingratiating themselves become perceived as familiar and similar to us. They become liked "insiders" rather than stereotyped "outsiders." Joining with them to form a group seems a natural and riskfree next step.
- Ingratiation activates the "norm of reciprocity." When someone behaves in a positive fashion toward us we are inherently motivated to reciprocate their behaviors. In cults, when people share with us their most deeply held attitudes, we feel a pull to reciprocate such disclosures, and to exaggerate the extent of our agreement with the ideas being expressed.
- Ingratiation works its black magic in both directions, to the advantage of the cult. Relationships are often characterized by an *imbalance of power*. This is especially true of cults. Normally, people of lesser status attach more importance to being liked than does the person of high status. This encourages them to agree with the high-status person's opinions, to ape his or her mannerisms, and to adapt to the belief systems such a person espouses. Those solicited by the cult find themselves inherently motivated to offer cult leaders the most positive feedback possible—agreement with their opinions and compliance with their demands. Meanwhile, potential recruits are showered with attention from precisely these figures. The two-way ingratiation process described here helps to explain both the conformity effects found within cults and our subservience to its authority figures, even when their sanctified image is only the most feeble phantom of the group's imagination.[22]

Politics and the Paranoid Personality

Conformity marches hand in hand with membership in any group. Disagreement threatens to shatter the illusions of unanimity, separateness, infallibility, and uniqueness, which are all vital if the members are to sustain a mood of total conviction. Dissent cannot be tolerated. Cults therefore relish conformity, and inflate it to absurd dimensions. The weed of obedience is watered thrice daily, and bathed in perpetual sunshine. Inevitably, those who cannot conform fall by the wayside, and either abandon activity or form their own groups. Political cults tend to become movements of fewer and fewer people, agreeing with each other about more and more issues.

In turn, the leader's sense of self-esteem grows ever more reliant on the acclaim of docile followers. But enough is never enough. In a familiar pattern of addiction, one sycophant must become two, then three, and then several world populations more. The leader becomes increasingly critical of the membership's inability to offer sufficient adulation, and demands larger audiences to whom they can dispense their sensational brand of wisdom. The failure to acquire real influence gnaws at the leader's entrails, calling forth bilious tirades against the inadequate efforts of the membership.

The possibility of such influence threatens to end the leader's total domination of the group. The more supporters he or she has, the harder it is to maintain control. Binges of recruitment alternate with bloody purges, in an exhausting spiral of effort that sees the group ascend to fresh peaks of demoralization. The perception that leaders and followers have of each other is distorted by the fatally flawed feedback systems that serve as the crux of their relationship. Locked in a disorienting cycle of over-the-top praise and devastating criticism, they are trapped in a symbiotic embrace that binds both sides to the debased belief systems and destructive rituals of the group.

Both the development of a healthy personality and constructive political activity are thwarted. In their place, the group dynamics of conformity, ingratiation, and unwonted obedience cultivate a hermetically sealed environment in which the social ecosystem is dominated by paranoia. The bizarre becomes commonplace, conspiracy theories run amuck, and today's friends could be tomorrow's bitter enemies, today's enemies tomorrow's vital allies. The cult, which often begins with noble ideals and high hopes, turns into a closed system of institutionalized paranoia.

Paranoia is characterized by guardedness, suspiciousness, hypersensitivity, grandiosity, centrality and isolation, fear of loss of autonomy, projection, and delusional thinking.[23] These lead the paranoid to incubate a powerful sense of uniqueness. Thus, the many left-wing cults that now exist each insist that they alone (hallelujah, comrades!) understand the dynamics of capitalism and are the anointed nucleus of a future mass revolutionary party. Furthermore,

> [t]he paranoid style is readily recognizable. Its users believe that a vast and subtle conspiracy exists to destroy their entire way of life. What is notable about the paranoid's view of history is not that he believes conspiracies exist and are important—after all, they do exist and may be important—but that he sees conspiracy as *the* motivating force in history and the essential organizing principle in all politics. Characteristically, the conspiracy is described as already powerful and growing rapidly. Time is short. Absolute and irreversible victory of the conspiratorial group is near. The few people who recognize the danger must expose and fight the conspirators. The conflict cannot be compromised or mediated. It is a fight to the death. The conspirators are absolutely evil, and so, as the opponents of this evil power, members of the paranoid

groups see themselves as the force for good. Indeed, they acquire in their own eyes the role of the defenders of *all* that is good. The struggle is cast in Manichaean terms as between good and evil.[24]

The central appeal of this approach, taken to an even more ludicrous conclusion in cults, is that it offers a surefire route to the reduction of uncertainty. Those who feel deeply discontented are reassured that the problem lies, in every respect, with the external world rather than themselves. They can therefore project their personal inadequacies onto others, while deriving comfort from the reassuring network of fixed beliefs that characterizes their inner world.

The cult maintains a necessary state of anxiety by echoing the message that the person's worst fears are an accurate depiction of the immediate future. The complete meltdown of the capitalist economy, plunging billions into poverty and on the road to revolution; invasion by an overwhelming mass of differently colored foreigners; the return of Lenin's Bolsheviks, under new leadership; the taking over of the United States by a United Nations–led conspiracy—these are all imminent prospects, in the folklore of one group or another. Happily, redemption is also on offer. Recruits are promised a glorious future, in which their personal pain will be eased by the victory of the group's triumphalist ideology. Holy certainty is offered. In return, true believers must agree only to deep-freeze their faculty for critical thinking.

Conclusion: The Engineering of Consent

Consent to any set of ideas, freely given, implies that people retain the right to ask questions, examine alternative sources of information, and review their initial commitment to the organization concerned. When group processes concerned with conformity, status, obedience to authority, and ingratiation are manipulated, we are witnessing an attempt to engineer consent. The hidden hand of compulsion lurks in the background, threatening people's right to withdraw their initial agreement and leave. Consent is extracted through pressure, the right to question leaders is withheld, alternative sources of information are ridiculed, and people are systematically pressurized into escalating their level of involvement with the group.

This outcome has been termed "mind control," and involves manipulating people's thoughts, feelings, and behavior to the greater gain of the manipulator, at the expense of the person being influenced.[25] Clearly, most human interaction consists of attempts to influence the cognition and behavior of others, while interaction within a positive reference group is inherently inclined to encourage the development of shared norms and behaviors.[26]

However, cults are characterized by attempts to close down choice, restrict information flow, discourage the expression of dissent, focus group norms along narrowly prescribed lines, exaggerate participants' sense of commitment by extracting public statements of loyalty (often after participation in humiliating rituals), and dominate the normal thinking process of affected individuals.

As we have argued in this chapter, the purpose of the exercise is to submerge recruits in a new belief system and prepare them for public activities that may well conflict with value systems they held before cult membership. Our susceptibility to the trappings of authority leaves all of us more vulnerable to the lure of various cults than we would like to think.

The underlying ideology of political cults is an active partner in this dynamic process. Political cults advocate programs of total social transformation. Partial gains and limited influence are interpreted as a defeat. The concepts of compromise, democracy, and debate are all viewed with contempt. Political cults see themselves as "movements," rather than simply as a normal political party. The effects of such a view have been summarized as follows:

> Membership in a movement requires the ability to see particular campaigns for particular goals as parts of something much bigger, and as having little meaning in themselves . . . (particular campaigns) are needed to provide a larger context within which politics is no longer just politics, but rather the matrix out of which something will emerge like Paul's "new being in Christ" or Mao's "new socialist man. . . ." This kind of politics assumes that things will be changed utterly, that a terrible new beauty will be born.[27]

Movements have sacred principles that cannot be compromised, they generate intense loyalties, they are officered by high priests proffering the divine interpretation of sacred texts, and they are possessed by a passionate conviction that anything is justified if it furthers the "cause." The infinite scope of the movement's ideology overwhelms the finite context of the outside world: an air of complete unreality infects all the group's pronouncements. The ends justify the means. Thus, once an organization becomes imbued with a conviction that it rests on inviolable principles, and is therefore a "movement," it is only a short step away from blind fanaticism, and the status of a cult.

It is possible to resist such malign group influence. In addition to the suggestions we have offered at various points of this chapter, Zimbardo and Anderson[28] have provided a twenty-point checklist of "ways to resist unwanted social influence," which we believe is of great use. Their suggestions include a willingness to step back and reject a conceptual framework before debating specifics; skepticism regarding the instantaneous love of others and an acceptance of the hurt involved in rejecting such love; and, above all, a willingness to question authority. It is useful to remember that *belief plus commitment minus doubt equals fanaticism.* On the other hand, healthy organizations are characterized more by debate and disagreement than by the absence of conflict.

No one in the modern world can avoid becoming a member of many groups, teams, organizations, and even "movements." Most of these will be completely benign. They will make invaluable contributions to the welfare of society and will benefit their own members. Such groups are characterized by vigorous debate and a nonphobic attitude toward dissent. Their leaders are restrained by democratic accountability. Their ideas are open to revision in the light of the group's experiences in the real world. Such experiences take precedence over theory, faith, or prediction. It is our hope that this chapter will help readers identify danger signs in those groups to which they belong. In the struggle to contain the dark side of group dynamics, our greatest weapon is awareness.

Part Two

Cults on the Right

Chapter 3

Christian Identity: A Heritage of Hate

*From time to time illustrated papers bring it to the
attention of the German petite-bourgeoisie that some
place or other a Negro has for the first time become a
lawyer, teacher, even a pastor, in fact a heroic tenor,
or something of the sort. While the idiotic bourgeoisie
looks with amazement at such miracles of educational
skill, the Jew shrewdly draws from it a new proof of
his theory about the equality of men that he is trying
to funnel into the minds of nations. It doesn't dawn on
this depraved bourgeois world that this is positively a
sin against all reason: that it is criminal lunacy to
keep on drilling a born half-ape until people think
they have made a lawyer out of him, while millions of
members of the highest culture-race must remain in
entirely unworthy positions.*
—Adolf Hitler, *Mein Kampf*

Introduction

In 1967, an obscure farmer in North Dakota stopped paying his taxes to the
Internal Revenue Service (IRS). His name was Gordon Kahl. He had concluded that the U.S. government was in the grip of a satanic conspiracy, and
he told the IRS that he "would no longer pay tithes to the Synagogue of
Satan." Later, Kahl killed two federal marshals in an armed shootout. He
wrote a statement after the murders, in which he explained that "our nation
has fallen into the hands of alien people. . . . These enemies of Christ have
taken their Jewish Communist Manifesto and incorporated it into the Statu-

tory Laws of our country and thrown our Constitution and our Christian Common Law (which is nothing other than the Laws of God as set forth in the Scriptures) into the garbage can." He then fled to Arkansas, where he was himself killed by the Federal Bureau of Investigation (FBI) in 1983.[1]

The tragedy of Gordon Kahl and his victims shows the hazards of adhering to an absolutist belief system that preaches that every event is the product of a conflict between the forces of pure good and a satanic, evil conspiracy. When one is possessed by the conviction that all modern institutions are directly under the aegis of Satan, the act of taking up arms against the state, or planting bombs outside its offices, becomes a minor next step. A thin red line marks the divide between legitimate anger and madness. Gordon Kahl was a perpetrator of unspeakable violence and prejudice, but he was also its victim.

Today, increasing numbers of Americans are seeking comfort in theological explanations for their problems. These explanations are based on the same belief system as that of Gordon Kahl. In this philosophy, Armageddon is imminent. Jews, blacks, gays, and all identifiable minority groups are the handmaidens of a devilish conspiracy against a pure, Christian, and white way of life. Catastrophe can be averted only by racial separation, achieved through conflict. Furthermore, the U.S. government itself is hopelessly enmeshed in the conspiracy. An uprising against the government is therefore inevitable and must be actively prepared for.

This theology is known as Christian Identity. It acts as a theoretical and emotional justification for the activities of the many white supremacist cults now active within the United States. Not every member of White Aryan Nations, Posse Comitatus, the Ku Klux Klan, or the innumerable militia groups that have mushroomed throughout the country openly espouses this ideology. However, such is the scope of its ambition and the explanatory power of its assumptions that their organizations and leaders have been inescapably influenced by its beliefs. They are drawn to it, just as a moth is attracted to the brightest light in a room. Christian Identity has become the Marxism-Leninism of the far right. It is a complex theoretical system with a long history, a packed pantheon of heroic pioneers, and a deep conviction that only its analysis stands between the chosen white race of North America and annihilation. Salvation requires the rapid conversion of many millions to its ideas. Understanding where it comes from is a vital step in grasping the mind-sets of those who are organizing to deliver white supremacy in America.

In this chapter, we look at the origins of the Identity movement and explore what it preaches. We also relate this to the psychology of prejudice and consider how prejudiced ideas assume tangible form in the minds of so many people. How can people maintain that they are Christians and yet see all difference as the mark of innate inferiority, to be feared, despised, and destroyed? Recognizing that these paradoxes are rooted in the general dynamics of prejudice formation will also help us begin to understand how both the individuals affected and our wider society can be inoculated against its noxious effects.

The Evolution of Christian Identity

Christian Identity is also sometimes known as British Israelism, Israel Identity, or the Kingdom message. Its origins lie in mid-nineteenth century Britain. The most basic idea animating its adherents is that white Christians are the true Israelites of the Old Testament and are God's chosen people. In its modern, American incarnation, Christian Identity argues that the United States is the true "promised land" spoken of in the Bible. This leap of geographical imagination is easily explained. Identity supporters believe that ten lost tribes of Israel migrated to Europe, Great Britain, and eventually the United States. They argue that fundamental differences distinguish one race from another and therefore that the races should not comingle. Miscegenation is the ultimate horror, threatening to dilute the pure blood stock of the Aryan master race.

This prejudice is cast in biblical mode. Nonwhites were created with other animals before Adam and Eve were driven out of the Garden of Eden. They are not fully human at all—an echo of Hitler's description of blacks as "half-apes." The theory of different origins enables many believers to claim that they are not racists at all. In contradiction to the general thrust of their propaganda, they argue that the races are not necessarily inferior or superior. They are just different, in the same way that cattle are different from dogs or humans, and have different roles, rights, and entitlements. Tim Houser, an Identity follower, has said: "Identity is not racist. Jews and blacks are what they are. God chose to . . . make blacks with the animals, we didn't. I have to believe God, and he spelled it out clear in the Bible. I'd give the shirt off my back to a black man if he came to my door. But I can't make him the same as me."[2]

The majority have fewer qualms about claiming that white Christians are superior to all other races. A white supremacist Web site inquires rhetorically after the whereabouts of Africa's philosophers, intellectuals, scientists, writers, and artists—a frequent refrain in such circles. Any human endeavor that departs from Western traditions is assumed either not to exist at all or to be so inferior that it is worthy only of ridicule. Invisibility is awarded as a badge of dishonor. Nonwhite races are regarded as a subhuman species, having more in common with animals than the rest of humanity. However, special attention is reserved for Jews. They are conceived as having a distinct and altogether worse point of origin.

Jews are regarded as the direct biological offspring of the Devil. Either the Devil or one of his underlings had sex with Eve in the Garden of Eden. Cain was the progeny of this union, and Jews are viewed as his direct descendents. This means that they have an unalterable capacity for evil. It is in their blood, and even conversion to Christianity is not sufficient to change it. This strand of Identity theology has a long genealogy, but was firmly in place by the early 1960s. Since then, it has become ever more dominant. As Michael Barkun has pointed out, it distinguishes the bigotry of Christian Identity from even the most virulent plagues of anti-Semitism in previous periods of human history. In the past, it was frequently argued that Jews were the products of interbreeding between people and animals. Their continued existence would lead to the defilement and degradation of the human race. Nevertheless, they were at least granted a common point of origin among the species of this world. The distinctive contribution that Christian Identity makes to anti-Semitism theory is viler and potentially more destructive than any of its racist precursors.

Its analysis has been given a political expression by organizations such as Aryan Nations. A creedal statement produced by it and the tautologically challenged Church of Jesus Christ Christian declares:

> WE BELIEVE that there are literal children of Satan in the world today. These children are the descendants of Cain, who was a result of Eve's original sin, her physical seduction by Satan. We know that because of this sin, there is a battle and a natural enmity between the children of Satan and the Children of the Most High God. . . .
> WE BELIEVE that there is a battle being fought this day between the children of darkness (today known as Jews) and the children of light (God), the Aryan race, the true Israel of the bible.[3]

In part, this explains the fascination with the person of Hitler that is displayed by so many on the far right. His photographs frequently adorn white supremacist sites on the Internet, an act of homage that accurately documents their ideological ancestry. However, not only are Jews demonized for their alleged satanic origin. It is also argued that they are engaged in a tightly organized and well-advanced conspiracy to take over the world. In some cases this conspiracy is presented as having already come to fruition. Thus, the U.S. government is often referred to as the Zionist Occupation Government (ZOG). Hate literature offers what its authors take to be indisputable evidence for this assertion—such as long lists of Jews who have belonged to President Bill Clinton's cabinets. Clinton himself has frequently been designated "President Klinton."

Anti-Semitism, deeply rooted in many circles, received a huge boost in the United States in the 1920s, when Henry Ford was given a copy of the "Protocols of the Elders of Zion." This was a Czarist police forgery from the nineteenth century, purportedly documenting a decision by a meeting of Jewish elders to take over the world. One of Ford's newspapers printed a series of articles based on the forgery. These were then published as a book called *The International Jew*, which enjoyed a huge popularity and sold over 500,000 copies. It is still retailed by some far-right groups in America, and its text is posted on their Web sites.

The book blamed Jews for every conceivable problem. These included the Russian Revolution ("The downfall of Russia was prepared by a long and deliberate program of misrepresentation of the Russian people, through the Jewish world press and Jewish diplomatic service"), what was seen as social degeneration ("It is the peculiar genius of that race to create problems of a moral character in whatever business they achieve a majority"), plus the advent of jazz music ("Jazz is a Jewish creation").

The book was praised by Hitler, translated into German, and distributed in millions of copies throughout the country. Hitler himself described Ford as "the leader of the growing fascist movement in America."[4] In 1938 Henry Ford received the highest award possible for a foreigner, the Grand Cross of the German Eagle.

Moreover, these activities helped pull public opinion within America in a more anti-Semitic direction. A 1938 poll found that 41 percent of U.S. adults agreed that Jews had "too much power in the United States." By 1945 this figure had reached 58 percent.[5]

Aryan Nations produces a newspaper entitled *Calling Our Nation*, which has regularly published accounts of Jews committing human sacrifices as a normal part of their religious rituals. In this subculture, rumors of all kinds abound about what Jews are supposedly up to.

Once such attitudes are acquired, those infected by them seek out evidence that supports their belief system and ignore anything that suggests they might be mistaken. This cognitive defect is shared by many people. Researchers have found that most of us interpret minor differences between groups, such as skin color, as a barometer of much greater difference. It has also been found that even those whites outside the Identity tradition, who observed or heard about a solitary black person's negative attitudes, had their critical outgroup perceptions strengthened.[6] They were also more likely afterward to avoid contact with black people or to minimize the duration of such contact when it proved unavoidable. Furthermore, a single negative event involving a black person was sufficient to lead participants into expressing in-group favoritism. Bad news about someone, the essence of gossip, seems to influence our perceptions more than good news.

The scope of the Jewish conspiracy is now assumed to be vast. It involves the International Monetary Fund; the Federal Reserve; the United Nations; the Trilateral Commission; and, of course, the IRS. Taxation is generally viewed as a threat to individual freedom. Gordon Kahl was not alone in refusing to pay his taxes. The primary aim of the conspiracy is to erode white rights. Many Identity followers believe that plans are well afoot to establish state-run concentration camps and that coded route directions to the camps are concealed on the backs of road signs throughout the United States. Gun control is designed to render whites helpless in the face of the enemy.

No organization is immune to the contagion of the conspiracy. Traditional Christian churches are viewed as impure. They may have begun with noble intentions, but have all succumbed to corruption, instigated by the Jews. The clearest sign of this is their acceptance, based on a flawed interpretation of the Bible, that Jews were God's chosen people. Christian Identity theology has determined precisely the opposite. Exactly how small numbers of Jews managed to corrupt the many millioned ranks of Christendom is not explained.

The End Is Nigh . . .

Christian Identity theology is saturated with the expectation of imminent doomsday. In this respect, its adherents excel the prophets of Marxism. They have dabbled in predictions that the "end times" were imminent for some decades. Occasionally, they have made the mistake of attaching precise dates to such speculations, with unfortunate results. Unsurprisingly, the 1930s and 1940s was a rich period for those with apocalyptic imaginations. In 1942 W.G. MacKendrick published a book entitled *This IS Armageddon*, in which he declaimed, "This is the war of God's Great Day—the final war of this age of wars." He predicted that Hitler would fall before the end of 1943, and that the climactic battles would not occur in Europe or the Pacific, but in Palestine. Today, believers once again imagine they are living in the "Last Days," and that human society in its present form is racing toward destruction. Dan Gayman, of the Church of Israel, put it like this:

> The fall of the American government is imminent. We are living already in the preparatory throes of a national and world wide revolution . . . as the agents of Satan who head their world wide conspiracy of anti-Christ, plot and plan the total demise of Christian civilization and of the white race. . . . A blood bath will take place upon the soil of this great nation, that will end only in victory for Christ or Satan. We of the Nordic race who believe in Jesus Christ are determined that this nation will remain ours.[7]

Such expectations lend a frantic urgency to the hunt for out-groups who can be stigmatized, demonized, and blamed for every calamity that besets the modern world. Unemployment, poverty in the rural Midwest, declining moral standards, and the reluctance of many to teach so-called creationist science in schools are all taken as evidence of the Jewish conspiracy against Christian and American values. If you doubt this, it suggests that you yourself are part of the conspiracy, and may need to be watched closely.

At the core of the Identity belief system lies the notion of racial obliteration. The white race is about to be overwhelmed by Jews, blacks, and other subhuman species. Identity believers want to relocate all minorities to about 10 percent of the U.S. landmass, and reserve the rest for white Christians. These must also be not gay, left wing, feminist, pro-abortion, or multicultural in outlook. Difference, the spice of life, will give way to bland uniformity. The landscape for all seasons is white, white, and more white. Dissent must bow its head in submissive conformity. Furthermore, most of recorded history is reinterpreted as a heroic fight for survival by an endangered white race. The present threat is one that stretches back to the origins of humanity, in the Garden of Eden. One Identity believer, David Lane, put it like this: "The political entity known as the United States of America has attempted with near single-minded determination, almost from its inception, to destroy any White territorial imperative, of any size and on any continent where such a State could be found. Genocide of the White Race has been the aim and the result of the American political entity."[8]

Thus, the real genocide experienced by Native Americans and the slavery inflicted on African Americans are excised from the history books. Moreover, hate groups are not content merely to demonize an out-group, compel it to adopt a subservient position, or even wipe it off the face of the earth. They must feel good about doing so. Each group possesses an "Almighty" reflex of self-righteousness. The "Word of God" is on everyone's lips. A welcoming smile and an eager embrace awaits those permitted to attend the services of the Church of Jesus Christ Christian. The warmth afforded those who belong to the in-group camouflages the hate at the core of its belief system. How can such an environment of love be depicted as one dominated by hate? Only those seduced by the Devil, or one of his serpents, could advance such an uncharitable interpretation.

Self-righteousness is deepened by yet another paradox. On the one hand, the sufferings of the stigmatized out-groups are described as nonexistent. On the other hand, the members of such groups are themselves blamed for any problems that are reluctantly acknowledged to exist.

This problem extends beyond those who belong to hate groups. Two researchers investigated white stereotypes of African Americans, Hispanic Americans, and Asian Americans.[9] They found that whites needed to "explain" the disadvantaged condition of the minority being observed—more precisely, to find explanations that justified it. Many alternative explanations for black disadvantage are available (for example, that the disadvantage is primarily the product of white prejudice and discrimination). However, to accept this would require self-criticism, and criticism might in turn be extended to social institutions with which many whites identify more closely than do members of minority groups. Thus, it was found that whites tended to assume a causal connection between the stereotypical traits ascribed to the minority groups and their social situation: that is, it was their own fault. In short, it was much more convenient to assume that their position of social disadvantage reflected their naturally inferior position than discrimination practiced by the white society. We would describe this as a perspective of "illusory causality." The tendency to blame those at the receiving end of bias for its effects is particularly pronounced among members of extreme hate groups.

Most white supremacists argue that if something like the Holocaust happened (the figure of six million dead is invariably laughed at), or if minority groups face other problems, the fault lies with those affected. Tom Metzger, a leader of White Aryan Resistance, has said, "I found so many Jews, and even when nobody was giving them any trouble they thought they were being persecuted, they're always looking for somebody to persecute them, and I think that many times they end up getting persecuted because of it."[10]

The apocalyptic ideas that go with this mind-set were greatly strengthened in the postwar period by the existence of the Soviet Union. One Identity writer, Bertrand Comparet, described the imminent Final Days in the following terms: "The Russian Gog will form a coalition of its own satellites, including Ethiopia, Afghanistan and Libya." He argued that these would also be aided by "the mixed breeds of Asia and Africa and India, who . . . will ally themselves with anything which promises them that they can pillage and rape in the lands of the White man."[11] The Russian hordes were then expected to seize the eastern Mediterranean and the Suez Canal, to disrupt the flow of oil to the West, and to attack the United States across the Bering Straits while also deploying missiles, submarines, and aircraft.

Typically, the only evidence offered for such predictions consists of biblical quotations, selected precisely because their vagueness means that they can be press-ganged into the service of any and every theological construction. The collapse of the Soviet Union has not noticeably dented anyone's sense of certainty. In a seamless transition that passes unnoticed by most true believers, the focus of the conspiracy theory is simply shifted onto new enemies—principally, ZOG. Thus, the underlying apocalyptic perspective is encased in titanium and located in bombproof shelters, where it withstands all refutation from the outside world. Yesterday's failed predictions are rationalized into insignificance. For long-term cultists, amnesia is an occupational disease. Right-wing cultism, in this respect, has much in common with those Marxist sects who eagerly insist that each new economic blip is the beginning of the final collapse of capitalism. Just you wait and see. The fact that the prediction has surfaced countless times before is concealed from new members and is consigned to the dusty vaults of memory by the old. Members are in turn too occupied by frantic activity to seriously think through the contradictions of their position. The conspiracy is too close to victory for debate, doubt, or questions. Action alone can save us, and it must be prepared for now.

Guided by their belief system, Christian Identity followers perceive every political event as further evidence that their conspiratorial interpretation of the world has been confirmed. Furthermore, in many cases, their expectation becomes a self-fulfilling prophecy. A believer in Christian Identity will view blacks, Jews, and gays as mortal enemies who threaten the survival of the white race and who should therefore be relocated to small reservations, or exterminated outright. They will engage in public protests and demand retribution against the designated out-groups.

The fact that members of such groups respond angrily to such suggestions, and even organize counterdemonstrations, becomes further evidence to the cultist that he or she is surrounded by enemies, and is facing a major onslaught. The drawbridge forming a link to reality is raised. On the other hand, if there is no public reaction, it merely constitutes evidence that the conspiracy has grown even more devious in covering its tracks.

Thus, the belief system is immune to falsification. Whatever happens, whatever could possibly happen, is taken as evidence of its essential correctness. Paranoia is the nearest thing we have to a perpetual motion machine. It requires no further impetus than a starting point and a modest injection of determination. The more self-contained its social environment and the fewer inputs it receives from the outside world, the stronger it is likely to become. As Joel Dyer has put it, "The power of conspiracy rests in faith: in the ability to believe in things unseen, to be sure of something that cannot be proven by our senses or by documentation. Faith has always been a stronger force in the world than mere reason, and because of that, debunking conspiracy theories is almost impossible."[12]

The conspiracy theory can sink such deep roots because members of hate groups tend to see those in minority categories as interchangeable with all other members of the category. However brilliant their achievements, the fact of their group membership is the most important thing about them—a black man may be a lawyer or a tenor, but is principally a "born half-ape." In this world, we do not live in communities composed of individual people.

Rather, we are besieged by homogeneous hordes of aliens, devils, feminists, half-apes, and sodomites, all out to get us.

Identity Theology, Paramilitarism, and Politics

Identity supporters have campaigned to get American law changed to reflect what are seen as biblical norms. Their efforts may be regarded as eccentric, but are mostly legal. However, not all those influenced by Identity theology conduct themselves within such parameters. Some argue that lawfulness means adherence only to their own interpretation of the Bible. This reading suggests that Jews are the direct descendents of the Devil. It follows that they can be killed with a clear conscience.

Furthermore, the movement's eschatological credo provides paramilitary and survivalist groups with an ultimate justification for their existence and an inexhaustible fuel for their overarching sense of self-importance. All that civilized people hold dear is in peril. Now is the time to organize, now is the time to repel the alien hordes, now is the time to win salvation, through rigorous self-sacrifice and a noble struggle. Accordingly, many Identity believers have embraced self-sufficient survivalist communities that eschew the larger societies.

The term "survivalism" describes a lifestyle of physical withdrawal and self-sufficiency geared to surviving some imagined future catastrophe. Survivalist writer Kurt Saxon has said that a survivalist is "one who anticipates the collapse of civilization and wants to save himself and his loved ones and bring something to the movement, if you would, which will contribute to the advance of the next generation."[13]

The sense of urgency is acute. Survivalist William Fowler has advised: "If you GET YOUR GUNS AND AMMUNITION NOW and prepare for war, you have nothing to lose." At best, such communities hover on the fringes of legality. In some cases, however, they are actively preparing terrorist campaigns and, ultimately, secession from the United States. A number of people have already proclaimed the "Republic of Texas" as a separate nation, and maintain that lawful authority within the state is to be located only within their compounds. Others have argued that organizing insurgency now will spark a wider popular rebellion against ZOG—a fallacy which, in slightly different forms, is often repeated on the left.

Radical withdrawal into self-sustaining communities promotes a siege mentality. Enemies are everywhere and the final battle for salvation has already begun. People become afraid to go into the woods at night. We noted, earlier, that Identity theology leads in many cases to a self-fulfilling prophecy. Survivalism is particularly prone to this outcome, promoting as it does the very confrontation with authority from which its advocates have been theoretically seeking to defend themselves. Bloodshed, uprising, and revenge against all impure enemies is inevitable and to be encouraged.

Thus, Identity believers have been deeply influenced by William Pierce's novel *The Turner Diaries*, a seminal text for the far right in America. Pierce holds a doctorate in physics from the University of Colorado and once taught at Oregon State University. He was for a time an aide to George Rockwell, leader of the American Nazi Party. His novel describes a post-apocalyptic America in which the Identity vision has been realized.

One chilling passage illuminates the extent of the novel's bloodthirsty vision and the nature of the final solution it envisages. The diary's putative chronicler describes walking the streets to see bodies hanging from every lamppost, sometimes "four at every intersection." In semipornographic detail he describes seeing a woman dangling from a tree and wearing a placard on which is scrawled "I defiled my race." As Pierce writes: "Above the placard leered the horribly bloated, purplish face of a young woman, her eyes wide open and bulging, her mouth agape. Finally I could make out the thin, vertical line of rope disappearing into the branches above. Apparently the rope had slipped a bit or the branch to which it was tied had sagged, until the woman's feet were resting on the pavement, giving the uncanny appearance of a corpse standing upright of its own volition."[14]

This is the ultimate vision of the Christian Identity movement: a theocratic state, in which all impurities have been purged, and in which their desiccated remnants dangle as a terrifying warning to all transgressors of the inescapable fate that awaits them. Among those influenced by this text was Timothy McVeigh, architect of the Oklahoma bombing in 1995 in which 190 people were killed. When arrested, he had photocopied portions of the book in his possession.

A white supremacist group named The Order has modeled itself on a body known in *The Turner Diaries* as "The Organization." Paranoia, hatred, archaic language, and Nazi mythology have been fused into a ferocious new strain of activism. Fresh members swear an oath that reads in part:

> I, as a free Aryan man, hereby swear an unrelenting oath upon the green graves of our sires, upon the children in the wombs of our wives, upon the throne of God Almighty, sacred be His name . . . to join together in holy union with those brothers in this circle and to declare forthright that, from this moment on, I have no fear of death, no fear of foe, that I have a sacred duty to do whatever is necessary to deliver our people from the Jew and bring total victory to the Aryan race.[15]

However, as Michael Barkun has noted, "the orientation of such groups towards combat introduces an element of uncertainty into assurances of salvation, for what if preparations are inadequate or believers insufficiently resolute?"[16] On the one hand, organizing reduces uncertainty. Temporarily, the disempowered feel empowered. The presence of others, on country retreats, in public demonstrations, in private confabs nourishes a sense of absolute conviction. It promises redemption, triumph, and public acclaim, when the conspiracy is defeated. Certainty in the justice of the "cause" increases. Yet such is the all-embracing scope of the conspiracy that it can never be fully vanquished. Paranoia needs enemies, as an infection needs diseased tissue. If one tentacle of the conspiracy is lopped off, another must be found immediately. The purpose of paranoia is paranoia.

Thus, the fact of struggling also increases uncertainty about the eventual outcome. The more one fights against the conspiracy, the more visible its agents become. The enemy is assumed to be everywhere, cunningly aided and abetted by agents within the government, the major churches, and even within other groups on the far right. The fevered imagination of the right-wing cultist is haunted by the specter of sellout and defeat. Thus, the struggle to reduce uncertainty combined with its undying presence further inflames cultists' sense of righteousness, isolation, and peril, ensuring a constant recommitment to the certainties of the struggle. Normal political action is quite compatible with question marks. For right-wing cultists, on the other hand, doubt is as welcome as daylight in a ghost story. Their rituals, incantations, and monster stories are all designed to hold it at bay.

Identity theology has also now reached the fringes of mainstream political organizations. Among those endorsing many of its tenets is Pat Robertson, a frequent contender for the Republican Party's presidential nomination at the primary stage. He has his own evangelical program on cable TV. Each show prominently features miraculous faith healings; but these are the least of it. Identity theology is laden with expectations of doomsday and a predisposition to interpret natural catastrophes as eruptions from an angry God, warning humanity of the looming end. Robertson has said that his prayers are so powerful they have averted cyclones and tidal waves on the western seaboard of the United States.

Expectations of the end time combine with commercial savvy and the enduring desire for healthy profits. Thus, he also announced that he has obtained exclusive rights to televise the Second Coming, and hired technicians to develop special TV lenses "that would be able to cope with the Messiah's holy radiance."[17] In preparation for this momentous event, Robertson's people have been scouting out the best positions for cameras in and around Jerusalem.

David Duke is another well-known figure. He attracted international attention as a presidential candidate in 1988. Duke has maintained close ties with Identity figures over a lengthy period, although he has sought to minimize or deny these as his career advanced. At one stage, he was a leading member of the Ku Klux Klan (KKK). In 1980 he appointed an Identity preacher to the post of KKK national chaplain.

Duke's first running mate for the presidency was "Bo" Gritz. Gritz, frequently described as the original role model for the character of Rambo, has well-documented Identity connections and was an intermediary between the FBI and Randy Weaver during the Ruby Ridge standoff in 1991—an event so central to paranoid thinking on the right that we discuss it in detail in chapter 4. His run as Duke's vice president closed only because he withdrew to campaign, unsuccessfully, for a congressional seat.

Duke's presidential ambitions barely ignited, but he had more success standing for state office. In January 1989 he won the Republican nomination for a special primary election for a seat in the House of Representatives in Jefferson Parish. Eventually, he won the seat by a margin of 234 votes out of 16,688.

Both Duke and Robertson demonstrate that the influence of Identity theology, and right-wing cultism in general, cannot be dismissed as something safely corraled on the margins of political discourse. More recently Pat Buchanan has launched a presidential bid that evokes many of the concerns of those influenced by Christian Identity philosophy. We expect he will attract a significant portion of the extreme right to his banner, thus giving these cultists a much-needed legitimacy.

Many right-wing cultists seem to imagine that they are auditioning for the title role in *Dr. Strangelove* (1964; a classic movie in which a paranoid general carries out his plan for dropping an atomic bomb on the Soviet Union), this time for real. Their success grows when they downplay the crudest elements of their racist past. In this guise, Identity theology can nevertheless infect the wider body politic. Its doctrines of demonic conspiracy and apocalyptic battle have already gained a following in places where they were unknown before. When such visions become a standard feature of the traditional political landscape the dangers of a social explosion are enormously accentuated.

There is no shortage of volunteers eager to press the button.

Uncertainty, Stereotyping, and Cult Recruitment

We argue, in the introduction to this book, that the social and economic transformations now under way have greatly heightened uncertainty, unease, and despair among wide sections of society. These moods render people much more vulnerable to the lure of political cults than is commonly supposed. Our concern now is to explore how such moods interact with the recruitment practices of the extreme right, to create a social environment that is increasingly receptive to their ideas.

In particular, the psychological ramifications of rising uncertainty are well known. People in general value habit in their lives. For example, in terms of work, most of us prefer to do a job the way in which it has been learned, performed, and reinforced in the past.[18] The pioneering social psychologist Gordon Allport pointed out that "the very values that sustain our lives depend for their force upon their familiarity. What is more, what is familiar tends to *become* a value. We come to like the style of cooking, the customs, the people, we have grown up with. Psychologically, the crux of the matter is that the familiar provides the indispensable basis of our existence."[19] Change makes our world less familiar, predictable, and comfortable, and we therefore react instinctively against it. The desire to increase predictability and to maintain a sense of order ensures that we attach great importance to the reduction of uncertainty during our interactions with others.[20]

Our assessment of many situations is therefore driven by both explanatory and predictive needs—that is, the need to *explain why things are as they are*, and *what is likely to happen next*. Normally, based on our predictions, we then select response options that enable us to accrue maximum gains. The most effective response options are those that are most in line with our self-image, and that offer us the greatest potential for reward.

In order to reduce uncertainty, we develop an increased tendency toward hasty generalizations, the formation of rapid judgments about people, crude social categorizations, stereotyping, and the ready embrace of simplistic political slogans. All of us bring considerable existing knowledge with us to any new interaction. Such knowledge includes person prototypes *(what this person is typically like)*, role schemas *(what someone playing this role is most likely to do)*, and typical event sequences or scripts *(what most often happens in this situation)*. In particular, the fastest way to reduce uncertainty in an unfamiliar social context is to stereotype the other people involved, by assuming that they belong to a readily identifiable category.[21] We rely less on person prototypes, and more on role schemas and typical event sequences. Stereotypes assume that individuals share more behaviors, personality traits, and beliefs with other people in their category than they actually do. Stereotyping helps us to simplify social reality, and so reduces uncertainty.

Furthermore, once the process of stereotyping starts, we try to infuse some kind of essence into what are essentially arbitrary social categories. For example, people may assume that academics differ from private sector managers and try to understand this difference by attributing a different essence to both categories.[22] It is then assumed that members of the designated category share this essence with each other. In turn, this strengthens the tendency to exaggerate similarities between the members of the social category concerned, while underplaying their differences. We also assume that members of the category concerned are more different from people in other categories than is actually the case. Instances of such behavior abound in our culture. For example, a magazine interview with a well-known British TV personality finds him declaring that the French "eat garlic and the women don't shave under their arms"; the Spanish "murder bulls and can't cook"; the Germans are "ready for another war"; while the Welsh are "so inbred they don't know the difference between a tractor and a Ford Capri."[23]

Stereotyping underpins the whole process of ethnic generalization and prejudice formation. In particular, it has obvious implications for our understanding of right-wing extremism, with its evident bias toward racism.

The impact of stereotyping individuals, groups, and events can also be understood in terms of attribution theory.[24] This proposes that we constantly attribute both *intention* and *disposition* to the actions of other people. The problem is that we cannot directly discern what their intentions and dispositions are. To our frustration, what goes on in people's heads remains largely inaccessible. Not to be defeated, we bypass this difficulty by taking the route known as creative theorizing. In social situations, this assumes the form of gossip and rumor. The purpose, again, is to reduce uncertainty. Rather than admit that we do not know what is happening, most of us have a tendency to speculate. When we share such speculations with others we engage in self-persuasion. In addition, research suggests that we have a tendency to believe that whatever is repeated is more likely to be true.[25] Furthermore, if those we talk to acknowledge that what we say might be correct, we grow even more convinced that our musings have some basis in fact. The more people who share an opinion with us, the more convinced we become that it must be accurate—an entirely vacuous reasoning process, known as "consensual validation."[26]

In particular, we tend to form generalizations based on our observations of other people's behavior, however short or limited such observations might have been. The extent to which we do this, and the wayward paths of misperception it leads us to, was well illustrated by a newspaper report on the appointment of General Boonthin Wrongakmit as assistant police director in Thailand some years ago. Speaking after his appointment, he said "I shall be introducing an all-round shoot-to-kill policy towards our criminals. As police chief of North-East Thailand for 37 years I always used this policy." Asked how he could be sure his men always shot the right people, the general replied: "You could tell by the look of them."[27]

By the same token, we have a well-documented tendency to judge behavior and situations by the expectations we have formed in advance: what psychologists term the "expectancy effect." For example, one study[28] required subjects to observe a videotape of a heated argument, which climaxed with one person pushing the other. If the "shover" was black, his behavior tended to be perceived by white observers as "violent." On the other hand, if the shover was white, his behavior was generally regarded as "playing around." In short, we see people and events not as they really are, but as our theories about them suggest they ought to be. When cults provide us with a theory of everything, it is little wonder that conflicting evidence from the real world is so readily set aside.

Our underlying desire in making such attributions is to establish causality, orderliness, and lawfulness in the world, and in so doing to reduce uncertainty. There is a need to believe that people and events are more predictable than they often are. We are helped to accomplish this if we assign people to categories, and then assume that mere membership of that category makes future behavior more explicable than it would otherwise be.

Conspiracy theories are a form of social categorization, in which the attribution process becomes a means of assigning predictable intentions and dispositions to large numbers of people. We no longer need to know precisely what particular individuals really think, believe, and intend to do. It is sufficient to know which category they belong to. In the process, all political life is conceptualized as nothing more than the orderly working out of whatever theory the cult's worldview has ordained as "the truth." Evidence is irrelevant.

Christian Identity and the Psychology of Prejudice

The word prejudice is derived from the Latin praejudicum, meaning a judgment formed in advance. Christian Identity's strength as a complex and self-contained belief system, liberated from normal standards of proof, evidence, and the laws of gravity, explains its appeal to those on the far right. The nature of this appeal can be better understood if we also look at some of the psychological dynamics that underlie prejudice formation, and that are at play in the Identity milieu.

One approach holds that prejudiced individuals share a common personality profile. This notion was memorably summed up in the title of an influential book published by Theo Adorno and a number of his colleagues in 1950, called *The Authoritarian Personality*.[29] This proposed that people who were strongly prejudiced against the members of one out-group (for example, Jews) were also likely to be prejudiced against most other out-groups as well. The numbers of people denounced by Identity theology are indeed legion, as we have seen, and would seem to exclude all but the tiniest proportion of the world's population. It was also suggested that those with an authoritarian personality would be rigid and ideologically conservative, would punish those who rejected conventional values, would be out of touch with their own feelings, and would have a generalized sense of hostility toward others.

In these terms, this is an accurate description of the belief system and attitudes displayed by most Identity supporters. Traits like these were assumed to represent a permanent disposition, and as such were thought to be impervious to education or other attempts at social engineering. This is a seductive explanation that seems to fit the facts with reassuring ease, and suffers from but one small defect: it is, in the main, not supported by the research evidence.

As one leading researcher has observed, "There is . . . no empirical evidence at all that people who are prejudiced are any more pathological than the general population, and also no evidence that particular pathologies subtend either prejudice as a 'generalized attitude' or specific prejudices."[30] Plainly, some of the Identity movement's most notorious enthusiasts, such as Timothy McVeigh, do hold generalized attitudes of hostility to others and have proved that they are indeed more pathological than most people. Few of us feel compelled to murder 190 people, in the service of a belief system. However, most Identity supporters have not yet emulated the militant militarism of Timothy McVeigh. Thus, researchers have generally found that those who score high on the measures of authoritarianism devised by Adorno and his colleagues tend to score within a normal range on a whole range of other personality attributes. It is hard to see how one aspect of someone's personality could depart so far from the norm, and leave the rest of it intact. An earthquake rarely limits its damage to only one street.

The notion of an authoritarian personality is comforting precisely because it implies that most of us can be grouped in one category—the normals. The bigots can then be sidelined in another—the fruitcakes. It will be noted that this is itself a process of social categorization, which involves a fair amount of stereotyping and is mostly geared toward satisfying our need to reduce uncertainty. Yet it was Hannah Arendt who coined the expression "the banality of evil," having witnessed the trial of top Nazi Adolf Eichmann in the 1960s. Eichmann's very normality defied easy analysis. Eichmann turned out to be just like the rest of us.

Milgram's obedience studies, reviewed in chapter 2, also reinforce this point. Many people might well be born with a disposition towards hatred and violence, but for the most part this will not go beyond an obsession with violent videos or other activities that, while distasteful, threaten no one. Prejudice is less a personality trait, and rather more the product of disposition, group dynamics, and the learning experiences that individuals accumulate in such social institutions as the family and school. To think of prejudice as a trait is to imply an unalterable destiny. It is to suggest that you can be born beautiful or ugly, tall or short, open-minded or prejudiced. On the other hand, if it is merely disposition, and one that moreover requires the presence of particular social triggers, it is possible that we can do something about it. An authoritarian personality, if such it be, is more likely a consequence rather than a cause of prejudice, bigotry, and a fascination with fascism.

On the other hand, it is also true to say that a unidirectional environmental impact has not been found either. A group of people can be placed in the same environment and each will behave differently. The heroism of Oscar Schindler was a striking demonstration of this process. Thus, some people will respond to adversity by looking for scapegoats, but others in identical circumstances will not. Whether we display a leaning toward prejudiced judgments, and hence feel drawn towards an Identity-type milieu, is the result of our disposition on the one hand, our social environment on the other, and the daily interaction between the two.

No one can know for certain why Timothy McVeigh was so drawn to Identity theology, and driven to give it such a brutal expression. However, whatever his natural inclinations, they might well have remained dormant in a different social environment. For example, he joined the U.S. military and saw service in the Gulf War. He often boasted of killing many Iraqis, and openly longed for the thrill of other killing fields. With this outlet denied him, McVeigh turned his rage and frustration on his fellow citizens. But even in this extreme case, it is possible to suggest that enough time in different social contexts might have drawn other sides of his character to the fore and repressed his tendency toward violence.

Robert Jay Lifton has coined the term the "Protean self," after the Greek sea god of many forms, Proteus, to describe the changes in self-concept that he believes have occurred in the twentieth century.[31] His perspective suggests one way of viewing the immutability of prejudice, and therefore of combating its effects. Lifton argues that humans are currently evolving a new sense of self, more contingent on circumstance and events than ever before. Principally, this is due to the unprecedented speed of change confronting the modern world, not all of it pleasant. Lifton chronicles the stories of many Vietnam War veterans who went to war psyched with gung-ho notions of patriotism, summed up in the films of John Wayne, and came back with their worldview and sense of self fundamentally changed. Just as our jobs and lives outside the home are bombarded with change, so how we view ourselves and the belief systems to which we adhere must also change. Hence the often strange spectacle of former communists in Eastern Europe embracing free market economics. Despite their struggles with the unfamiliar syntax of democracy, this still represents a fundamental shift in the attitudes of many millions of people and their leaders. Yet this transformation was so unthinkable up until the late 1980s that many commentators assumed communism had shaped a new collectivist personality trait on the part of the peoples of the Soviet Union.

Today, whole communities have been devastated by the fallout from globalization. The social ecosystem suffers from its own form of global warming. Those sweltering in the heat of injustice, real or imagined, hunger for explanations and solutions. When it comes to what impacts on the most important aspects of our private lives, the majority of us still believe that explanations of a causal nature must be at hand. Chaos theory might be acceptable for the natural world, but we find it oddly discomforting and unconvincing when it comes to human affairs. There has to be a reason for why things are as they are, and there must also be someone to blame. The disposition to reduce uncertainty interacts with a highly uncertain environment, and detonates the passions of prejudice in a cacophonous thunderstorm of fury and violence.

Earlier in this book, we suggested that the centrist stand favored by most major political parties often appears as a declaration of irrelevance. Given this, it is not surprising that many people are attracted to the slogans of Christian Identity, and have inched toward the open arms of the increasingly militarized far right. Behind every Timothy McVeigh stand a dozen dispossessed and shattered families, reluctant to abandon the mainstream but enraged to the point of feeling that they have nothing left to lose. Where has rationality led them? How many problems has it solved? What once appeared as madness can sometimes seem the only way left to escape from the gathering storm. But belief systems, and despair, are not immutable. This is the age of the protean self. We can recover from our mistakes, and even learn how to grow up. This offers hope that under certain circumstances, and with a revitalized political system, prejudices can be overcome.

Conclusion

Suffering is not ennobling and does not create a monopoly of virtue. The theology of Christian Identity is likely to evoke an opposite but equally powerful reaction from many of those it stigmatizes. A variety of attitude measurements taken in the past have shown that Jewish students who felt themselves the victims of prejudice were more rather than less likely to display anti-Negro sentiments. Catholic students who were surveyed and felt that they had been victimized ranked higher on tests of both anti-Semitism and anti-Negro prejudice than those who did not.[32] Those at the receiving end of prejudice themselves feel frustration, and in turn direct this against other minority groups. A spiral of social disintegration can be set in motion, in which a fragmented society turns in on itself, allowing all sorts of bizarre cults to seize this time as their time, and impose a separatist agenda on our society. In the heat of the night, white supremacist movements may yet find real phantoms stepping out of the shadows to greet them.

The example of Timothy McVeigh shows one end point, visible from the crossroads where we now stand. The loss of life in Oklahoma was devastating in its own right. It is also clear that McVeigh's arrest was largely accidental. The initial assumption of the media and most commentators was that the bombing was probably the work of Arab terrorists. Had McVeigh not been apprehended, his Identity-inspired actions could have seriously destabilized relations with the Middle East, and inflamed a wider racist mood within the United States. Identity theology has driven its adherents into the cultic firmament, by virtue of its emphasis on conspiracy as the driving force of history. Timothy McVeigh internalized this analysis, and took one logical course of action. Pat Robertson, David Duke, and others take another route, which is less immediately dangerous but which also seeks to detonate the existing political system.

It is a message that has a growing appeal for many people.

Chapter 4

Soldiers of God

*AMERICA'S RULERS—THEY ARE ALL RACIST
JEWS! THE RACIST JEWISH MAFIA CONTROL
AMERICA 100%! And will betray America in a
heart beat whenever it becomes either politically
expedient or will pay in huge money dividends for
the Jews are always for sale, as any study of the
Jews will prove.*
—Pastor James Wickstrom,
Leader of Posse Comitatus,
quoted in the Web site *Hatewatch*,
http:/www.hatewatch.org

All You Need Is Hate

Inspired by the theology of Christian Identity, and drawing strength from the problems rampant in society, hate groups have grown substantially in recent years. New technology has come to their aid. The Simon Wiesenthal Center estimated that, at the time of Oklahoma bombing in 1995, there was one hate site on the Internet. Within four years, this had risen to two thousand. Some of these hate sites were aimed at children under ten.[1] Nor are their activities confined to cyberspace. By the century's end, the Southern Poverty Law Center calculated the total of hate groups within the United States at five hundred thirty-seven, and growing. These groups claimed two hundred thousand members.[2] Rosemary Reuther, a professor of applied theology, estimates that there are about fifty thousand people who call themselves Identity Christians.[3]

What is certain is that the number of neo-Nazi and Ku Klux Klan (KKK) groups rose by 40 percent in one year, to three hundred fourteen.[4] Militia groups have also mushroomed, and are reckoned to be active in at least thirty-six states.⁵ Some crave publicity, making their activities relatively easy to track. Others prefer to toil in obscurity for their vision of the "promised land," to be achieved through an end-of-days confrontation with the U.S. government.

The dominant mood is one of paranoia. One report into militia activities summarized the prevalent belief system in these terms: "Some speak of government plans to shepherd dissidents into 43 concentration camps. . . . Some claim that the government plans to murder more than three-quarters of the American people . . . that Hong Kong policemen and Gurkha troops are training in the Montana wilderness in order to 'take guns away from Americans' on orders of the Clinton administration; that UN equipment is being transported on huge trains and that Russian and German trucks are being shipped to attack Americans. . . ."⁶

Such perspectives are indispensable to the nurturing of a cultic environment. The long list of enemies can only be defeated by intense effort on the part of the group members. Those who resist this truth are dupes of the conspiracy. As night follows day, more organization, more effort, and yet more certainty around the core belief system are sure to result. The leader grows ever more convinced of the group's ideas, feeds this certainty back to the members, and takes their assent as corroboration of the theory's correctness. How, it is reasoned, could so many people be wrong?

The ideology of right-wing cultism delights in the misfortunes of the many groups it imagines to be its enemies. Dave Holland, a leader of the Southern White Knights of the Ku Klux Klan, captures the mood perfectly, in this peroration on the AIDS pandemic: "'praise God for AIDS!' AIDS is wiping out the undesirables . . . it's taking out blacks by the thousands; before long it'll completely depopulate Africa. You know they're over there, they're living like savages . . . the government says they're equal to the white man. And I don't believe that, there's no way that could be possible."⁷

Consistent with Identity theology, it is denied that such proclamations in any way constitute "hate." The Reverend Fred Phelps is the founder of Westboro Baptist Church in Topeka, Kansas.⁸ His approach is typical of the genre. Phelps often pickets the funerals of gay people. Among the funerals so treated was that of Matthew Shepard. Shepard was a gay college student who was beaten and killed in 1998. Phelps and fifteen of his followers protested outside the funeral. Inevitably, Phelps has a Web site. It features a photograph of Matthew Shepard bobbing in the flames of hell. Phelps does not consider any of this distasteful. He says, "I simply feel an urgency and a necessity to preach the gospel to them. Nobody else is, and I hope they will listen to me and repent." It is, perhaps, another example of "compassionate conservatism."⁹

Such incitement is increasingly enacted in violence on the streets. Between 1991 and 1995 there were 4,046 pipe bomb incidents in the United States.[10] Members of Aryan Nations have been accused of murder, conducting armored car robberies and staging over twenty bank robberies, to finance a white supremacist revolution.[11] In an all too typical sign of the times, August 1999 saw a member of Aryan Nations, Buford Furrow Junior, charged with murdering a Philippines-born postman and attempting to murder three boys, a sixteen-year-old girl, and a sixty-eight-year-old woman in an attack on a North Valley, southern California, Jewish Community Center. The organization's leader, Richard Butler, distanced himself from Furrow, but also described the attack as "understandable," in the face of what he called a "war against the white race."[12]

The far right is subdivided into countless tiny sects. In this chapter, we discuss two of them in some detail—Posse Comitatus and Aryan Nations. They are among the best known, and are also representative of the milieu. The story of their relative progress over recent years does not begin in the smoke-filled rooms of a cult meeting. Rather, it takes us to Ruby Ridge, in the mountainous and almost empty terrain of Boundary County, Idaho. The events that occurred there in August 1992 have entered the folklore of the right, and are viewed as a defining moment in its history. To a right-wing cultist, Ruby Ridge is what Roswell, the area of New Mexico where a UFO reputedly crashed in the 1950s, is to believers in unidentified flying objects (UFOs). UFO cultists continually watch the skies. Their right-wing counterparts are fixated on rural Idaho and refer to it constantly in their literature, on their Web sites, and at public gatherings. The facts have been buried in a dense thicket of speculation, rage, and invention. Unraveling the reality illuminates the paranoid mind-set that lies at the core of cultic belief systems and organizations.

The Turning Point of Ruby Ridge[13]

Rural Idaho may seem to be an unlikely setting for an apocalyptic conflict between the races. Randy Weaver thought otherwise. He was a former Green Beret who moved to Idaho in the early 1980s, while he was in his mid-thirties. The location was not an accident. Increasing numbers of neo-Nazis and supremacists had hopes of turning the Pacific Northwest into an exclusively white area and making it the capital of a rejuvenated Aryan America. What about the other people who already lived there? A simple answer was to hand. Asian Americans were to be relocated to Hawaii, Mexicans to Alta California, blacks to Florida, Native Americans to Oklahoma, Jews to Long Island, and immigrants from southern Mediterranean areas to New York (minus Manhattan and Long Island).

Weaver was immersed in this culture and had a previous association with Aryan Nations. He built a ramshackle cabin, without electricity or running water, at Ruby Ridge. It was a perfect setting for survivalism. Weaver and his wife, Vicki, already had three children, and a fourth was born after they moved there. This setting, however, was far from tranquil. Like many white supremacists, Weaver disdained the notion that he ought to pay taxes, and consequently he owed back taxes on his property. Further trouble loomed. In 1990 he was indicted after attempting to sell two sawed-off shotguns to a Federal Bureau of Investigation (FBI) informant. He refused to turn up for his trial and instead took refuge in his remote and inaccessible shack. Despite knowing his whereabouts, the authorities seemed reluctant to do anything, until sections of the media began to wonder whether such tolerance would be extended to a black supremacist who flouted the law in a similar manner.

On August 21, 1992, U.S. Marshal William Degan and five fellow officers put Weaver's cabin under surveillance. Weaver and his fourteen-year-old son, Sam, emerged from the cabin and spotted the marshals. They unleashed their dogs and the panicked agents fled, eager to escape a confrontation. Then shots rang out. Precisely who fired first or with what intent has been the subject of controversy ever since. But there is no controversy over the fact that Degan was immediately killed. Three of the agents managed to escape, while two others were pinned down for several hours before they could be rescued and Degan's body recovered. He had been shot through the heart. A siege began, with over a hundred FBI agents, twenty-six Idaho national guardsmen, and scores of other law enforcement officers and U.S. marshals in attendance.

A long stalemate developed. As we have noted, the siege mentality of the far right can easily become a self-fulfilling prophecy. This had now happened at Ruby Ridge. Several days after the initial confrontation, the authorities discovered the body of Weaver's son Sam in a small outbuilding. He had evidently been shot in the firing when Degan was killed. This further outraged many locals. They argued that Weaver had been entrapped into the gun sale, for which he was indicted in 1990, and were far from concerned about his avoidance of property taxes. Why not leave him alone to lead his eccentric life in the vast mountain spaces where he was doing no one any harm? Sam Weaver had become a martyr to this argument and attracted a sympathy that was noticeably withheld from the law enforcement officer who had been killed. Protesters assembled with placards denouncing the state's intervention, and were soon reinforced by chanting members of Aryan Nations.

The white supremacist James "Bo" Gritz appeared and positioned himself as an intermediary between Weaver and the authorities. It emerged that

Weaver and a friend who had been with them, Kevin Harris, were both wounded, the latter seriously. Worse still, Weaver's wife was also dead, shot through the head. It seemed that, after Sam had been shot, Weaver had put his body in the outbuilding. The following day he went back to it. He and Harris were shot as they tried to open the door. They fled back to their main shack. Vicki was at the door, holding the couple's youngest baby in her arms. A shot hit her in the head, killing her instantly. The authorities at no stage alleged she was bearing firearms or threatening federal agents; but she was killed anyway. The far right had acquired another martyr—this time, a mother holding her baby.

By August 30, Harris, now dangerously ill, had surrendered. Weaver gave himself up the following day. At their trial it was established that Harris was the one who had killed Degan. He was charged with murder, conspiracy, and firearms violations. His defense argued that the state had used undue force and had failed to observe standard rules of engagement. Weaver, meanwhile, was convicted of minor charges, for which he received an eighteen-month sentence. Given that he had served a year, he was released immediately—as was Harris.

This mild outcome did not appease the right. Ruby Ridge became incontrovertible evidence that the state was intent on smashing white resistance to the Zionist conspiracy. A similarly distorted perspective attends to the far right's interpretation of the 1993 Waco standoff, in which more than eighty Branch Davidians perished after a long siege by the FBI. One long-time supremacist, Eustace Mullins, penned the following critique of what occurred: "The Waco Church Holocaust, in which many worshippers, including innocent children, were burned alive while worshiping in their church [was] an atrocity which surpasses the worst accusations made against the Nazis in Germany."[14]

The lack of perspective is typical, and alarming. In the world of the far right, the Holocaust is the "Holohoax," and never happened. On the other hand, the significance of any confrontation that they have with the state is immediately exaggerated. In particular, the cock-up theory of history, which accepts that many events are the products of accidents or incompetence, is invariably rejected in favor of conspiracy theories, the more outlandish the better. Undoubtedly, the authorities bungled the sieges at Ruby Ridge and Waco. However, their limited understanding of how to manage such situations does not constitute evidence of an assault on white rights inspired by the Zionist Occupied Government (ZOG). In the world of cultism, major overgeneralizations based on limited evidence are the norm.

Ruby Ridge had a profound impact. Within two months of the standoff, Christian Identity leader Pete Peters called a gathering of 150 far-right leaders from around the country.[15] Those assembled included Richard Butler, of

Aryan Nations, and many other stalwarts of the Identity movement. In a dramatic coalescing of the far right, it also included Larry Pratt, who in 1996 became for a time Pat Buchanan's right-hand man during his presidential campaign. The gathering accused the authorities of "genocide" against the Weaver family—an accusation that has been repeated often in the years since.

This meeting was significant, since it brought together so many disparate forces on the far right. It also sparked an enormous increase in militia activity and in the level of coordination of their activities. Moreover, the right finally had martyrs to the cause, and incontrovertible proof of a Satanic Jewish conspiracy against their beliefs. Who could now doubt that a final confrontation with ZOG was imminent?

Joel Dyer has argued persuasively that Ruby Ridge—and the despairing message of the far right—resonates so sharply because of the crisis afflicting rural lifestyles in America. Many small family farms have gone over the edge and into bankruptcy. Official figures show that nearly two-thirds of farm families in the United States were driven in the 1990s to seek off-farm incomes. A study in Oklahoma found that suicide had overtaken accidents as the leading cause of death, by a factor of five to one. Furthermore, the suicide rate of farmers was three times that of the general population.[16]

In a stable environment the hate-filled message of the right would attract only the deranged. Today, it is a cry of hope to people like Arthur Kirk, a Nebraska farmer who like many others ran into financial trouble in the late 1980s.[17] Gradually, he became embroiled in Posse Comitatus. When deputies served him papers from the bank he chased them with his guns and was eventually killed by a Special Weapons and Tactics (SWAT) team. Arthur Kirk, Gordon Kahl, and Randy Weaver are not alone. Mona Lee, a counselor working in the rural Midwest, summed it up well:

> As the local storefronts are being boarded up, as the rural institutions such as schools, hospitals, churches and banks are being closed, whole communities develop the same symptoms as a depressed individual. They become angry, withdrawn communities whose guilt gives them the need for someone to blame.[18]

The far right knows precisely whom to blame. For many such people, Ruby Ridge has become a beacon of resistance against a powerful Zionist conspiracy. They are increasingly convinced it is out to destroy their lives.

Posse Comitatus

Today's militias and white supremacist organizations trace their origins to the middle of the last century. The grandfather of them all is the Ku Klux Klan (KKK), formed in 1866 by a group of defeated Confederate soldiers from Tennessee. Within two years it had over half a million members.[19] The Klan's fortunes have ebbed and flowed ever since. It had between three and four million members in the 1920s but had shrunk to under ten thousand in the 1950s. The black civil rights movement of the 1960s rekindled hatred and suspicion, and the Klan was revitalized. By the decade's end it once again had about fifty thousand members. Its consistent message has been that hated and feared outsiders are attempting to destroy white rights.

The most recent precursor of the militia movement is Posse Comitatus, an armed right-wing group formed in Portland, Oregon, in 1969. Its title is derived from the Latin for "Power of the County." One of its publications declares:

> Our nation is now completely under the control of the International Invisible government of the World Jewry. Our United States Constitution, our Bill of Rights and our Christian Law has been trampled under the mire and filth of the International Money Barons of high finance who now control the government of these United States.[20]

Posse's leader is James Wickstrom—or, as he prefers to be known, Pastor James Wickstrom, minister of the Church of Christ Israel. Wickstrom's seminary was the road of hard sales—he is a former tool salesman from Munising, Michigan. Today he is renowned as one of the most aggressive anti-Semitic preachers in the Christian Identity movement. Wickstrom's "sermons" can be downloaded from his Web site. Their tone is fairly conveyed in the epigraph that opens this chapter. Wickstrom has also used it to argue that concentration camps are about to be opened throughout the United States, to be used to imprison the white race, and has defended the murder of doctors who perform abortions.

Posse believes that all power above county level is an illegitimate usurpation of the people's democratic rights. It has declared that anyone attempting to impose the authority of powers higher than the county is obstructing "the Common Law of this country and should be considered a domestic enemy of the United States—this includes IRS, FBI, CIA or other usurpers of common law. Such interference constitutes an act of war and is treason under authority of the Constitution itself." The threat of violence is clear. Gordon Kahl, whose fate we discussed in chapter 3, was among Posse's members.

The organization has sent death threats to U.S. senators and local officials, spread wild rumors of impending Soviet attacks during the 1980s, and distributed some of the crudest hate literature available. A typical article from one of its publications is headed "Scientists Say Negro Still in Ape Stage." Its appeal has been to the dispossessed and the fearful, and it has a clear message about who is to blame—blacks, Jews, and the U.S. government. The solution lies in resisting the power of federal government, and in separating whites from the minority groups perceived as threatening their rights. Holed up in its own retreats, utterly obsessed by the notion that one simple explanation holds the answer to all life's problems, and centered on the inspired leadership of Pastor Wickstrom, Posse Comitatus has all the makings of an archetypal cult.

However, Wickstrom is not content to vegetate on the margins. He has electoral ambitions.[21] In 1981 he ran for the U.S. Senate in Michigan and finished third among five candidates. Undaunted, he ran the following year for governor of Wisconsin, and received 0.2 percent of the total votes cast. The gap between aspiration and reality pushed him back into the power trip of underground organizing, where rejection by ungrateful electors is less likely to be a regular occurrence.

Such organizing brings confrontation. In 1983 Wickstrom was arrested when Posse formed an illegal compound of around thirty mobile homes. In the same year he was sentenced to eighteen months for impersonating a town clerk and municipal judge. When released on bail he fled and in 1984 was arrested in Tulsa, Oklahoma, for being a fugitive from justice. He was convicted on two charges of impersonating a public official and one of jumping bail. He served a total of thirteen and a half months.

In January 1990 Wickstrom fell foul of the law yet again. He was charged with the possession of $100,000 dollars in counterfeit money, conspiracy to counterfeit, and conspiracy to buy firearm silencers. He was sentenced to thirty-eight months in prison and three years probation for the counterfeiting charges. With so much held to be at stake, legality is clearly the least of Wickstrom's concerns.

His organization is on the far fringes of the survivalist right. Wickstrom has urged "ALL Christian Americans [to] purchase at least nine months of food for Everyone in the family, munitions, guns, and other supplies."[22] He preaches a message of hate that is extreme even by the normal standards of the genre. However, it would be foolish to dismiss the threat that he poses. First, in times of stress, organizations like Posse can suddenly acquire a large following. Death threats may become reality, as eager new members seek to graduate from the propaganda of the word to the propaganda of the deed.

Second, the overexcited milieu created by the survivalist right is likely to produce deranged loners, hyped to the point of hysteria by the prospect of white supremacy, and convinced that the time to act is now. There are already many instances of precisely such behavior.[23] In September 1994, a Missouri state trooper was shot and wounded by a man whom the Bureau of Alcohol, Tobacco, and Firearms (ATF) termed a "white supremacist with militia leanings." Later the same year, a Tennessee man gathered an arsenal in preparation for war with the government. When pulled over for drunk driving, he wounded two officers before he himself was shot and killed. In February 1995, a young Oregonian with militia connections shot State Police Trooper Lisa Boe and Explorer Manolo Herrera, who were inside a patrol car. Fortunately, they survived the incident. Posse Comitatus and other similar organizations might strive, for now, to avoid the worst excesses of illegality and therefore the prospect of suppression. Their problem is that the movement is populated with people who share the same mind-set as Timothy McVeigh. They are easier to recruit than they are to restrain.

Aryan Nations

Among the best known of the white supremacist movements is Aryan Nations. Richard Butler founded it in the mid-1970s, when he moved his Church of Jesus Christ Christian from California to northern Idaho.[24] Naturally, he also prefers to be known as a pastor. Butler imagined that Idaho would be the capital of a future all-white nation carved out of the United States. In his eighties and suffering from heart trouble but undaunted, he continues to energetically promote his message of hate.

As its title suggests, Aryan Nations is in many respects a fan club for Adolf Hitler—but one that seeks to turn his program into modern-day reality. Butler has opined that when Germany lost the war in 1945 "the white race lost the war."[25] It is his goal to ensure that such a shameful defeat never happens again.

Despite his age and his well-attested lack of charisma, Butler remains one of the most dangerous figures on the far right. Most observers agree that he played a pivotal role in the late 1970s and 1980s in bringing white supremacists from Nazi and Klan backgrounds together, and infusing them with a new spirit of militancy and cooperation. Perhaps inevitably, Butler is a keen believer in the philosophy of Christian Identity, and views it as an indispensable theoretical underpinning of the supremacy movement. In his world-view, the white race must conquer the Jewish communist enemy, or itself be destroyed.

The mood is best captured in the organization's "Oath of Allegiance," as follows:

> My brothers let us be His battle-ax and weapons of war. Let us go forth by ones and twos, by scores and by legions, and as true Aryan men with pure hearts and strong minds face the enemies of our faith and our race with courage and determination.
>
> We hereby invoke the blood covenant and declare that we are in a full state of war and will not lay down our weapons until we have driven the enemy into the sea and reclaimed the land which was promised to our fathers of old, and through our blood and His will, becomes the land of our children to be.[26]

From such premises, it follows that conflict with the state is inevitable. Aryan Nations is obsessed with the distresses caused by paying tax, a preoccupation common to the supremacist right. Its Web site asserts that taxes are used to control and destroy the future of the white race. Tax avoidance is encouraged: "Methods are not important, when you understand that all tax enforcement today is directly, or indirectly, supporting your destruction as a White Separatist. All tax avoidance, in any way, helps to bleed and weaken the Beast. Your sweat and hard-earned wages are the source of power that is used against you." It was precisely this message that first set Randy Weaver on his road to confrontation with the authorities.

The threat of violence is never far below the surface. Raphael Ezekiel attended an Aryan National Congress in northern Idaho and has produced a chilling account of the proceedings.[27] Here is one speaker and the response of his audience:

> "We must get rid of the Federal Reserve System and of the income tax. We must repudiate the national debt. We must tell the people at the top: *There will be treason trials! You will be strung from the trees!*"
>
> The room explodes in loud applause. Cries of "*Hail Victory!*" Cries of "*White Power!*"[27]

Such gatherings display all the colors of a cult in full bloom. By comparison, Republican conventions are a love fest for minorities. The congress observed by Ezekiel was held at a compound in Hayden Lake, away from any outside scrutiny or the possibility of corrective influence from anyone unimpressed by supremacist theology. A sign near the entrance read "Aryans Only," setting a tone of exclusivity from the beginning. All new arrivals had their credentials checked by guards posted at the entrance. The message was: This is a gathering only for the initiated, the trusted, the select few. Nazi music played throughout the weekend, broadcast from loudspeakers located in a convenient watchtower. There was no escape from the incessant message of hate. Nazi flags were prominently displayed, while all arrivals were quickly habituated to the frequent exchange of Nazi salutes. Meanwhile, an endless succession of speakers pounded away at the same message: The Jewish threat is moving toward conclusion; blacks are gaining power everywhere; the U.S. government is in the pay of the conspiracy. The refrain is relentless: "White Power! White Power! White Power!" For those present, the return trip to reality must be traumatic.

Aryan Nations members are also heavily armed. They oppose gun control with the same vehemence as they refute the state's right to levy taxes. Many live in fortified compounds, where they toil in preparation for Armageddon. Others still live in the wider society, but refuse to pay taxes and therefore incur confrontation with the state. Their ideology, rooted in fear, paranoia, and aggression, is tailored to capitalize on any mood of millennial madness that may seize the country. Aryan Nations is frequently much more disorganized and ineffectual than its impassioned leaders like to pretend. Nevertheless, it can provide enough incendiary material to ensure that some loose cannons are fired into action. In the modern age, terrorism requires few people, and even less intelligence, to have a destructive impact. Aryan Nations may seem too bizarre, and even too insane, to worry about.

This is not a conclusion that the (alleged) victims of Buford Furrow Junior would be likely to share.

Conclusion

Many are no longer content simply to voice their hatred of minority groups. In 1997, the FBI recorded 8,049 hate crimes.[28] This underestimates the reality, as the story of Billy Jack Gaither shows. Gaither was a gay man from Alabama who seemingly made advances to two male drinking acquaintances in February 1999. They lured him down an alley and beat him to death with an ax handle. His body was then dragged to a creek bank and set alight on a pyre of old tires. Yet Gaither's death is not registered as a hate crime. For that matter, the most recent reports compiled by the FBI record no such crimes anywhere in Alabama, Mississippi, or Arkansas.

There are many reasons for this strange reluctance. One clearly is that hatred thrives in high places. For example, state legislators in South Carolina, Alabama, and Mississippi have refused to consider removing the Confederate flag from official buildings.[29] The groups surveyed in this chapter certainly take such hate to extremes. However, they derive their strength in part from the fact that their message receives an encouraging nod from the mainstream. Many on the Republican right have openly dabbled in race propaganda. The implicit message to the supremacist movement is "You are not alone." Dr. Samuel Johnson, the noted eighteenth-century literary figure, once famously defined patriotism as the last refuge of a scoundrel. Today, for many in American public life, practicing the politics of hate has become the quickest way to establish one's patriotic credentials. If it is expressed with more subtlety than is found in the words of James Wickstrom and Richard Butler, it is at least recognizably bred from the same stable.

Supremacist organizations and cults thrive on a diet of Armageddon, of imminent "end times," of a final confrontation between the races. If they alone adhered to such a perspective, their influence would undoubtedly remain limited. However, apocalyptic visions of the future are widespread in American society. A recent survey found that 59 percent of American adults feared that the world would come to an end, while 12 percent of those surveyed believed it would happen within the next few years.[30] These figures represent a lot of people who, when they think of the future, tremble in fear. Each day, the propagandists of hate play with matches in a room packed with explosives.

The dangers we are discussing are not limited to the United States, or even the English-speaking world. Bjorn Soderberg was a trade union representative in a company in Stockholm, Sweden. In October 1999 he publicly denounced the election of a neo-Nazi as a trade union representative. A week later he was dead, shot in the head at point-blank range. Two days later, three youngsters known for their neo-Nazi sympathies were arrested and their firearms seized.[31] Throughout the world, it seems to be easier than ever to procure weapons, and to move toward turning the nightmare fantasies of the supremacist right into reality.

Not all supremacist organizations are cults. Some do not meet the criteria for cultic organizations that we describe in chapter 1. However, they do possess what we would describe as a cultic mind-set. In some cases, the forms of organization adopted on the far right lag slightly behind the mentality of their members. We believe that cults are best viewed as a continuum. At one end stand healthy, well-functioning groups, in which dissent is respected, people participate in decision making, and members at all times retain a foot in the real world. At the other end we find totalitarian enclaves in which conformity is prized above all else and people are frequently manipulated against their will for the greater good of the cult leader. Totalistic belief systems encourage such formations. People and organizations can move back and forth on this continuum, depending on events. Thus, organizations are not necessarily either cults or not cults. They can be both, at different times and in different places.

Identity theology is particularly prone to activate the process of cultic formation. David Neiwert has accurately described its belief system as "so far astray from those of mainstream Christianity—and so repellant to average Americans—that they induce in the religion's followers a cult-like closed mind-set: a sense of persecution coupled with self-righteousness."[32]

For those fired by the passions of prejudice, Posse Comitatus, Aryan Nations, and the other groups on the supremacist right offer a warm embrace, a welcoming smile, and the certainty of absolute conviction. Here, there will be no challenge to set convictions, but there will be plenty of simple answers to complex problems. Above all, at long last, there will be someone to blame.

In the eyes of many, it is a welcome refuge from the torrent of change now engulfing the outside world.

Chapter 5

The Travels of Lyndon LaRouche

Once we have begun the permanent colonization of
Mars on a sound basis, as we might approximately
forty years from now, the philosophical standpoint
. . . reflected here, would be hegemonic for humanity.
—Lyndon LaRouche

The Early Days

One morning in late March 1946 Don Morrill was chipping paint off one of the forward hatches of the *SS General Bradley*. It was the last troop ship but one to leave India for the United States. Three young soldiers approached him. One of the men introduced himself as Lyndon LaRouche, from Lynn, Massachusetts, Morrill's hometown. The four immediately fell into a political discussion. Morrill explained that he had been a supporter of Leon Trotsky prior to the war.

Morrill remembers LaRouche as a brilliant fellow who spoke French and German fluently. His parents, Morrill discovered, were prominent Quakers. He was an excellent chess player, taking on four tables simultaneously and winning. Morrill and LaRouche soon became close friends, spending their time talking politics. It was a heady time. Fascism had been defeated and millions around the globe had hopes of a new and better world emerging from the carnage of war. Morrill and LaRouche had witnessed the revolutionary turbulence of the peoples of the Indian subcontinent who were in the throes of casting off their imperial masters. They were not the only soldiers considering socialist ideas. By the time the boat reached the American shore, LaRouche was a Trotskyist.

Sometime in 1947 LaRouche joined the Lynn branch of the Socialist Workers Party (SWP), the main American Trotskyist group, taking on the party name Lyn Marcus. The branch was composed primarily of workers from the nearby General Electric plant. Morrill was an active union militant. LaRouche, however, displayed little interest in union affairs and divided his time with the nearby, larger Boston branch. By 1952 LaRouche had moved to New York City, where he found employment as a business consultant.[1] Morrill lost touch with him.

Little is known of LaRouche's activities between 1952 and 1961. This is probably because he preoccupied himself with his career, playing little role in the internal life of the SWP. By 1961 he was almost totally inactive in the party, was earning his living as an economic consultant for the shoe industry, and lived in a large apartment on Central Park West.[2]

LaRouche was very much of a loner in those days, already immersed in his own intellectual pursuits, isolated in a party with strong working-class pretensions, which had little use for intellectuals of any kind and none for him. LaRouche looked then about the same as he does now; he was slightly thinner in the face, but already his hairline was receding and he wore glasses. He was in his early forties.

Building the Fifth International

In the summer of 1965, LaRouche launched a political struggle inside the SWP against the leadership. He was supported only by Carol Larrabee (who also used the names Schnitzer and White), with whom he was then living. He had already developed many of the basic ideas that flowered in his prosperous days as an independent leftist—ideas that he has adapted to his rightist politics.

In this period LaRouche lived with Larrabee in a small apartment crammed with books and documents in the West Village. LaRouche struck those who met him as extremely brilliant and exuded self-confidence. He was convinced he could master any subject and had thoroughly studied Marx's *Capital*, Rosa Luxemburg's *The Accumulation of Capital*, and Hegel's *Logic*.

He drew an elitist view of the world from Lenin, particularly from his famous pamphlet *What Is to Be Done?* This he interpreted to mean that an intellectual layer, the "professional revolutionary," had the key role to play in the process of social transformation of society. The task of this revolutionary cadre was to gain hegemony over the intellectually backward masses.

He borrowed from Gramsci his view of "hegemony." [3] He saw this as a twofold process: a struggle of competing intellectuals on the left for dominance, while the left seeks working-class leadership by defeating the "bourgeoisie's" hegemony over the minds of workers. However, he did not accept Gramsci's more equalitarian notion that the working class would develop its own leaders, "organic intellectuals."

He was also influenced by Georg Lukács' concept of "class consciousness," particularly his emphasis on the active role of thought and therefore thinkers in the revolutionary process.[4] Of course, he saw himself as *the* revolutionary thinker with a critical role to play in the hegemonic struggle to lead the masses to power.

Another element of his thinking was a deep belief in conspiracy theories. He believed that Nelson Rockefeller and associated liberal, internationalist-oriented capitalists were conspiring to corrupt black revolutionaries through antipoverty programs, while saving capitalism internationally through various aid schemes.[5]

LaRouche left the SWP that year and joined a small Trotskyist group associated with Gerry Healy (see chapter 10), then called the American Committee for the Fourth International (ACFI).[6] This brought him into contact with Healy when he came to Canada to meet with his American supporters. Healy was not impressed. Gurus generally find other gurus intolerable.

LaRouche stayed with ACFI for only six months and then moved on to another minute Trotskyist group, the Spartacist League. Unable to win this group over to "LaRouchism," LaRouche and Larrabee left after a few months. He sent out a letter pompously announcing that all factions and sections of the Trotskyist Fourth International were dead and that he and Larrabee were going to build the Fifth International. In a way, this is what he has done.

LaRouche and SDS

The year was 1968 and the student strike at Columbia had been broken a few months earlier. There were around thirty students in the room, sitting on the floor. They surrounded a tall, stoop-shouldered man sporting a shaggy beard. It was Lyndon H. LaRouche Jr., and he was lecturing his followers, members of the National Caucus of Labor Committees (NCLC). At the time the group was an affiliate of the Students for a Democratic Society (SDS). LaRouche had gathered these students around him when he played a very active role in the recent student strike at Columbia.

The meeting started at three P.M. and went on for seven hours. It was difficult to tell where discussions of tactics left off and an educational presentation had begun. LaRouche encouraged the students and gave them esoteric assignments. One was assigned to search through the writings of George Sorel to discover the anarchistic origins of Mark Rudd, the future leader of the Weathermen. Another volunteered to study Rosa Luxemburg's *The Accumulation of Capital*. Since SDS was strong on spirit and action but rather bereft of theory, LaRouche definitely filled a void.[7]

We can see here the embryo of a social-political grouping which would, in time, evolve into a political cult. The group was based upon this single intellectual leader. LaRouche had become a kind of intellectual and political guru and was training these students as his disciples. Yet the rational still dominated his thinking and that of the group, its structure was informal and its discipline minimal, and it was not without influence among broader New Left intellectual strata.

LaRouche trained his disciples to view themselves as a gifted elite, the only people on earth who fully grasped the nature of the epoch and who had the program that could solve all of society's ills. "One must start with the recruitment and education of a revolutionary intelligentsia," LaRouche wrote in 1970. "By necessity, rather than choice, the source of such cadres is mainly a minority of young intellectuals, such as student radicals, rather than working class, black militant layers, etc., themselves." He expected these student recruits "to commit themselves to a total re-education and life of the most intensive study as well as activism."[8] These members were trained to view themselves as an elite and to have a very low opinion of the "swinish"[9] workers they had been self-appointed to lead.

Lyndon LaRouche developed a Marxist worldview in his early leftist NCLC days, which has stayed with him as he evolved into a rightist. LaRouche, basing himself on Marx, believed that the capitalist system needed to continuously expand in order to survive. Once capitalism reached its limits and could no longer grow, it would go into crisis and collapse. LaRouche also shared a modernist outlook with Marx. He believed progress in the form of the growth of the world's productive forces was the central purpose of human activity.

Marx viewed capitalism as a passing phase in societal evolution. Thus capitalist crisis created the conditions for working-class revolution, which in turn would produce a socialist society. Under socialism the productive forces, no longer constricted by capitalist relations, would continue to develop. LaRouche developed a series of proposals aimed at what he viewed as the contradictions of capitalism.

He called this approach the "Theory of Reindustrialization." Capitalism, he claimed, had entered a "third stage of imperialism" and desperately needed new opportunities for capital investment. The Vietnam War was being waged by the United States because it needed the country as a rice bowl to feed India. India, in turn, would be the next area of rapid capital accumulation. This led him to predict the imminent collapse of the system unless his advice was followed. Present leaders of capitalist nations stood as impediments to progress, while only LaRouche, and those who followed him, could prevent catastrophe.[10]

Operation Mop-Up

In the late 1960s and early 1970s, LaRoucheite writings and agitation were presented in an increasingly frenetic manner bolstered by predictions of economic doom. He sounded very much like Gerry Healy in this respect. (See chapter 10.) The fate of the world rested with his group and its great leader, Lyndon LaRouche Jr. The resources, both technological and human, were present for a glorious economic transformation. The problem lay with the stupidity of the nation's leaders and the swinishness of the masses. The obvious solution was to bring Lyndon LaRouche Jr., swiftly to power.

LaRouche, like most of the rest of the left, expected the 1970s to be a period of growing discontent in the United States, a continuation of the student movement of the 1960s, this time extended and reinforced by a labor radicalization. Instead a conservative mood engulfed student and worker, leaving pretty slim pickings for the remaining radical groups. Many groups—LaRouche's among them—turned inward, rejecting a world that rejected them.

It was in 1973 that LaRouche began a process that consolidated his followers into a cult while moving the group politically from the extreme left to the extreme right. By this time he had broken with SDS. The process began with "Operation Mop-Up," which raged from May to September 1973.[11] His supporters, armed with bats, chains, and martial arts weapons, launched physical attacks on members of the Socialist Workers Party and the Communist Party.[12] LaRouche announced to the world that he intended to remove these two parties as competitors.

Not content to attack these two organizations, he extended his efforts to the "New Communist" groupings, the Revolutionary Communist Party (RCP), October League (OL), and Progressive Labor Party (PLP). "If Rockefeller's Maoist Police dogs are still running loose a few weeks from now," his press declared, "you had better kiss your family goodbye. These gangs of rapists, strike breakers, terrorists and brainwashers—RU [Revolutionary Union], PLP, and OL—are the best thing that Rocky has going for himself in his mad push for fascist rule. . . ."[13]

The Labor Committee physically assaulted various groups sixty times between April and September 1973.[14] LaRouche had decided to gain hegemony through physical beatings. People on the left began to wonder about whether LaRouche could still be considered one of them.

Next came a series of actions about as bizarre as any undertaken by religious cults. In the summer of 1973, learning from the confrontational therapy of the New Age psychology cults, LaRouche began holding "ego-stripping" sessions.[15] (See discussions of this same process as used by the Workers Revolutionary Party [chapter 10], the Democratic Workers Party [chapter 9], and the New Alliance Party [chapter 7].) Anyone who failed in a political task was subjected to "pure psychological terror," as one victim, Christine Berl, later described the process.[16] Everyone in the group would start attacking the individual, delving into every aspect of their past and their personal life.

In this period LaRouche launched a campaign against the sexual impotence of his membership.

> The principal source of impotence, both male and female, is the mother. . . . [T]o the extent that my physical powers do not prevent me, I am now confident and capable of ending your political—and sexual—impotence; the two are interconnected aspects of the same problem. . . . I am going to make you organizers—by taking your bedroom away from you until you make the step to be effective organizers.[17]

The Manchurian Candidate

LaRouche became convinced that the Central Intelligence Agency (CIA) was determined to assassinate him. After all, LaRouche reasoned, he alone threatened the entrenched ruling powers in the world. It was therefore to be expected that the ruling elite would enlist the services of the CIA to remove him.

In 1972 Carol Larrabee left LaRouche and married a young British disciple, Christopher White. The couple settled in England and worked, rather unsuccessfully, at building the NCLC in that country. Berlet and Bellman believe that Larrabee's leaving is what so completely unhinged him, contributing to the frenzy of "Operation Mop-Up," as well as the insanity of his rantings about impotence and his extreme paranoia.[18]

LaRouche recalled the couple to the United States to attend a national conference in December 1973. White, realizing he was headed for an ego-stripping session and not being particularly mentally stable, broke down during the flight to America. As he left the plane, he started shouting that the CIA was planning to kill both Larrabee and LaRouche. Larrabee called LaRouche, and the deranged fellow was dragged off to a deprogramming session. White confessed to being a "Manchurian candidate" who had been tortured in a London basement by the CIA and British Intelligence. He claimed he was programmed to kill his wife and set LaRouche up for assassination by Cuban exile frogmen. The whole group was caught up in a frenzy, press releases were issued, and members were given training on how to detect other "Manchurian candidates" and how to withstand CIA torture.

One member, Alice Weitzman, could not swallow the CIA business. Her skepticism was sufficient proof to LaRouche that she must be a CIA agent.

He sent six members to her apartment, near Columbia University. She was held captive and forced to listen to Beethoven at high volume. LaRouche had a high regard for the composer (he was German, after all) and believed his music could deprogram "Manchurian candidates." Weitzman was able to toss a note out her window. A passerby picked it up and alerted the cops. She was rescued but refused to press charges against her captors.[19] The incident cannot help but bring to mind Irene Gorst's experience in Gerry Healy's Red House just two years later (see chapter 10).

The significance of the 1973–1974 period in the evolution of Lyndon LaRouche's NCLC is not to be underestimated. Only his most unquestioning and devoted followers could possibly have survived the madness of their leader. Those capable of independent judgment and thought were effectively weeded out. The remaining members traveled with LaRouche from the extreme left to the extreme right without even being aware of the political distance involved. The membership of the NCLC had been transformed into cultists.

Life in the LaRouche Cult

Linda Ray, a former member of the LaRouche group, described a group lifestyle that parallels closely the lifestyles of religious cults:

> Leaders exploited normal family tensions to separate LaRouche members from their parents, lovers and spouses. Two members of LaRouche's elite convinced me that my father was laundering money for the drug trade. . . . The LaRouche organization tried to control all aspects of my life. I was told which apartment to live in, when to buy a car, when to quit my job, what to read, what movies not to see, which music was o.k., how to ask my parents for $2,000 for dental work when I needed money to pay the rent, and when to split up with my boyfriend.[20]

From 1974 on, the group became increasingly right wing. It abandoned recruitment efforts on the left and substituted Moonie and Hare Krishna–style solicitation at airports and bus terminals. Remarkably, the political transition was so gradual that most members did not even notice what was happening. Linda Ray herself, a 1960s radical who joined in 1974, hung on until 1981. The red, white, and blue replaced the red. Members were told that "Hamilton's economic policies represented the same ideals of progress and industrialization in this country that Marx represented in Europe," while Plato and Dante replaced the Marxist reading list. In 1980 members were instructed to vote for Reagan.[21]

Members no longer had time to read, think, or even sleep. They were working twelve-hour shifts and living on stipends of $100 or $125 a week, which were not always paid. "It seemed that we were constantly in a state of mobilization, our bodies filled with adrenaline, ready for fight or flight." In 1981 some 300 to 600 people left the organization, including many, but not all, of the old leftists. Those that remained were committed cult members, completely under LaRouche's control.[22]

The New American Fascism

LaRouche's politics became extremely right wing though still populist. Consistent with his views on reindustrialization, he became a strong advocate of nuclear power as well as of Stars Wars technology. This permitted him to raise considerable funds from the industries devoted to those technologies. He became a bitter enemy of "entropists" such as environmentalists. Preaching imminent doom unless his policies were followed, he claimed that only he could save the nation.

Dennis King has documented in detail Lyndon LaRouche's fascist and neo-Nazi connections. "In the early and middle 1980s LaRouche utilized SDI [the Strategic Defense Initiative, also called Star Wars] and beam weapons to draw together the scattered forces of European and American neofascism to defend Nazi war criminals and promote revanchism."[23] Berlet and Bellman have shown LaRouche's connections with the Aryan Nations,[24] while McLemee documented his relations with the extreme right anti-Semitic and proto-fascist Liberty Lobby.[25]

He laced his program with a combination of anti-Semitism and conspiracy theories. For example, much of LaRouche's venom has been directed against the British. The Rothschilds, according to this view, ran Great Britain, creating "the Zionist-British organism."[26] He is a Holocaust denier, and the New York State Supreme Court ruled it is "fair comment" to call LaRouche an anti-Semite.[27] Rockefeller remained high up in LaRouche's enemies list, while special hatred was directed against Rockefeller associate Henry Kissinger (who is Jewish). LaRoucheites sought out Kissinger and hounded him. Richard Lobenthal of the Anti-Defamation League (ADL) characterized LaRouche's NCLC as the "closest thing to an American fascist party that we've got."[28]

The power of LaRouche's cultist hold on his followers is illustrated in the case of Ed and Nancy Spannaus, as well as Tony Papert, all three well-known young New Left activists in the 1960s, who have remained in the LaRouche group as his chief lieutenants. Just as impressive has been LaRouche's ability to hold on to his Jewish followers, including his former companion Carol Larrabee, despite his blatant anti-Semitism.

LaRouche operated through a series of interlocking front organizations. For example, he organized the Fusion Energy Foundation, which received support from people in and around the nuclear energy and aerospace industry. He put out a journal called *Executive Intelligence Review*, claiming to operate a private intelligence service directed against terrorists and drug cartels.

The federal government under Ronald Reagan was hoodwinked. Top officials of the National Security Council (NSC) and the Central Intelligence Agency met with LaRouche in 1982 and 1983. He even had White House access.[29]

LaRouche entered the Democratic Party primary in New Hampshire in 1980. Jonathan Prestage, a reporter for the Manchester *Union-Leader*, asked LaRouche about his organization's intelligence-gathering network. He was threatened by NCLC supporters. He wrote the article anyway. "Prestage said the day after the story ran, he awoke in his large old house in rural Barrington to find one of his cats dead on his back doorstep. In all, three cats were left dead on the doorstep over three days."[30]

He infiltrated the Democratic Party again in 1986, setting up the National Democratic Policy Committee. His people actually won the primary slots in Illinois for lieutenant governor and secretary of state forcing the party's candidate for governor, Adlai Stevenson III, to disassociate himself from them and contributing to the party's losing the election.[31] He has been a perennial candidate for president, using the United States Labor Party mantle. Other front groups include the Club of Life (which is antichoice on abortion), the Lafayette Foundation for the Arts and Sciences (which promotes LaRouche's cultural tastes), and the Schiller Institute (which publishes LaRouche's writings.) This method of operation closely parallels the methods used by New Alliance Party (chapter 7) and by Gino Perente's NATLFED (chapter 12).

In the 1980s LaRouche launched the Proposition 64 initiative in California, which would have established restrictive public health policies regarding acquired immune deficiency syndrome (AIDS). Proposition 64 was opposed by virtually all public health experts and public officials. It was rejected by a three to one margin by the voters. However, the measure did a lot of damage by causing a good deal of unnecessary fear among the population. In 1987 LaRouche wrote "that unless repeated mass screening and isolation of AIDS victims are undertaken, 'other ways of reducing the number of carriers will become increasingly popular.' Lynch-mobs, he says, 'might be seen by later generations' historians as the only political force which acted to save the human species from extinction. . . . [T]he only solution is either public health measures including isolation as necessary, or "accelerated deaths" of carriers.'"[32]

LaRouche quickly learned how to recruit the disoriented children of the wealthy and to separate them from their money. LaRouche's most famous recruit is Lewis duPont Smith, a duPont heir to an estate worth millions. He gave $212,000 to LaRouche and moved to rural Virginia to be near the master. However, his family went to court; had him declared mentally ill; and put him on a $5,000 a month stipend, protecting the rest of his $10 million fortune.[33] Other large donations included $2 million from Charles Zimmerman, a retired Bethlehem Steel executive, and more than $1 million from Elizabeth Rose, another retiree. The *Wall Street Journal* estimated in 1986 that LaRouche's various groups were spending about $25 to $30 million a year.[34]

LaRouche developed quite an empire, centered on a 172-acre estate in Leesburg, Virginia, which he purchased for $2 million. In 1986 between 250 and 500 people lived and worked at the complex, which included phone banks, offices, and a printing plant. The facility was guarded by armed men with walkie talkies twenty-four-hours a day.[35]

The LaRouche empire reached its high point in 1986. However, LaRouche's hunger for publicity brought him to the attention of the public and federal officials, while his phone bank operators, working to meet increasingly high quotas for funds, began making unauthorized withdrawals on credit card accounts.

> Outside the Boston federal courthouse, a photographer discreetly snaps pictures of certain persons entering the building. In the echoing halls, private security guards whisper into tiny two-way radios. Those entering the second-floor courtroom pass through the gleaming arch of an electronic metal detector. When the main defendant leaves the courtroom, husky bodyguards surround him as he is hustled into a car waiting in the basement parking garage.

So went opening day of the 1987 trial of LaRouche on credit card fraud and conspiracy to obstruct justice. While that proceeding ended in a mistrial, a later criminal trial in Virginia convicted him on charges of illegally soliciting unsecured loans, mail fraud, and tax code violations.[36]

LaRouche entered a Federal penitentiary in 1989. After being paroled in 1994, he returned to Leesburg.[37]

The Colonization of Mars

In order to occupy himself while in Federal prison for defrauding old ladies, LaRouche wrote a short book, *In Defense of Common Sense*. It is a rather strange book, typical of his current writings, that combines obscure geometric illustrations, a defense of Platonism, a eulogy to the seventeenth-century astronomer Johannes Kepler, and denunciations of Kant and most philosophers since Plato with an essential restatement of LaRouche's modernist, Marx-derived worldview. "Scientific and technological progress," LaRouche stated, "reflects a quality of the human individual which sets mankind apart from, and above all other living creatures." Our very nature leads to "potential population-density."

LaRouche was totally opposed to any kind of "entropic" view which might suggest a limit upon the constant expansion of human technology and population. He coined the word "negentropic" for his advocacy of continued industrial and population growth. However, what do we do with all the technology, pollution, and people? No problem! "Once we have begun the permanent colonization of Mars on a sound basis, as we might approximately forty years from now, the philosophical standpoint in statecraft, which has been reflected here, would be hegemonic for humanity."[38]

While their leader was thinking deep thoughts in prison, his minions were far from inactive. In addition to the usual phone bank solicitations and airport tabling, the NCLC took what looked on the surface like a lurch to the left. They joined with other antiwar demonstrators to oppose the Gulf War in 1990 and 1991. The NCLC was by no means a lone voice from the right among the left-wing demonstrators. Pat Buchanan, the Populist Party, the Liberty Lobby, and related ultra-rightists and neofascists also joined in. Ultra-nationalism and neo-isolationism brought elements of the right into a "united front" with elements of the left.[39]

An Offer to President Clinton

Lyndon LaRouche has made a career out of predicting the collapse of the global economic system. Understandably he felt vindicated by the world economic troubles which occurred during 1998. He, of course, has felt no need to explain to his followers how this system has survived, and in fact prospered, over the past forty years despite ignoring LaRouchian nostrums. He simply raised the volume on his rhetoric. "The world is now in a crisis which is best compared to a world war," he stated. We are threatened with a "New Dark Age" and "headed toward Hell."[40] "There is no economic catastrophe in all modern history," LaRouche wrote, "which compares with the global disaster which, unless prevented, will strike world-wide, within a period more likely countable in weeks, rather than months."[41] There is only one solution: "We appeal to you, President Clinton, to appoint Lyndon LaRouche immediately as economic advisor to your administration."[42]

LaRouche's reasoning is of interest. He has developed a theoretical framework for contemporary fascism. LaRouche drew from Marx his modernist identification of human progress with the growth in the productivity of labor through industrial development. This growth is seen as dependent on the development of the "machine tool design sector" of the economy.[41] He called his policy the "American system"[44] and claimed it was rooted in the views of Alexander Hamilton and the practice of Franklin Roosevelt. This approach, he claimed, was abandoned following the death of Jack Kennedy. Its last great accomplishment was the "German-American"[45] space program.

It was now time to abandon "crisis management," and "shilly-shallying"— in other words, democracy. LaRouche believed in "the inherent tendency of popular opinion toward mediocrity. The very tendency to rely upon collective (e.g., 'collegial') decisions, rather than decisions based upon validation of principle, is itself a well-spring of mediocrity."[46] He further explained, "To propose to assemble a virtual rabble of decision-makers, usually featuring those parties who are still advocates of the policies which have caused and advocated the crisis, is scarcely a noble enterprise, nor a fruitful one. Some relatively few, in the position to issue influential directives must pre-empt the situation."[47] Just in case there should be any question as to LaRouche's concept of governance, he declared China to be "probably one of the best governments in the world today, in terms of quality of leadership, the kind of leadership required to get through crisis."[48]

He proposed "directives" in the "Classical military sense." As LaRouche saw it: "Every sovereign nation has available to it, those inalienable emergency powers inhering in the right of any sovereign nation-state republic to continue to exist." Such powers were "acknowledged, and specified, with varying degrees of explicit reference" in the United States Declaration of Independence and in the Preamble to the Constitution. He opposed all forms of international organization because "there exists no higher political authority on this planet, than a perfectly sovereign nation-state republic."[49]

Once the leader of the nation-state—LaRouche addressed his appeal to President Clinton—assumed emergency powers, he was to impose a protectionist trade policy, to set prices, to introduce rationing if necessary, and to institute a large-scale government investment program aimed at strengthening the aforementioned machine tool design sector.

The parallel between LaRouche's thinking and that of the classic fascist model is striking. LaRouche, like Mussolini and Hitler before him, borrowed from Marx yet changed his theories fundamentally. Most important, Marx's internationalist outlook was abandoned in favor of a narrow nation-state perspective. Marx's goal of abolishing capitalism was replaced by the model of a totalitarian state that directs an economy where ownership of the means of production is still largely in private hands. The corporations and their owners remain in place but have to take their orders from LaRouche. Hitler called this schema "national socialism." LaRouche hopes the term "the American system" will be more acceptable. Berlet and Bellman believe "Lyndon LaRouche represents the most recent incarnation of the unique twentieth-century phenomenon of totalitarian fascism."[50]

All this may sound quite far-fetched, especially when President Clinton is viewed as the man to implement these proposals, with LaRouche's advice. Yet, in an uncanny way, LaRouche has constructed a theoretical basis for a contemporary fascism. At a time when many people see global corporations exporting jobs and undermining wages and social benefits, an autarchic economic program can have its appeal. Pat Buchanan's and Ross Perot's nationalist attacks on globalization sound very much like LaRouche's. His rejection of all international restraints on the nation-state connect up with similar views held by supporters of the militias and by related rightist extremists (see chapter 4). When politicians of both parties are held in such low repute, talk of assuming "emergency powers" could have an appeal in some quarters.

On August 18, 1999, Lyndon LaRouche filed papers with the Federal Election Commission asking for federal matching funds for the presidential election. He planned to run in the Democratic primaries against Al Gore and Bill Bradley. He claimed to have raised more than $1 million and to have some 7,000 volunteers. The latter figure was surely an exaggeration. The main theme of his campaign is to be—surprise!—the "advanced state of the global economic crisis." At the time of the filing LaRouche was living in Germany recovering from double bypass surgery.[51]

Conclusion: A Long Journey

It is quite possible that, given a different set of circumstances, LaRouche could have continued to lead the uneventful life on the fringe of radical politics that occupied him during the first two decades after he returned on a troop ship from India. What unhinged him?

Lyndon LaRouche in the 1960s was an egotist who showed signs of instability. Yet, for all that, he was an intelligent fellow who attracted serious intellectuals committed to the betterment of society. Some of his thinking was a little strange, but, on the whole, he was rational.

We view LaRouche as a grotesque product of the sixties ferment. The adulation of some of these students created the conditions for him to assemble a grouping around his ideas and personality. The collapse of student radicalism in the 1970s set the stage for his political evolution from left to right. His followers' loyalty encouraged him in his madness, reinforcing his psychotic view of the world and of his role within it.

We may never know with certainty what caused LaRouche's transformation from a committed leftist for two-and-half decades into a virtual fascist or how he rationalized it. Our guess is—and it is only a guess—that he felt a deep bitterness toward the left because of its lack of appreciation of his brilliance. Convinced he deserved to be worshipped, he had to find a new group of parishioners.

LaRouche's political evolution permits us to bring into focus those aspects of leftist ideology that lend themselves to rightist interpretation. *Catastrophism* is one such element. The extreme left and the extreme right share a common belief that the world economic and political system is on the verge of collapse. More significant is *elitism*. LaRouche was by no means alone in drawing from Lenin the concept of an intellectually elite professional cadre of revolutionaries, with an understanding of the world that is superior to that held by ordinary folk. This elite layer is destined for a special leadership mission in the revolutionary process. Inherent in this view is disdain for the majority of the population and therefore for the democratic process itself. The masses are to be manipulated and mobilized for their own good. LaRouche did not need to change anything in this outlook as he traveled from left to right.

Gathering an elite praetorian guard led to cultic practices that parallel the most extreme religious thought control groups. The LaRouche organization practiced ideological totalism, regimented its followers, had an authoritarian structure, and certainly believed that its members alone possessed the truth. LaRouche perfected methods for breaking the will of members, altering their sense of self. Paranoia clearly delineated the group's boundary with the outside world. Adherents were separated from their families, driven to work extreme hours with little sleep, and maintained on little money. LaRouche's core membership is rather small, perhaps no more than a thousand these days, yet he has been able to have influence far greater than this membership figure would suggest.

LaRouche's millennialist vision, which inspires his members to conduct feverish activity and binds them to him, has political roots quite distinct from religious cults. Even in its current fascist form, the group's beliefs have more in common with "Marxist-Leninism" than with the Bible. Yet the concept of a small cadre group that possesses the critical knowledge needed to save a world threatened with imminent collapse can drive political cult members as powerfully as a dream of a messiah descending from heaven.

Part Three

Therapy Cults and Politics

Chapter 6

Scientology, Maoism, and the Reevaluations of Harvey Jackins

*If desired a man can be completely changed . . . and
after such a change has been accomplished, he will
be suitable for any purpose.*
—Bertolt Brecht

Introduction

During the 1960s, the slogan "The personal is political" was embraced by millions of people. Interest soared in both personal development and political action. New psychotherapies emerged, catering to the lucrative mass market for happiness as well as social justice. In consequence, psychotherapy has become for some a secular religion. It offers an updated version of the myths that inspired earlier generations. Thus, we have original sin, perceived as the source of all adult discontent (usually, childhood trauma), the birth of a "savior" (the founder of the therapy concerned), the need to be "born again" (by internalizing the therapy's all-embracing belief system), and the promise of redemption (when all humanity puts the therapy's precepts into action).

Today, you can find counselors or psychotherapists listed in any phone book in almost any city in the world. In many countries, such as the United Kingdom, there are no formal registration or licensing requirements. Accordingly, you can now undertake past-life therapies, in which hypnosis promises to regress you to a previous existence, quite probably as an Indian Princess or an omnipotent Pharaoh. There are even "future-life therapies," in which you may be fast-forwarded to life stages you have not yet experienced.[1] A common theme in all of them is sweeping promises of total effectiveness.

Each therapy promotes itself as a breakthrough, superseding all previous theories of human psychology. Those who sign up are promised that the therapeutic tools employed will transform their lives, making them more effective in the world than they ever dreamed possible.

Charlatanism is rife. The proponents of all "innovative" therapies strongly resist experimental testing and external inspection, since these procedures would reveal that there is no evidence to support their claims. This freedom from scrutiny ensures that cult formations are rampant. Charismatic therapists can simply proclaim a theory, unsubstantiated by evidence; pronounce a belief in its effectiveness; and set up shop. Given the levels of misery in the world, there is no shortage of customers anxious to buy into each new brand of radiant optimism. They want to believe that the soul can be washed whiter than white.

In this chapter, we explore one supposedly innovative therapy that, like a number of others, combines promises of what it calls "individual reemergence" with a radical program of political action. Reevaluation counseling (RC; also often known as cocounseling) has been in existence since the early 1950s. Although information about its size and influence is a closely guarded secret, one writer estimates its number of supporters at around 10,000, mostly concentrated in the United States.[2] Given RC's propensity to expel dissidents, a trait it shares in common with all other cults, this calculation is probably overly generous. Throughout its history, the organization's inspiration and guru has been Harvey Jackins.

He promised techniques to cure all mental ailments, and even many physical ones (including, in his more expansive moments, the problem of mortality). He also linked his "insights" to the need for action to transform the external world, and encouraged his followers to take leadership roles in what he called "wide-world" liberation movements. In recent years, his organization has been beset by crisis, splits, and familiar accusations of sexual intrigue. It is a story in which the personal and the political truly meet.

Jackins, well into his eighties and in poor health, passed away on July 12, 1999. As in the case of the cult founded by Gino Perente (chapter 12), there is every sign that the cult will survive the death of its founder and leader.

The Murky Trail of Harvey Jackins

The life of Harvey Jackins, like the lives of other gurus, is shrouded in myth and secrecy. He was born Carl Harvey Jackins on June 28, 1916, in northern Idaho.[3] In the late 1930s he attended the University of Washington and studied mathematics, but, for reasons that are unknown, he did not graduate. During the 1940s he became a labor organizer and was also a member of the

Communist Party. At some point, he was expelled from the Communist Party, again for reasons that are unclear. However, the tendency to worship the alleged architects of socialism, a habit absorbed under the tutelage of Comrade Stalin, remained. For decades, Jackins was an ardent admirer of the "Great Helmsman," Mao Tse-Tung. His speeches and articles were peppered with admiring references to Mao's achievements, including the disastrous Cultural Revolution of the 1960s. In one of his publications, Jackins urges his followers to: "read Mao. . . . He cared much more effectively about humans than the other great leaders. Find *Selections from the Writings of Mao Tse-Tung.* . . . You will be deeply moved and informed by what's in it, and it will guide you in what else you want to read. He's someone you'll wish you had known; you feel this as you read it."[4]

In the aftermath of his adventures with the Communist Party, Jackins became embroiled with L. Ron Hubbard, the founder of Scientology. Again the details of the story are obscure. Jackins advanced a particular history of reevaluation counseling, in which Hubbard's image was completely erased. However, there is ample evidence that Jackins was indeed closely involved in the origins of Scientology, when Hubbard promoted what he then termed the "science of dianetics." A 1952 photograph captures the embryonic organization's governing body, the Hubbard Dianetic Foundation, in a group pose. It includes a smiling Harvey Jackins among its members. In a letter that has survived from the period, Jackins proclaimed that, having used dianetic techniques, "the results have been nearly uniform and positive. Apparently the auditor (listener or therapist) can be very forthright and direct in seeking out the past traumatic experiences which are continuing to mar the rationality and well being of the person. Once located, the exhaustion of the distress and re-evaluation of the experience apparently leads uniformly to dramatic improvement in ability, emotional tone and well-being."

Today, reevaluation counseling is administered from a converted church building in Seattle, which houses Personal Counselors, Inc. Personal Counselors was founded in 1952. Its articles of incorporation provide further evidence of the Scientology connection. These express its purpose as "to engage in, conduct and teach the art and science of dianetics." Subsequently, Jackins split from Hubbard, but neither ever spoke publicly about the reasons for their separation. We may speculate that it was a case of two gurus disliking one another. It may well be that, at this stage, Jackins simply wished to found his own empire, without the need to acknowledge the preeminent genius of anyone else. Whatever the precise motivation, the origins of reevaluation counseling can be traced back to the 1950s, and from this period on it has blazed an independent trail on the outer fringes of obscurity.

The "Tools of RC"

An alternative version of RC's origins was promoted by Harvey Jackins, clearly embarrassed by his link to Hubbard. In the folklore of cocounseling, it all began when Harvey was visited by a friend called Charlie, who was in great distress.[5] (In RC literature, and at RC events, Jackins is referred to simply as "Harvey.") Charlie had lost his job and had just split with his wife. He was in floods of tears. Reasoning that his crying could do no good and might even be harmful, Harvey told him to stop. But Charlie was too distressed to listen and kept on crying. Harvey eventually got him to keep quiet so that he could go to work, but Charlie resumed his crying when he got home. He kept this up for a week or two and then began to shake. Eventually, his shakes gave way to yawns. When these too ran their course, to Harvey's amazement, Charlie seemed perfectly normal, and went back to his wife, apparently "cured" of the miseries that had been ailing him.

Thus, Jackins concluded that much behavior we normally interpret as distress (e.g., crying, shaking, and making loud noises) are attempts by the human organism to rid itself of negative feelings, in a process he later termed discharge. However, our culture seeks to interrupt precisely such discharge: "Big boys don't cry." The goal of all therapy should be to listen attentively and to encourage discharge behaviors, despite the widely held assumption that they represent great pain and misery.[6] This charming story is marred only by the fact that not a word of it is true. Nevertheless, it is regarded as the foundation stone of all subsequent RC theory.

It is a characteristic of cult organizations that they make immodest claims for the scope of their theory. Jackins embarked on this particular course of embroidery as far back as the 1950s. In testimony before the House Un-American Activities Committee in 1954 he proclaimed, somewhat incoherently, "We have discovered, a human—any limitation on his ability, his enjoyment of life, his ability to be intelligent in any situation—is purely the result of the experiences of hurt which he has endured, including emotional distress."[7]

The implication is clear. What Jackins usually described as the "tools of RC" can lift any mental disturbance from people, thereby freeing them to take full command of whatever situation they find themselves in. It is an axiom of RC theory that we use only a limited part of the mental resources available to us, and will function much more effectively if we discharge and reevaluate our early experiences. How is this to be done?

RC's basic approach is to promote a form of egalitarian counseling between two people who exchange the role of counselor and client.[8] For this reason it is often known as cocounseling, and adherents use the two terms

"RC" and "cocounseling" interchangeably. The relationship between counselor and client is considered to be the key to success. The goal of the counselor is to facilitate discharge. This is accomplished by offering contradictions to whatever feeling of distress is held by the client.

It is assumed, *pace* Freud, that most adult trauma is rooted in early childhood experience. Adult experiences that remind us of these early traumas are, in RC jargon, restimulations.[9] These interfere with the natural zest and creative intelligence of the person. Negative feelings or recurrent dysfunctional behaviors, such as drug addiction, smoking, and wife beating, are described as patterns.

If a client feels worthless, the counselor may suggest that she repeat loudly, "I love myself." The contradiction between such affirmations and the underlying negative feeling (or pattern) theoretically brings on voluminous discharge, which eventually frees the client from distress. This is defined as reemergence. The holy grail of cocounseling is complete reemergence from all feelings of turmoil, from self-doubt, from sexist conditioning, and from participation in systems that oppress others.

Like other cult leaders, Jackins was at pains to insist on the novelty of what he offered. Such claims, as is also the norm, were much exaggerated. In foregrounding the counselor-client relationship he was echoing the mainstream ideas of Carl Rogers, founder of client-centered therapy. Thus, within RC, basic (and uncontentious) counseling skills such as listening and repeating back the essence of what the client has said are among the key behaviors employed by the person in the role of counselor. The notion of discharge can be traced back as far as Freud, although he later recanted some of the hopes he had invested in its transformative powers. Later schools of thought, in particular the "primal scream" movement, have reiterated their faith in its efficacy.

None of this prevented Jackins and his coleaders from claiming that their approach has a unique ability to transform the lives of all humanity. Many former RCers we spoke to in doing research for this book told us of RC leaders who habitually assured their classes that everyone present was a genius and was only prevented from realizing it by the distresses imposed by a dysfunctional, classist, racist, and sexist society. This is a very alluring message. Few of us are immune to flattery or bribes. It is consoling to imagine that one might be an unheralded genius in the mold of Darwin, Einstein, or Leonardo. It will take only one more heave to break through to the sunny uplands of public acclaim.

On another level, the notion that an untapped well of genius lies within encourages people to believe that, whatever the paltry results obtained so far, unimaginable gains lie in wait, if they will only persist with the therapy a little longer. They may be in a hole, but are urged to dig deeper. Many Scientology survivors have encountered similar arguments. Higher levels of what Scientologists call "auditing" are always available. Those discouraged with their experiences at one level are urged to pay more money by trying the next level up. RC takes a similar tack. Given its origins in dianetics, this is scarcely surprising. When participants complain that they still feel poorly, they are told that they need to undertake further classes. Thus, in the guise of preaching empowerment, RC discourages people from trusting their own perceptions of the social world and the therapeutic environment around them.

Thus during a cocounseling session, a client might report that his wife has just abandoned him, causing distress. After discharge on this immediate issue, the counselor is likely to insist that the real source of his pain must be something else, of which he may be unaware on a conscious level. Accordingly, he will be asked repeatedly: "What is the restimulation?" and "When was the first time you had this feeling?" Since, after a certain age, we rarely encounter miseries that we have not previously experienced in some form, most feelings call up echoes of similar moods in childhood. This tends to mean that, whatever the initial presenting problem (perhaps sexual dysfunction, unemployment, or racial discrimination in the workplace), clients are encouraged to focus obsessively on early childhood memories. More and more time is spent weeping over memories, real or confabulated, of child-parent interaction.

In this case, the client will be pressed to identify points of similarity, perhaps between his relationship with his wife and his mother, for example. If he resists he will be told, somewhat caustically, that he is "refusing to take a direction." He will then be urged to elaborate on his recollections of such episodes, in a process that clearly has the potential to uncover highly detailed but inaccurate "false memories."[10] Like the leaders of many therapies that engage in such practices, RC leaders seem largely unaware of this potential for damage.

The Turn to Politics

From the mid-1950s on, Jackins devoted himself to building the RC organization throughout the United States, and then internationally. His own press (Rational Island Publishers) has produced a ceaseless flow of books containing the collected sayings, poems, attempted witticisms, workshop demonstrations, and speeches of Harvey Jackins.

Much later, the theory was extended to encompass a vast range of political issues, and to create a movement with an overtly political agenda. The origins of this shift were pragmatic. Initially, Jackins argued that his therapy would remove all feelings of distress and improve people's overall functioning. When this failed to happen, he offered the hypothesis that, however much people discharged their primary hurts, new ones were added daily by a fundamentally racist, classist, and sexist society. Social and political problems must also be faced, to achieve reemergence.

This became known as "liberation theory." Over time, it has been refined into a primary focus on the iniquities of capitalism. In a now-familiar process of intellectual grave robbing, this shift was clearly rooted in Marxism. Jackins elected, in the late 1980s and 1990s, to make this connection much more explicit, on at least one occasion reportedly claiming the Communist Manifesto, published by Marx and Engels in the 1840s, as a founding document of the cocounseling movement.

Thus, RC practice has steadily evolved since the early 1970s. In addition to anguished soul searching for "early memories," RC members have been hectored into engaging in "liberation work" on an increasing variety of issues. Such activity has taken two main forms. In the main, it has meant the creation of innumerable RC support groups—for example, groups that offer support on being either male or female, on the nature of early sexual memories, on being raised Catholic, on working in industry, and even on the pain of working as a lawyer. These have involved intensive counseling sessions, which again tend to focus on the earliest memories people can summon up of their membership in the designated group. Much counseling of this sort has occurred in groups—a pernicious aspect of RC practice to which we will return later in this chapter.

Second, people have been encouraged to "naturalize" RC, by adapting the organization's basic theory into a full-fledged liberation program for every category of people they can think of. The ambitions of the organization have been extended in all possible, and many impossible, directions. Those RC members who see themselves as belonging to multiple designated categories, as most people would, come under pressure to participate in a bewildering number of liberation "support" groups. In these, they can uncover an ever-greater range of issues about which to feel anxious.

As RC evolved into an openly political movement, scandal began to trail its activities, usually centering on the personality of Harvey Jackins himself. In particular, more and more female members alleged, with increasing insistence, that he was using the counseling rationale of the organization as a means to seduce scores of vulnerable young women. All such developments are rooted in the most basic theories of RC. We believe that these were always bound to lead in the direction of cultic organization. A more detailed examination of the difficulties with these theories will unveil the full extent of their impact on the day-to-day practice of RC and the degree to which they have placed greater and greater power in the hands of Harvey Jackins.[11]

Key Problems of RC Theory

(1) *Restimulation:* The theory of restimulation contains many ingredients of individual and group manipulation. Cults and destructive groups in general attempt to shape the consciousness of members by reframing their most personal experiences in cult jargon and ideology. Many cults compel members to recall the past so that it can be reinterpreted in the light of the group's totalistic ideology, thereby escalating members' emotional commitment to the group.[12] Racist political cults, for example, encourage members to recall past experiences with members of minority groups, in such a way that the underlying ideology of the group is affirmed. Positive behaviors by such people will be discounted; instances of "bad" behavior will be exaggerated and retold many times. The process of selective recall and interpretation eliminates the autonomous self, and is a particular danger in the context of psychotherapy.

There is, for example, some testimony from former RCers to the effect that ideas or experiences that do not fit neatly into RC's theoretical framework are dismissed as "restimulations" of past trauma, rather than addressed in their here-and-now validity. Such is the fate of those who raise criticisms of Harvey Jackins. They will be told that they are "dramatizing their distress." This inflicts a body blow on independent thought: clients' perception of reality is invalidated, their right to express their own ideas is rebutted, and their attention is directed inward to old traumas rather than toward current observation and analysis.

It may be necessary for people to pay some attention to past experiences that influence feelings of distress—for example, the reality of sexual abuse in early childhood. However, it is also possible that therapies that seek to frame all current experience within a simple causal nexus of past to present influence will miss opportunities for "Present Time" change, while disabling people's ability to challenge therapeutic theory or practice.

(2) *Discharge:* The central role allocated to discharge is precisely one of the features of RC that makes it most vulnerable to allegations of abuse and manipulation. Artificially engineered peak experiences have long been known to induce extreme conformity. In the case of RC, the supremacy of emotion over thought means that the discharge process is exalted as the most important part of the counseling experience.

A great deal of the discharge involved in RC occurs in groups conducted by various leaders. It is quite evident to all involved that powerful displays of emotion, along the lines pioneered by the much mythologized Charlie, are what is required. The client who performs as expected is rewarded with loud applause and general enthusiasm. This increases the possibility that such behaviors will be repeated in the future, and will be emulated by the next in line for counseling. It is not unusual to see people, at RC events, begin to sob and shake as they approach the front of the room, even before their counselor has said a word.

Research suggests that when people engage in embarrassing behaviors in front of a group they are inclined to exaggerate the benefits gained from group membership.[13] Given what they have been through, they are in urgent need of some justification for their behavior. Who wants to admit having just made a prize fool of oneself? Counseling individuals in front of large crowds at workshops, while encouraging the strong display (or dramatization) of extreme emotion, unleashes precisely this dynamic within RC.

(3) *Liberation theory and catastrophism:* RC stresses the necessity of widespread social change. It is evolving into a movement whose primary purpose is social and political transformation rather than individual recovery from emotional distress. These broader social issues are often raised with great urgency. For example, Jackins has asserted that "The survival of the human race is now crucially dependent on the transformation of the present society to a rational one, world-wide."[14]

Failing this, nuclear holocaust and incalculable horror is in prospect. Furthermore, it follows that the rapid growth of RC, or at least the spread of its influence in important "wide-world" organizations, is necessary to prevent catastrophe. This doom-laden analysis, with the implication that the current small group of RC activists bear an inordinate responsibility for saving the planet in the immediate future, is characteristic of all cult organizations. It is a primary lever for extracting maximum commitment, alongside a minimum critique of the group's analysis, from the members. Time is too short for anything but frantic activity, in the form of recruiting more people. Membership in the group is a privileged opportunity to save the world. Those who criticize the organization's leaders or challenge its ideas can be dismissed all the more readily as despicable traitors whose nefarious activities are endangering the survival of the planet.

(4) *RC and homophobia:* Bizarrely, for an organization committed to what it describes as liberation, one of the dominant strains in RC thinking over recent years has been rampant homophobia. It is yet another characteristic of cult organizations that all its core ideas must be seen to originate with the inspired founder of the group. Jackins was also entitled to the credit for "discharging" the contagion of homophobia into the RC organization. He wrote as follows in 1974: "We conclude that homosexuality (as distinct from the desire to touch or be close) is the result of distress patterns (often very early

in origin and chronic) and will disappear by the free choice of the individual with sufficient discharge and re-evaluation."[15]

This article goes on to claim that clients who have used RC enough "find their attitudes and actions changing from compulsive homosexuality towards relaxed heterosexuality (not toward compulsive or distressed heterosexuality)." He repeated this position frequently during the intervening years, including in the pages of his last book.[16]

Gay RCers have been encouraged to undertake much counseling in this area, to free themselves from what Jackins saw as their "patterned" addiction to homosexual behavior. As with so many other issues, no evidence was ever presented to support Jackins's views. His conclusions rested solely on the observations he elected to make during counseling sessions with gay and straight clients. In reality, RC theory here provides cover for antigay prejudice and ensured that gay people come under systematic pressure to either imitate heterosexual behaviors or adopt a life of celibacy. A former RC activist, interviewed by one of our students, recalled, "I have watched various people in workshops saying that they always knew that homosexuality was a distress. A lesbian I know actually said that she was trying not to have sex anymore."

In 1990 Jackins took this position a step further. He began to argue that people suffering from AIDS should be quarantined. Despite opposition from within the normally docile ranks of RC, he repeatedly returned to the theme, evincing a peculiar obsession with homosexual activity.

The Seductive Dance of Recruitment

Typically, people encounter RC through personal contact with other participants. In general, the organization is averse to publicity, and steers clear of the media. Would-be recruits are invited to join what is called a "fundamentals class." At this stage the attraction is clear: low-cost help for people in distress, alongside the opportunity to learn some simple communication skills of wider social use. The introductory fundamentals class will meet once a week for tuition in cocounseling techniques, demonstrations of counseling in front of the group by a teacher accredited by the RC organization and will coordinate informal cocounseling sessions between class members from week to week. By its nature, much of this activity is harmless or even downright helpful. People certainly benefit when they are listened to respectfully. A great deal of such activity occurs in RC classes, and at this level provides a considerable amount of support.

However, during and after fundamentals classes, participants will be invited to local, national, and international workshops. They will also be urged to attend ongoing classes, or "support groups" organized around themes such as resistance to women's oppression, religious and age discrimination, and difficulties experienced in a variety of work occupations.

Its recruitment methods are, in essence, similar to those described by other researchers[17] as being typical of cults. An immediate benefit to joining is offered. However, the original commitment is rapidly escalated. Furthermore, if members point out that the promised benefit is yet to materialize, they are told that they need to increase their involvement in the group—in this instance, by attending ever more workshops, of the regional, national, and international varieties. If this fails to produce reemergence, the answer is simply that the recruit needs to engage in more liberation work, on a wider range of primary oppressions. And so it goes on, until the person is investing virtually all of his or her time and money in the process. At this point, for the most dedicated activist, such a powerful commitment has been made that reevaluating the initial decision has become unthinkable.

In addition, the overall method of organization found in RC is strongly influenced by the principles of democratic centralism, which are derived from the example of Lenin's Bolsheviks and which we encounter in many forms throughout this book. In each locality groups of cocounselors meet more or less regularly as an organized "community," headed up by an appointed Area Reference Person (ARP). Groups of such districts are formed into regions, under the direction of an appointed Regional Reference Person (RRP). Every four years there is an international conference, and between conferences total authority to dissolve regions or areas, and to accredit or remove accreditation from teachers, is vested in the International Reference Person (IRP). Unsurprisingly, this post was held by Harvey Jackins, who, in line with the feudal principle of monarchical succession, nominated his son Tim Jackins as his deputy and heir apparent.

The point of entree into the RC hierarchy is to become certified as an RC teacher. Such certification is awarded by the ARP. Ultimately, ARPs were directly and indirectly accountable to Jackins, and, after his death, to his son. In theory, he was answerable to the regular World Conferences. However, such conferences consist entirely of the various reference persons whom he himself appointed. Meanwhile, between conferences,

> Jackins has the power to appoint and remove all Reference Persons and other leaders; he can bar people from RC events or expel them altogether; he can create and dissolve whole areas and regions. Through Rational Island, he controls the many RC publications . . . there are no independent checks on Jackins' power."[18]

This reinforced its artificial sense of distinctiveness and strengthened the spiritual authority of Jackins over a vast range of issues. The implications of this mentality for what we would term the manufacturing of consent are discussed below.

Manufacturing Consent

RC placed enormous emphasis on the founder and leader, who was given total authority over the organization. All the major RC publications and books were written by Jackins. He was a regular contributor to *Present Time*, particularly of articles billed as articulating landmark developments in RC theory. These were usually followed up in subsequent issues with enthusiastic testimonials from members, asserting that this new theory had been tried by them with outstanding results. The theory, if such it be, was seldom developed in such contributions: rather, they served the role of emphasizing Harvey Jackins's tremendous level of insight into the human condition.

Criticisms of RC theory do not appear in *Present Time*, nor in any other RC publication. The opportunity for renewal through democratic debate is sacrificed in the interests of conformity.

The superiority of RC over all other therapies is also an axiom of the organization. Its ideas are held to be unique, and indispensable for the salvation of humanity. Thus, Jackins claimed that "Re-evaluation counseling can be confidently viewed as the very leading edge of the tendency toward order and meaning in the universe."[19]

For this to be taken seriously, RC would have to extend its application to virtually all areas of human activity, in a vainglorious display of intellectual imperialism. Such attempts have frequently been made by followers of Marx, Darwin, and Freud. Jackins clearly sought to join such illustrious company. The following examples illustrate how this works, and show the dangers it poses.

One of Jackins's obsessions was what he derided as the mental health system. Ignoring the vast amount of research showing that, for many mental conditions, such as depression,[20] drug therapy is highly effective, he wrote in 1990, "it is very misleading to treat any mental dysfunction as a medical condition."

The solution, of course, is cocounseling. Like his mentor Hubbard, Jackins evinced a powerful hatred of psychiatric medication, and encouraged his followers to disregard it. Writing in the mid-1970s, he approached senile dementia in a similar spirit: "'Senility,' except in the rare instances where it has a basis in the physical deterioration of the brain from disease, is simply the piling up of distress patterns to a 'topple-over' or chronic point. Senility can be recovered from by discharge and re-evaluation just as any other distress."[21]

Attempts have been made to extend this mode of analysis beyond purely mental issues, and into areas where physicians are in almost unanimous agreement that physiological causation is totally involved. Thus, Jackins wrote, "if we had more counseling resource, I think epileptic seizures would turn out to be simply terror recordings. Several people that I've worked with have gotten over them."[22]

In consequence, what we are increasingly minded to term "survivors of RC" have reported that RC members are often encouraged to stop taking their drugs. One workshop participant has spoken of being persuaded to disregard her asthma medication for a weekend, and to counsel her way through the ensuing asthma attacks instead. There is a strong tradition of cult organizations urging their followers to abandon medication, in favor of whatever panacea the leader currently promotes. In this way, the authority of the leader intrudes ever more deeply into the lives of his followers, producing a debilitating dependence. As a result, many people have died of neglect or suffered permanent physical damage. So far, to our knowledge, RC has produced no such fatalities. However, its overly ambitious attempt to promote the primacy of counseling when basic medical needs are at stake suggests that it is, potentially, a dangerous activity in which to engage. Worse may await us, before the full extent of its activities unravels.

The most bizarre area where this approach has been revealed was in Jackins's approach to death. He argued that a great many of the ailments we associate with the aging process are simply the accumulation of distress patterns and are therefore amenable to counseling. Thus, with sufficient counseling, "perhaps a 'natural' time of death would be in the 130s or 140s."[23] He did not suggest that this by itself would render his followers immortal, but he argued that, as humanity acquires sufficient rationality, techniques will be found to postpone death indefinitely.[24] In the meantime, those of his followers who apply his ideas with sufficient precision should enjoy a vastly prolonged life span. Like other gurus who boast techniques capable of extending the human life span, Jackins's own demise somewhat undermined the argument.

It is also clear that the "unconditional positive regard" at the core of much humanistic counseling can be manipulated by unscrupulous organizations into a form of "love bombing." RC is particularly vulnerable to such a critique, since many participants testify to overwhelming displays of closeness between people who barely know each other at RC events. Total strangers are encouraged, on meeting for the first time, to embrace each other in full-length body hugs. During RC meetings, people often sit holding hands with individuals they have never met before. They are expected to exchange "appreciations"—that is, to identify what they like or love in others however little they really know them. These practices are posited as a "contradiction" to inherent distress, capable of unleashing "discharge."

Such behaviors toward people when they are already highly vulnerable manipulates them into signing up for the entire RC ideology and experience, regardless of its real capacity to effect positive change in their lives. By encouraging people to engage in forms of touch that would ordinarily be expected at a much deeper stage of relationship development, RC undermines the capacity of participants to assess the real levels of intimacy in their relationships within and without RC, thereby rendering them more vulnerable to manipulation.

Quite clearly, there is also the potential for RC to monopolize the time of its participants—one of the dominant traits found in a variety of psychotherapy cults.[25] An article in *Present Time*[26] outlines a level of activity that the organization's leaders plainly feel is necessary to achieve reemergence. This includes attendance at a weekly class, at least one- and maybe two-hour cocounseling sessions per week (filled with discharge), at least four weekend workshops per year, participation in support groups, regular reading of RC literature, and the shouldering of some organizational responsibility for running the RC organization. It is assumed that these activities will form a long-term commitment. If taken seriously, this is a recipe for therapy as obsession. It assumes that people are living to counsel, rather than counseling to live.

RC's intense insistence on its uniqueness inflames these problems still further. We have already traced links between underlying RC theory and Marxism, client-centered counseling, Freudian psychoanalysis, and primal therapy. By reformulating well-established ideas without acknowledging their origins, the organization seeks to exaggerate its sense of uniqueness, the depth of its insight, and the closeness of its members. For example, the excessive use of a common jargon ("patterns," "restimulation," "discharge," "wide world," "liberation theory") might jar outsiders, but inside the group it has the effect of convincing its members that they are much more alike and have more in common than is actually the case. The result is the manufacturing of consent around a spurious ideology, and the internalization of a stultifying conformity.

RC, Sex, and Learning to Love Father

One survey of mainstream psychotherapists[27] found that 10.9 percent of respondents admitted to having sexual relationships with clients. Other surveys have estimated that, in the United States and Australia, 25 percent of male therapists have had sex with their patients.[28] So great is the problem that, in parts of the United States, workshops on the topic "How to Avoid Sleeping with Your Patients" have been organized for trainee psychologists.

The question arises as to whether boundaries, evidently difficult to maintain under optimal professional conditions, are even more porous within RC, which places so much stress on closeness between participants. In principle, the organization has attempted to address this question. There are strict rules in its guidelines against even normal socializing between members, in order to preserve the primary integrity of the counseling relationship. These also prohibit the development of sexual relationships between cocounselors, and are considered sufficiently important to warrant a three-page explanation in the *Fundamentals of Co-Counseling Manual*,[29] issued to all new participants. However, many participants in RC regard themselves as the victims of sexual abuse.

In particular, scores of former female RC activists have now alleged that Harvey Jackins seduced them, in the pretense of offering counseling assistance. During the late 1980s two former RC members, Holly Hurwitz and Steve Dickens, conducted extensive interviews with many such women.[30] The unsavory picture that emerges is in line with what we have found in a wide variety of cult organizations.

It appears that Jackins for decades urged vulnerable women to have sexual relations with him, on the basis that it would help them resolve issues about their relationships with men in general and their fathers in particular. The overall climate of veneration of Harvey, inculcated in RC, made this piece of spurious nonsense quite believable to many. In the heightened emotional atmosphere created by a cult's group dynamics, there are few things that cannot be made to seem plausible for some people at least some of the time.

Given Jackins's preeminent position, his seductions caused intense distress. Each woman imagined that she had a unique and particularly close relationship with him. When the truth emerged, she was generally devastated. A considerable number of these women also alleged that a high proportion of the most prominent female leaders in RC developed a rota arrangement, whereby they took turns sleeping with Jackins.

One of the most important female leaders in RC, Nancy Kline, made a major contribution to the development of its liberation policy for women. She was expelled in 1988 for raising the issues discussed here and demanding that Jackins cease his multiple relationships with female clients. An analogy to the Workers Revolutionary Party (WRP) in Britain, discussed in chapter 10, springs irresistibly to mind. It appears that Jackins, like Gerry Healy, transformed a supposed "helping" organization into his own private brothel.

This degenerate process left its mark on wide swaths of RC theory and practice. Increasingly, Jackins advanced the notion that distress around sex is the primary oppression from which people must free themselves. This sits alongside the conflicting view, inherited from Marxism, that the source of all oppression resides in class.

Given the view that the miseries we face have their origins in childhood, it naturally follows that sexual distresses have an early origin. Thus, Harvey Jackins argued that the key to individual reemergence was work on "early sexual memories" (or, as RCers say, "ESMs"). This approach served as a theoretical justification for Jackins's own personal obsession with the subject. It also prepared many of the women he worked with for later sexual intimacy with the guru himself.

The following testimony from one former RC woman activist illuminates only too clearly what "working on ESMs" means, and the hazards it opens up:

> I was first introduced to ESM work at a lesbian workshop. I had been doing RC for a year at this time. The workshop lasted for a weekend, and three or four times during this weekend we had to stand in a group of four people called an ESM support group. In turns, we each had to answer the question "What is your earliest memory connected with sex in any way?" We were told to answer with the first thing that came into our heads, even if it was not connected with sex, even if we thought it was not true. . . .
>
> I have always been blessed with a vivid imagination and my mind went wild. At the beginning of the weekend I had no early memories connected with sex, and by the end I remembered being sexually abused. Listening to other people's memories of abuse in my support group aided this process. After the workshop was over, in order to make sense of this memory, I joined a support group of people who were "working on sexual abuse." In fact they were all working on incest memories and I soon started to do so too.
>
> In my personal life however, I became very disoriented. I began to get memories of being sexually abused as a child continually. I wasn't able function at work or at home. . . . I found that continually flicking backwards and forwards between a horrific past and a superficially happy present numbed my feelings. I was unable to respond emotionally when I heard about sexual abuse in "the wide world." This is called "not getting restimulated."[31]

In reality, there is no evidence to suggest that traumatic experiences, such as incest, are repressed by people, in the way in which RC theory suggests occurs. The evidence supports the view that although all memories, including those of trauma, become degraded and lose their initial clarity, people remain only too well aware of what they have endured and remember at least its broad outlines. For example, research has found that children who have witnessed a parent being murdered often have a distorted recollection of the event, but never repress the memory of the experience.[32]

The promotion of the contrary view within RC engenders a systematic fear of the outside world. The only safe place to be, or so it appears, is within RC and particularly in the company of other "survivors." If the person's primary family is now seen as the source of incest, or as having colluded with its practice, it is also likely that relationships there will be sundered.

Again, this reinforces the individual's attachment to RC. Where else is there to turn?

Paradoxically, this mood was more likely to facilitate sexual overtures from Jackins. An attitude of dependence, reverence, and blind faith in the guru ensured that all his actions, however abusive, were benignly interpreted as being in the victim's own best interests. As one letter in *Present Time* put it, Harvey was, after all, "a lover of all humanity." Whatever he did was a "contradiction" to a "distress pattern," exclusively intended to produce "discharge."

Repelling "Attacks"—RC on the Defensive

Many RC members have been greatly concerned by the issues we have discussed in this chapter. However, it is impossible to debate them within the organization. A distinctive feature of RC theory is its stress on protecting and defending leaders. The writings of Jackins are replete with warnings that leaders of "progressive organizations" will become the victims of government-inspired attacks. This obsession with repelling attacks, in a most fortunate coincidence, seems to have begun precisely at the point when many people started to question Jackins's relationships with young women participants in RC. Now, if people want to raise criticisms, they must first prove that they are not paid agents of the FBI.

Thus, the "Policy on Attacks" was adopted by the World Conference of the Reevaluation Counseling Communities in 1989.[33] We argued earlier that RC's theory of restimulation can be used to dismiss all criticism as the "pattern" of the critic, devoid of external validity. The "Policy on Attacks" ensures that criticism is regarded as a distress that requires the counseling of the critic, rather than as a "reevaluation" on the part of leaders, leading to change. The "Policy" states:

> Attacks . . . are not attempts at correcting mistakes, but rather dramatizations of distress. . . . It is the job of all members of the RC community to interrupt such attacks; this includes the interruption of gossip.
> Any Co-Counselor who has an issue with a Co-Counseling leader's behavior shall communicate the criticism directly to that person, and not express such criticism to anyone else inside or outside of RC.

One RC member, Deborah Dixon, was so enamoured of the policy that she produced a strong defense of it in *Present Time*.[34] She declared, "There are several reasons people attack leaders." The possibility that the leader may be wrong, mad, bad, or daft, and therefore merit some criticism, is not one of the options considered. Instead, Dixon reasons that:

> Leaders sometimes say or do things that bring up our distress recordings. This is particularly true when leaders are acting boldly to challenge common distress patterns. We are sometimes pulled to "dramatize" the distress that leaders' actions bring up, acting out these distresses in the form of an attack as a way of trying (subconsciously) to get help discharging the original distress. For example, if a leader does something that reminds you of something upsetting that one of your parents did when you were very young, you may be tempted to attack the leader in order to get help discharging that earlier experience.[35]

Leaders of other cults would give much to have such a policy on their statute books. The consequence is that criticisms of RC, or attempts to raise the question of Harvey Jackins's sexual proclivities, are viewed as reflecting a fundamental problem on the part of the person raising them.

RCers are accordingly prevented from taking a "public position" on their criticisms of RC leaders—that is, organizing to discuss and advance their views. Under this logic, if RCers were to overhear RC leaders conspiring to detonate a nuclear bomb, they would be prevented from doing anything about it. Such a phobic response toward debate is in accord with normal cult practice, which places all trust in the infallibility of the leader, and responds to his weaknesses either by ignoring them or by turning on those who attempt to discuss them.

Conclusion

There is no evidence that RC works. One authoritative researcher estimates that 67 percent of seriously ill neurotic patients will be fully recovered within two years, without any form of therapy at all.[36] This is known as spontaneous remission. It is therefore inevitable that a certain percentage of participants in RC will improve after exposure to the organization's techniques. The same would be true if they experimented with any one of innumerable other therapeutic approaches—or none at all. Being listened to sympathetically, by a nonjudgmental friend, dog, or therapist, has never harmed anyone.

Yet Harvey Jackins went much further. Like many innovative therapists, he simply claimed that his techniques "worked" (with an unspecified number of his clients) and that their widespread adoption is vital if the world is to be saved from destruction. Using this approach to research, it would not be difficult to prove that people improved dramatically, even if their counselor did nothing more than stand in a corner, making white rabbits appear from a hat. However, RC is about much more than delivering simple forms of help to those in turmoil, and it certainly goes further than distracting them from their misery with a variety of harmless conjuring tricks.

Its increasingly political agenda distracts attention from simple peer group counseling activities. It also encourages people to embark on campaigns to change the world precisely at a time when their own judgment is most likely to be impaired, and when what they really want is some form of counseling assistance. Furthermore, the global reach of such ambitions may well increase people's sense of uselessness.

Given all these difficulties, dissent, schism, and separation have been the norm. In the late 1970s Mary McCabe, who founded cocounseling with Jackins, left the organization, enraged by his activities. Many of his British followers departed in the early 1980s. They set up a rival and more democratic alternative—the Co-Counseling International, which now coordinates the activities of those who are influenced by RC theory, but are unwilling to submit to its disciplinary regime, in a number of countries.

In the late 1980s Jackins expelled many of his European followers, when they introduced a revision to RC theory, which they termed "present-mindedness," and questioned RC's increasingly overt political agenda. Similar purges have occurred in Ireland, Kansas, the Twin Cities, and other parts of the United States. As with all the cults discussed in this book, in the conflict between control on the one hand and influence in the real world on the other, it is invariably the former that wins out.

Since his father's death, Tim Jackins, has eased himself ever further into the limelight. It has become a family business. Like many other family businesses faced with the founder's death, it has been preoccupied with the problems of succession. But the one constant remains. There is no sign that the new regime will be inclined to reevaluate the past or subject its heritage to any form of critical scrutiny. There are, it seems, perks and privileges to leadership in the RC community that few people are willing to relinquish. And why should they? In these desperate times, there is no shortage of new recruits, their hearts full of both hope and pain, who are ready to strike out on the trail of reemergence.

Under a new whip, administered with a smile and a hug, the saga continues.

Chapter 7

Fred Newman

Lenin as Therapist

Let Hitler take office—he will soon be bankrupt,
and then it will be our day.
—H. Remmele, Communist member of the Reichstag, 1933

Pat Buchanan and That Woman

In the fall of 1999 Pat Buchanan sat down to lunch with Dr. Lenora Fulani. A pretty, light-skinned African American woman, conservatively dressed, with close-cropped hair, Fulani was by no means a novice to politics. She had been the 1992 presidential candidate of the New Alliance Party (NAP). The party qualified for more than $1 million in federal matching funds and was on the ballot in nearly all fifty states. In the past Fulani had supported Jesse Jackson and had been a close confidante of Louis Farrakhan and the Reverend Al Sharpton. She had a reputation as an outspoken lesbian and a defender of abortion rights. Buchanan was on a tour promoting a book in which he expressed the view that the United States should not have interfered with Hitler, his subjugation of Europe, and the Holocaust. Some eyebrows were raised in the mainstream press corps.

During an interview later that day, Buchanan was asked about his relations with the "black-nationalist Marxist." His eyes narrowed and he answered: "I did not have sexual relations with that woman, Lenora Fulani."[1] Political relations, however, were a different matter. Fulani was about to launch her latest grand political maneuver, promoting Buchanan as the presidential candidate of the Reform Party.

Fred Newman runs the cult, which fuses politics seamlessly with psychotherapy. While Newman is little known, Dr. Lenora Fulani is a national media figure. The Newmanites prove that cults can affect mainstream politics in the United States in a dangerous way. At the same time Newman's distinctive method of cadre recruitment gives us an insight into the psychology of cult organization in general.

The Cult's Obscure Origins

Fred Newman, a Korean War veteran, was awarded a Ph.D. in the philosophy of science from Stanford University.[2] He has had no formal training in any branch of psychology. He turned to a Maoist version of Marxism in the mid-1960s. In 1970 Newman gathered together a tiny collective, which shared a communal apartment on Manhattan's Upper West Side. This was a moment when the left was searching for a road forward after the collapse of the Students for a Democratic Society (SDS) and the New Left generally, while a cultural revolution was in full swing. Newman's collective, much like Harvey Jackins' reevaluation counseling (see chapter 6), combined the radical politics of the sixties with the New Age therapy of the seventies. The result was a potent mixture of cultic consequences.

They named their collective "If . . . Then."[3] While Jackins stressed techniques of cocounseling in which therapist and patient exchange places, Newman developed a group version of radical therapy led by a therapist, which he called "social therapy" or "crisis normalization."[4] All members underwent therapy while they, at the same time, carried out political activity. By 1973 the group was called Centers for Change (CFC). "CFC is," Newman explained, "a Marxist-Leninist-Maoist organization."[4]

The origins of the group in a communal setting gave it a cultlike character from the very beginning. This aspect of Newman's operation did not change. Its core members have lived in shared facilities or are closely linked to such communes. Core members are expected to quit their jobs, sell their private possessions, and earn a meager living through such activities as soliciting funds on street corners.

In Bed with Lyndon LaRouche

For approximately one year, from the middle of 1973 until the end of August in 1974, Newman's group was under the influence of Lyndon LaRouche (see chapter 5). The "United Front," was formed, consisting of LaRouche's National Caucus of Labor Committees (NCLC), Newman's Center for Change, and a third group led by Eugenio Perente-Ramos (this later became another cult, the Communist Party U.S.A. (Provisional) (CPUSA [P])—see chapter 12).[5] Joint forums were held and activities coordinated. On June 1, 1974, Newman wrote, "We have traveled from a community based storefront, to a health service collective, to a cadre socialist organization. We have traveled from non-existence to existence and finally back to non-existence at a higher level. For CFC is disbanded. We move, not as a collective, but as self-conscious human beings into the National Caucus of Labor Committees."[6]

Fred Newman's comment about moving into the NCLC "not as a collective" proved to be a bit disingenuous. Then again, a cultist like LaRouche should have been sharp enough to spot another cultist. The group had been formed around the personality of Fred Newman, they all underwent continuous group therapy under his guidance, and they shared common living quarters. The Newman group continued to operate in lockstep while within the NCLC. It should therefore come as no shock that the fusion did not work out. The two gurus inevitably clashed. In late August 1974 Newman and thirty-eight followers walked out of the NCLC to form the International Workers Party (IWP). Newman announced that his tiny group had "now become the vanguard of the working class." Newman declared: "The organization of the vanguard party is, as Marx makes clear, the organization of the class. The formation of the IWP had grown from our attempt to organize the [NCLC] from within that it might move from a position of left hegemony to a position of leadership of the class."[7]

Newman's period of association with LaRouche was to have a major impact on his thinking and future development. It is significant that he joined up with LaRouche precisely at the moment when the NCLC was moving from left to right and engaging in some rather bizarre conduct. Newman contacted LaRouche within weeks of the conclusion of his "Operation Mop-Up," involving physical attacks on the left.

Newman declared in 1974 that "the former workers of CFC will organize in the spirit outlined by Marcus [Lyndon LaRouche]."[8] He wrote a book that contained extensive quotations from LaRouche. He echoed LaRouche's catastrophism, seeing the United States as facing "the grim reality of cannibalization and encroaching fascism."[9] He agreed with LaRouche that a "massive fascist brainwashing" was taking place. Like LaRouche, he dismissed most of the left: "Black nationalism, community control, feminism, the petty bourgeois movement, gay pride, worker participation programs, trade union parochialism, and so on, are concepts devised by the fascists to locate a group's identity in something other than the working class."[10]

In 1974 Newman declared that "Liberalism is fascism. . . . The liberal do-gooders are the fascists."[11] And, "'The Left Movement' or 'The Radical Movement' or 'The Movement' . . . is the CIA-developed deterrent to the development of a vanguard party. . . . Fortunately there are some around working to destroy the CIA controlled left movement. Lyn Marcus and the NCLC are such a group."[12]

While Newman never again publicly referred to the left in such terms, he was never really *part* of the left. His relationship was more that of a predator: from time to time running in Democratic primaries, moving into existing leftist organizations with the aim of taking them over, and utilizing prominent black leaders to advance his own aims.

Just as important, there was a concurrence between LaRouche and Newman on the critical questions of the role of leadership, cadre formation, and the mental manipulation of the membership. LaRouche brought to the "United Front" a far more developed distortion of Marxism than anything Newman had been able to extract from Mao Tse-Tung. Crucial was the linking of an apocalyptic crisis theory with the necessity of creating an elite cadre.

Newman contributed his knowledge of psychotherapy and experience gained in transforming his followers through these techniques into political operators. We suspect that LaRouche's rantings about impotency and his ego-stripping sessions were at least partially inspired by Newman, who claimed that "all psychic problems are correctly diagnosed as impotency."[13]

After parting, the political evolution of the two gurus was, on the surface, quite different. LaRouche transformed his hostility toward the left and its constituents into a new rightist ideology with links to fascism. Newman continued to function politically on the left until 1994, when he began to move into the right-centrist Perot movement. Yet both leaders shared a common disdain for ordinary citizens, who were to be manipulated; for their members, who were transformed into robots to be used to do the manipulation; and for the democratic norms of a pluralistic society.

The Theory of Proletarian Psychotherapy

Fred Newman developed, in his 1974 book *Power and Authority*, a theory of the mind and its relation to society that has served him well as a justification for the existence of his cult and has aided him in controlling his followers. Newman saw revolution as a two-level process: the external overthrow of the bourgeoisie and its state and the internal overthrow of the "Bourgeois ego."

We must learn, he insisted, to see "in both directions—inside and outside."[14] "Proletarian or revolutionary psychotherapy is . . . the overthrow of the rulers of the mind by the workers of the mind."[15] "Revolutionary therapy," he stated, "involves an act of insurrection; of overthrow."[16] Through this act the "bourgeois ego" is replaced by the "proletarian ego." "The proletarian or revolutionary therapist is . . . a leader."[17] This internal revolution is followed by "a long period of the withering away of the proletarian ego."[18]

Newman viewed the "bourgeois ego" as the automatic product of the capitalist system. Drawing from Marx via Lenin and LaRouche, he concluded that "the self-interested, rational *individual* is guided by a ruling class imposed conscience (or super ego) which she or he transforms into a self controlling bourgeois ego."[19]

This view could be interpreted as a reasonable distillation of Marx's concept of alienation. Capitalism tends to atomize people. People then relate to each other in the belief that they are acting autonomously in their own self-interest. Actually their relations are being determined by market forces and their thinking is influenced by the dominant capitalist culture and institutions.

Marx, however, noted countervailing effects of capitalist relations upon the worker. The very organization of the production process brought workers together collectively, creating the conditions for their common action, such as trade union organization and the formation of workers' parties. Newman, following upon Lenin and LaRouche, dismissed such processes as expressions of "trade union parochialism" and therefore reactionary. He proposed "therapy" as a substitute.

A difficulty arises out of Newman's efforts to "overthrow" the individual's "bourgeois" ego through a therapeutic act while the capitalist system remains intact and functioning. The discarded ego is actually the only *individual* identity a person is capable of developing and sustaining within a capitalist society. Its dissolution creates a vacuum that is filled by the ego of the therapist. The therapist's ego is no less shaped by the society within which he functions. The guru therapist's desire to control others, manipulate others, and drive others to carry out his wishes represents a demented form of the worse features of personality in contemporary capitalist society.

Newman developed a critique of Freudian and all other forms of psychotherapy, labeling them "bourgeois." Bourgeois psychology (read "all therapies excluding Newman's") "entails an act of transference (making the therapist into a substitute conscience and, at the same time, into a 'temporary' oppressive ruler) and eventually this transferential act itself must be analyzed and undone. . . . The bourgeois authoritarian leader allows a temporary and controlled regression to the bourgeois id and then leads the patient back again to her or his bourgeois ego."[20]

These therapies, in Newman's view, take a patient with a wounded ego; pass her or him through a process of transference; and, ending the transference, rebuild a healthy independent ego in the person. However, Newman believed, this process simply strengthened the "bourgeois ego," that is the mind control of a sick society. He believed the very concept of a "self-interested rational individual" was reactionary.

What then is to be done? As part of a group therapy practice, the "leadership" of the therapist is required to carry through an insurrection against individual egoism. Once the "proletarian ego" is installed, the therapy is by no means at an end. It continues and is coordinated with revolutionary activity. "Revolutionary therapy becomes more and more indistinguishable from revolutionary organizing."[21] The victory of the "proletarian ego" over the "bourgeois ego" is thus expressed in the patient's complete devotion to the political causes espoused by Fred Newman.

Normal therapy is designed to be completed during a limited time period. The patient may be emotionally bound through the transference process to his or her therapist for a period of time. However, health comes through the ending of the transference process and the restoration of the patient's own sense of self and emotional independence. Not so in Newman's "social therapy." *The process of transference, and therefore dependence upon the therapist, is never ending!*

The difficulty is that the "proletarian ego"—read "emotional dependence on Newman"—withers away only when the proletarian state withers away. Since the creation of a proletarian state does not appear to be imminent in the United States or any other advanced country, and further, since all attempts to create such states have so far led to growth rather than withering away, the patient must remain dependent on Newman indefinitely. In the case of Newman's oldest adherents, this dependency has persisted for more than twenty-five years!

The doctrines explicitly developed in this book continued to guide Newman's practice right up to the current period. Dr. Lenora Fulani, the group's spokesperson, wrote in 1989: "One of the earliest statements on the foundations of Social Therapy is contained in a book written by Newman in 1974 entitled *Power and Authority*. It states that psychic and emotional life in contemporary society reflects the political and economic degeneration of capitalism."[22]

The International Workers Party and the Federal Bureau of Investigation

Having founded the IWP, Fred Newman was not quite sure what to do with it. For a brief period he sought unification with various small Trotskyist groups as well as Marlene Dixon's Democratic Workers Party (see chapter 9). In June 1975 the Newmanites were admitted into the Peoples Party, a forerunner of the Citizens Party that ran Barry Commoner for president in 1980. A bitter internal struggle ensued, which almost destroyed the small party. The group was expelled in March 1978.[23]

It was in this period that Fred Newman developed a curious relationship with the Federal Bureau of Investigation (FBI). In April 1974 Jim Retherford left the therapy cult. He had had a child with Ann Green, a devoted member who stayed with Newman. After Newman took his followers into the NCLC, Retherford, not wanting his son to be raised by people he viewed as crazy, took him away without the mother's permission and left town. Green appealed to Newman who enlisted the help of two young lawyers, one named Harry Kresky, who were cult members. Together they developed a strategy that they hoped would enlist the aid of the federal government in finding Retherford and the child.

The lawyers contacted the FBI and arranged a meeting between Green and its agents. Green told them that Retherford was a former member of the Weather Underground and maintained relations with Jane Alpert, at that time a fugitive. Kresky met with representatives of the U.S. attorney in New York, giving them the same information.

The matter was brought out into the open in 1976. A meeting was held at St. Gregory's Church on the Upper West Side to form the New York State Working Peoples Party, a forerunner of the New Alliance Party. A group called the Communist Cadre, which had recently split from Newman's IWP, issued a statement primarily devoted to the Retherford matter.[24] They accused Newman of working with the FBI. The IWP, in an answer to the charges, admitted that the events had occurred but held three members, not Newman, responsible.[25] King, however, believes that it is "unthinkable" that Kresky and Green, loyal followers, could have acted without Newman's full knowledge and approval.[26]

This incident raises a question fairly early on in Newman's political evolution about the seriousness of his commitment to the left and its causes. Our study of political cults complements the conclusions reached by those who have studied a broader array of cult types: they operate in the interest of their leaders rather than for the purposes they are purportedly created to promote.

A West Side Story

In 1977 Fred Newman turned his attention to the politics of New York City's Upper West Side. The area was and is among the most sophisticated liberal political strongholds in the nation. His activities caused concern among political activists. Newman's group had resurfaced as the New York City Unemployed and Welfare Council.

He caused a stir when he ran a key follower, Nancy Ross, for local school board and actually won. The startled liberal politicos decided to look a bit deeper at Newman, his past, and his current practices. Dennis King, who was later to write a book about Lyndon LaRouche,[27] conducted an investigation of the group, interviewing over thirty people, including many former members. For the first time Fred Newman found himself publicly accused of leading a "therapy cult."

> There are about 35 individuals in the inner circle of the cult, most living in semi-communal apartments on the Upper West Side. Through the years, a combination of group pressure and Newman's directive therapy had induced most

of them to give up their jobs and to break off all meaningful personal ties out-side the group. Likewise they have been induced to turn over all personal prop-erty and savings to the cult. They regard themselves as full-time organizers for the cult's front groups, operating under tight discipline and secrecy. They eat and pay their rent through a variety of parasitical activities, such as street cor-ner solicitations, the practice of amateur psychotherapy, the dunning of past and present patients for "political contributions," and the occasional plucking of an inheritance or trust fund from a patient.[28]

Newman acted as a "benevolent despot," to use his own words. "Fred's ve-neer of compassion and his deep-set Rasputin-type eyes created strong trans-ference feelings in . . . [his] patients."[29]

"His groupies," King explained, "cut off from the outside world and with almost every waking hour spent either in 'busywork' or interminable meet-ings (so that independent thought could be kept at a minimum), had no feed-back from reality."[30]

When Nancy Ross campaigned for the school board, she insisted that the IWP had been disbanded. Newman's front organization, the New York City Unemployed and Welfare Council, issued a statement that the party had dis-banded shortly after the factional struggle in 1976. However, Jack Finn, an-other reporter for *Heights and Valley News*, discovered that the IWP continued to exist in a "clandestine" fashion. It issued at least a dozen issues of an internal bulletin, "Party Building." These bulletins referred to the ongoing work of a "central committee" and of "chairman Fred Newman." There were mention of the "Party" and the "work of the Party," while the IWP was called the "apparatus."[31]

We believe Fred Newman concluded from his brief experience attempt-ing to build the IWP that he had no need for an open vanguard formation. He recruited new members through therapy and gained political influence by working within other groups or creating broad front organizations. How-ever, he did have need for a clandestine vanguard formation, based on the Leninist model and made up of core therapy patients. As we will see, there is considerable evidence that the IWP continues to exist up to the present time.

The 1977 period of activism on the Upper West Side was a learning expe-rience for Newman and his followers. They became skilled at operating within politically ill-defined front organizations and raising funds from guilt-ridden middle-class liberals. Most of all Newman got a taste for electoral activity. This would shape the rest of his political life.

The New Alliance Party

Sometime in the late 1970s Newman had the great good fortune of running into Lenora Fulani, an attractive black woman who had been raised in Pennsylvania and was earning a Ph.D. in psychology at the City University of New York. She heard Newman lecture and "was very intrigued by the progressiveness of the politics guiding his thought." She dropped her black lesbian Gestalt therapist and joined a Newmanite social therapy clinic full time.[32]

In 1979 Newman and Fulani formed the New Alliance Party (NAP). While the politics of the new party were purposely vague, they generally reflected a progressive agenda similar to Jesse Jackson's Rainbow Coalition. Fulani ran as the NAP candidate for lieutenant governor of New York in 1982.

In 1984 the NAP ran Dennis Serrette, a black socialist and NAP member, for president. The party was on the ballot in thirty-three states and received 35,000 votes. A year later Serrette broke from the NAP, accusing it of having an all-white leadership that manipulated him. He took his charges to the *Jackson Advocate*, the only black newspaper in Mississippi. The NAP sued the paper in 1986 and lost.[33]

In May 1985 the NAP held its founding convention in Chicago, even though it had been formed six years earlier. Emily Carter, a black woman from Jackson, Mississippi, who called herself a "former organizer, now therapist," was elected chairperson.[34] In 1988 Fulani ran for the office of president of the United States. The party qualified for ballot status in all fifty states and received nearly $1 million in federal matching funds and a respectable 217,219 votes.[35]

Fulani's tactics in 1992 became increasingly complicated. She began the year by entering the New Hampshire primary on the Democratic Party line. Then the Newmanites in California joined the Peace and Freedom Party and battled to capture it. While Newman lost that factional struggle, he nearly destroyed the small leftist party in the process. That spring Newman and Fulani turned their attention to the growing movement around Ross Perot, the right centrist billionaire curmudgeon. When Perot withdrew from the race in July, Fulani commented that "we've been stabbed in the back." Fulani revived her presidential bid under the NAP label. Walter Sheasby has noted:

> Fulani offered herself and the Presidential campaign as the vehicle of a Perotism sans Perot. . . . Fulani claimed to represent "my base—the old 'New Deal' coalition base of African Americans, labor, Latinos, women and gays." And she said to the Perot followers "and there you are. In the radical and independent Perot base lies the potential for a new majority coalition."[36]

The NAP once again qualified for ballot status in all fifty states, and this time it received $2 million in federal matching funds. Fulani received 73,708 votes, a considerable decline from 1988 and no doubt part of the reason Newman turned toward Perot.

A Washington, D.C., newspaper has exposed the complexity of Newman's financial maneuvers that year. This involved running in the New Hampshire Democratic primary, where Fulani received only 402 votes out of 167,900 cast. She then switched tactics, running in several small party primaries, including California's Peace and Freedom. Finally she ran on the NAP ticket. The total budget for primary activity alone was $4,161,495, which included the matching funds.

Interestingly, some $901,495 of this money "went to organizations that share offices, phones, and leadership with the NAP." This permitted a process of "double-dipping," whereby members of the NAP, working for various front organizations, were paid with campaign funds and in turn made campaign contributions that qualified for federal matching funds. While campaign funds are required by law to be spent on campaigning or returned to donors, the NAP, by spending a large portion of its funds on individuals and organizations associated with Newman, saw to it that the core group prospered. For example, "Fred Newman Productions received $68,925 in retainers for Newman's services as campaign manager."[37]

Life Among the Newmanites

Loren Redwood, a lesbian who fell in love with a Newmanite, told her story in a letter to a gay newspaper in San Francisco:

> My experience with NAP was a nightmare. I am a white, working class lesbian and met NAP in Indiana where I was living at the time. NAP was in Indiana petitioning to put Fulani's name on the ballot there. I was so excited and so moved to find that a black woman was running for president that I immediately began working for the campaign. I also fell in love with a woman working on the campaign. When it came time for NAP to leave Indiana, she asked me to go with them, and I did. . . . I was given 48 hours to prepare. I quit my job, left my home, my friends, put my belongings in storage, found a home for my pet, and gave the use of my car to NAP in exchange for their taking over the payments. . . .
>
> As a working class lesbian, I thought I had finally found a political movement which included me. What I found instead was an oppressive, disempowering, misogynistic machine. All my decisions were made for me by someone else. I was told where to go, and who to go with. I worked seven days a week—sixteen to twenty hours a day (I had two days off in two and a half months). There was an incredible urgency which overrode any personal needs or considerations, an urgency that meant complete self-sacrifice. . . . I felt totally powerless over my life, forced into a very submissive role where all control of my life belonged to someone else. I had given up everything for the campaign, my job, my home and my support system, I felt desperate.
>
> Another strange aspect of NAP is what they call social therapy. This is political therapy founded by Fred Newman. . . . [I]t was expected that I enter social therapy and I did attend a few sessions. . . . My position on political

issues was dictated to me by NAP—independent thought was discouraged. We were all part of something bigger than ourselves and were of one mind. I felt personally threatened, like I was being absorbed into something and was losing myself. . . . I was completely exhausted, so tired I was unable to work well. Being unable to work I had no income, as I was expected to raise my salary myself in addition to raising money for the campaign. . . . I was very frightened. I was in a strange city, I knew no one really except my lover, who couldn't help me: I had no job, no home and no money. At this point I was feeling very suicidal.

It's been four months since I left the campaign and I am putting my life back together piece by piece.[38]

This report is interesting in a number of respects. First, it documents one method of recruitment to the Newmanite cult: a person is attracted to one of the political projects sponsored by Newman, in this case the NAP, and is then urged to take group therapy. Only those who combine political activism with therapy are considered solid core members of the group.

Second, we are given a picture of the intensity and time-consuming nature of the group's political activity. Loren Redwood felt "an incredible sense of urgency which overrode any personal needs." This in turn has a disorienting and numbing effect upon the recruit. Her feelings and experience is identical to that reported to us by members of such groups as the Workers Revolutionary Party, the Militant Group, the Democratic Workers Party, and the LaRoucheites. It helps explain how a politically oriented cult can produce the same degree of total control over members as religious cults.

Third, the Newmanites carry out a practice that is common among religious cults but not used as extensively by political cults. This is having members quit their jobs, move into common quarters with other members, and solicit funds from the public to support the organization as well as themselves. This increases the recruit's isolation from civil society as well as his or her dependence upon the group for survival. We have found this practice among the LaRoucheites (chapter 5), NATLFED (chapter 12), and Synanon (chapter 8).

Not all recruits have joined the cult through political activity and been steered toward social therapy. Many seek out therapy because of emotional disturbances, only to find themselves sucked into Newmanite political groups. Berlet reported this experience of an East Coast Latina activist:

I first came into contact with the Social Therapy Institutes through a friend who . . . said there was a group that offered therapy for people with progressive views so I went to see what they offered. . . .

Before and after the therapy session, they would say "why not sell the newspaper" or "maybe you could do us a favor and hand out those leaflets." The therapy offices were full of their political propaganda. In the group therapy sometimes we discussed politics and their political party.

> Some people get involved because they think the political work will help them get better emotionally. They told us societal problems are making people ill and the New Alliance Party is going to change things so people get better.[39]

Marina Ortiz, a single mother living in the Bronx, became involved in social therapy in 1985 in a similar fashion.

> The trouble wasn't "in our head," but "in the world," we learned. . . . Through Social Therapy, I was conditioned to relate to my personal history in exclusively political terms. My family's problems and subsequent poverty—and all my suffering—were all the result of the government's imperialist invasion of Puerto Rico. . . . But consciousness-raising in itself was not enough. Our individual development and growth, we were told, was dependent upon the group's. . . . Only by embracing this psycho-therapeutic doctrine could I hope to change what it meant to be a "poor, working-class Puerto-Rican woman. . . ." [T]he "cure" for my depression and anxiety was ultimately conditional upon my becoming a serious political activist.
>   When I finally left the cult in July of 1990—after finally becoming disgusted with the totalitarian internal structure which, in my opinion, basically relies on slave labor for profit in the name of justice and empowerment—I had to literally rebuild my life.[40]

Individual distress is manipulated to transform the patient into a political activist under the total control of the therapist or the revolutionary leader. The new "family" of fellow cultists replaces the traditional family and friends. The followers become completely dependent upon Newman for their sense of self-esteem. "When Newman was happy, everyone was happy," commented one former member. "When he was angry, everyone was terrified."[41]

Organic Leaders: Jackson, Farrakahn, Sharpton

Antonio Gramsci originated the concept of the "organic intellectual." In contrast to "traditional intellectuals," such as clerics, teachers, and other professionals, Gramsci believed each social class created *organically* out of its own members a stratum capable of generalizing that class's historic mission and projecting its hegemony over society as a whole. Since he believed that the capability of being an intellectual is in all human beings, he was convinced that the working class could and would develop its own organic intellectuals. This aspect of his thinking could be interpreted as more democratic than Lenin's approach.

Lenin—particularly in *What Is to Be Done?*—advocated building a party composed exclusively of full-time professional revolutionaries drawn from the traditional intellectuals. This vanguard would bring socialism from "outside" the working class into the proletarian milieu. It matters little the degree to which Lenin may or may not have modified this view in a later period. What is critical is that so many on the left, including virtually all cultists, have been influenced by this vanguardist "from the outside" theory. Newman learned his Lenin from LaRouche.[42]

Fred Newman operated on the basis of both concepts of leadership. He viewed his core group as a vanguard formation, made up overwhelmingly of white, middle-class, traditional intellectuals. His elite members were professionals in two ways: They largely worked full time for Newmanite fronts, and, in many cases, they were professional therapists.

Newman's concept of "organic leaders," borrowed from Gramsci, was given a decidedly undemocratic twist. For Newman the term "organic" became a code word meaning "people of color." Organic leaders were therefore prominent black spokespersons with real bases of support in the black community and wide media recognition. He embraced these "organic leaders" uncritically, but they were just so much window dressing to be used as a way of advancing the interests of the secretive vanguard made up of white traditional intellectuals. The result was a manipulative and undemocratic relationship.

The Newmanites' first major foray into organizing around an "organic leader" involved support of Jesse Jackson's Rainbow Coalition and his 1984 and 1988 Democratic Party presidential bids. Declaring "Two Roads Are Better Than One," Lenora Fulani announced support of Jackson while at the same time fielding her own independent candidacy under the New Alliance Party banner.[43] Then, in an interesting and self-serving twist, the Newmanites organized the Rainbow Lobby. The group, headed by Nancy Ross, had almost the same name as Jackson's organization and an identical program. However, it was not authorized by Jackson, was totally controlled by Newman, and raised its own independent funds to the tune of more than $1 million a year.[44] In 1992 the Lobby was closed down and the lobbying firm Ross and Green was formed. The "Ross" of Ross and Green is the very same Nancy Ross, former school board member from the Upper West Side and head of the Rainbow Lobby.[45] The "Green" was Ann Green, whom we met earlier working with the FBI.

The next "Organic Leader" to catch Newman and Fulani's attention was Louis Farrakhan of the Nation of Islam, noted for his anti-Semitic rantings. This is particularly interesting because, in the LaRouche cohabitation period, Newman shared NCLC's extremely hostile (bordering on racist) attitude toward black nationalists. The NAP moved its national headquarters to Chicago in order to be closer to Farrakhan. In 1995, *after* Newman's dissolution of the NAP and turn toward Perot, he ran a full page advertisement in the *Village Voice* entitled "Never Again! A New Pledge for the Jewish Community," saluting the Million Man March. It featured a photo of Newman, Farrakhan, and Fulani, and was signed "Dr. Fred Newman, Convenor, Jews for Farrakhan."[46]

Soon Newman added the Reverend Al Sharpton to the organic roster. Sharpton developed a particularly close relationship to the Newmanites during the period he was conducting confrontational marches through Howard Beach and promoting Tawana Brawley, whose tale of rape by white assailants has been proved to be a fabrication. Sharpton has developed a reputation as an antiwhite demagogue and has clashed with New York City's Jewish community. The Newmanites even rented office space to Sharpton and put him on their payroll as a $12,000 a year consultant.[47]

Noting the connections with Farrakhan and Sharpton, Dennis King wrote in 1992 that the NAP has "unsevered ties to anti-Semitism." Newman is Jewish but this did not prevent him from saying that "Jews 'as a people' have made a pact with 'the devil' to serve as the 'stormtroopers of decadent capitalism against people of color the world over.'"[48]

Overall the Newmanites gained a high profile and significant membership growth in the decade between 1982 and 1992. Newman expanded his base beyond the Upper West Side with therapy centers throughout New York City, as well as in Boston; Chicago; Los Angeles; San Francisco; Pennsylvania; New Jersey; Washington, D.C.; Jackson, Mississippi; and elsewhere. During its first ten years of operations Newman's core group numbered between thirty and forty people. By the end of the next decade, Newman had several hundred core followers and significant political influence. In 1992 NAP-related businesses employed fifty-six people and brought in at least $3.5 million a year. The East Side Institute for Social Therapy alone reported sales in excess of $400,000 a year.[49]

Lenora Fulani was a popular, media-savvy spokesperson who received considerable, and largely favorable, press attention. The potent combination of the NAP election campaigns with high-profile identification with Jackson, Farrakhan, and Sharpton made Lenora Fulani a well-known public figure. However, the political winds were shifting to the right. Discontent in America was finding a new path for expression: Ross Perot. Was this tiny white billionaire with his folksy manners and Texan twang a new "organic leader"? If so, of what class?

A Pact with Ross Perot

Beginning in 1992 Ross Perot developed a movement around his quixotic personality. He drew almost exclusively from whites, was particularly popular with small businessmen and people who lived in smaller cities and towns, and pulled support almost equally from the Democratic and Republican parties. His politics were generally right of center. He was antigovernment, strongly against political action committees (PACs), and for electoral reform; he favored a balanced budget and welfare reform. Perhaps his most popular position was his strong stance against the North American Free Trade Agreement (NAFTA) and the General Agreement on Tariffs and Trade (GATT). His economic nationalism gained him some support among workers hurt by job competition from south of the border. Many voted for him because he was very rich and therefore beholden to no special interests (except, of course, himself). The Perot movement definitely represented a radical departure from the traditional two party system. However, there is no evidence that this departure was in a left direction.

In 1993, immediately after the 1992 elections, Fulani met with Nicholas Sabatine III, a small-town Pennsylvania attorney, and helped form the Patriot Party. In April 1994 the NAP officially dissolved into the Patriot Party. The National Patriot Party was formed with Sabatine as national chair and Fulani as chair for New York State. The apparatus of the Patriot Party was, for all intents and purposes, controlled by the Newmanites.[50] The Patriot Party was, to quote Fulani, "based on the principles of democracy, fiscal responsibility, government accountability and a deep commitment to inclusivity and diversity." Many on the left view "fiscal responsibility" as a code meaning cuts in benefits to the poor. According to Sabatine the party supported privatization of Social Security and a flat tax, hardly progressive positions.[51]

In 1994 Fulani ran in the New York State Democratic primary against Governor Mario Cuomo. She received 142,000 votes, or 21 percent of the vote. She then switched her support to businessman Tom Golisano, helping to create the Independence Party. That party received 217,000 votes.[52] The Independence Party, like the Patriot Party, was a forerunner of the Reform Party.

In 1996, Ross Perot, who had resisted forming a third party, preferring to run as an independent, permitted the formation of the Reform Party. The problem facing Perot was how to get his party on the ballot in all fifty states in order to qualify for federal matching funds. His supporters were, by and large, enthusiastic but disorganized and politically untrained. Newman came to the rescue, throwing his cultists once again into a grueling nationwide ballot drive. Russell J. Verney, national coordinator of the Reform Party and a Perot confidante, stated to the *New York Times* in 1996 that "Mr. Perot was aware and appreciative of the role Ms. Fulani and Dr. Newman have played in helping the Reform Party. 'They are just one voice in a very big group of individuals.'" [53]

At Newman's and Fulani's urging, the Patriot Party and the New York Independence Party affiliated with the Reform Party. Verney recalled that, faced with the need to get 90,000 voters registered in the Reform Party in California, he called Jim Mangia, the chairman of that state's Patriot Party. Mangia was formerly a member of the New Alliance Party. Having succeeded in registering 120,000 voters, Mangia was made secretary of the state Reform Party.[54] In 1999 he assumed the same post in the national party.

In 1997 Richard Lamb, who was defeated by Ross Perot in his effort to become the Reform Party's presidential candidate, split away to form the American Reform Party. "They resented what they said was autocratic management of the party from Dallas," the *Chicago Tribune* reported. "In Illinois, additional resentment had grown over the presence in the party's governing structure of former supporters of Lenora Fulani and the largely defunct New Alliance Party."[55]

In 1998 Lenora Fulani organized the Democracy Slate of candidates for the State Committee of the Independence Party. Both Fulani and Newman were on that slate. She took over control of the party and then ran as the party's candidate for Lieutenant Governor.[56] The Independence Party's platform calls for "fiscal conservatism." It states, "Wherever possible, we prefer to minimize the role of government, transferring needed activities into the private sector through privatization." It favors an alteration of civil service requirements to make it easier to discharge government workers, a one-year New York residency requirement for welfare benefits, no welfare for illegal aliens, public funding for private schools, and more cops.[57]

From early on Newman has displayed little interest in the political programs of the parties he participated in, such as the Democratic Party; or set up and controlled, as in the case of the NAP; or supported, like Farrakhan and Sharpton. Still, until 1994, all his political machinations involved figures and parties generally considered to be on the left of American politics. Since there is nothing even faintly liberal or progressive, not to mention socialist, about the politics of the Reform Party and affiliates, what trick of dialectics did Newman employ to justify his moving into the Perot movement?

Bill Lynch, an aide to former New York City Mayor David Dinkins came up with a cynical answer: "We could never figure out what the New Alliance agenda was. The one common thread was that they were always trying to move in and take over someone else's political operation."[58]

Alliance with Pat Buchanan

Political relations between the Newmanites and Pat Buchanan date back to 1996. In an article entitled "Black Empowerment: What Does the New Populism Mean for African-Americans?" Fulani claimed that Buchanan was being "demonized," comparing him to Louis Farrakhan, Ross Perot, and Jesse Jackson. Buchanan's views were characterized as "anti-government, anti-big business, pro-people." Fulani saw the Reform Party as "populist, not centrist," a populism that "cuts across the traditional labels of right, center and left."[59] She and Newman had already prepared the theoretical groundwork (read: rationalization) for embracing Buchanan as a candidate for president on the Reform Party ticket.

Chip Berlet is one of the few political commentators to note Fulani's shift to the right and to begin to develop a theoretical understanding of its broader implications. He notes that the extreme right wing has developed a "producerist narrative" which pits "hard-working productive middle class and working class" people against a rich elite and a socially parasitic welfare class. This movement is sometimes called "Middle American Nationalism" or the "Radical Center" or "Middle American Radicals." It is narrowly nationalist and isolationist, opposes free trade, and is against big government and business. However, it also tends to be homophobic, racist, sexist, and anti-Semitic.[60] Some leftists have become confused by the "antiwar" and antiglobalist demagogy of these rightists. Fulani and Newman are contributing to that confusion.

Buchanan's interest in Newman and Fulani stems from their power within the Reform Party as well as from the proven ability of their cult followers to put the party on state ballots. At the 1999 Dearborn Convention of the Reform Party, Lenora Fulani received 45 percent of the vote for the position of vice-chair.[61] They dominate the New York, Illinois, and California parties, and have extensive influence elsewhere.

Fulani and Newman have thrown their considerable support behind Pat Buchanan's primary campaign. On November 11, 1999, Fulani announced that she would serve as cochairs of Buchanan's campaign. "In traditional political terms, Pat Buchanan stands for all things that black progressives such as myself revile," Fulani stated. "So how can we get to be standing here together with me endorsing his candidacy? Because we have a common interest in overthrowing the traditional political terms."[62] We are reminded of the German Communist Party in the early 1930s, which campaigned using the slogan "Hitler First, Then Us." There never was a second.

Fulani has framed Buchanan as "a mighty powerful spokesperson for issues of political reform" whose appeal goes "beyond ideology . . . beyond issues of left, center and right."[63] When asked on Cable News Network (CNN) about Buchanan's views on gay rights and abortion, she said that she could overlook them because Buchanan "can play a role as a unifier, bring everybody together."[64] In another interview Fulani said "We're hoping he gets 10 to 15 percent of the vote." Newman added that such a result "keeps the dollars coming in, and it keeps us as America's major minor party." When asked what would happen if Buchanan actually won the presidency, Newman cynically answered "Then we're all in trouble."[65]

It seems quite clear from the above that the Newmanite support for Buchanan is rooted more in opportunism than in ideology. This fits with a pattern of political opportunism that goes back for decades. Their past support for Farrakhan despite his anti-Semitism prepared them for their current role in Buchanan's camp. Hard as it is to believe, the core members of this group, believing themselves to be progressives, even Marxists, will carry out Newman's instructions to advance the agenda of a man whose most recent book claims it was a mistake to oppose Hitler.

The Clandestine Party

We have noted that in 1976 Newman claimed to have dissolved the International Workers Party. However, a reporter on the Upper West Side discovered that the party was never actually dissolved. The evidence suggests that the IWP continues to exist today. Cathy Hollandberg-Serrette, who left the NAP in 1985 with Dennis Serrette, reported that, at the time she left, "the IWP was alive and well with about 150 members in NAP." Sheila McCue, who was associated with Serrette, also confirmed the existence of the IWP.[66] Marina Ortiz reported that in the period between 1985 and 1990: "I was drawn in the group's underground web of pseudo-revolutionary cult activity—The International Workers Party. . . . Once indoctrinated, most IWP cadre are immediately divested of all assets and assigned mandatory fundraising quotas (ranging from $75–300 per week), and bi-weekly IWP 'dues,' which combined with Social Therapy fees, ranges from 15–30% of their income."[67] Wittes referred in 1994 to "a sub-rosa political core made up of the underground remnants of a self-declared Marxist-Leninist revolutionary organization." He stated that "at least five ex-members confirmed the continued existence of the IWP. . . ."[68]

The *New York Times* interviewed Newman in 1996, describing him as "a 61-year-old white-bearded man who looks like Santa Claus after a bohemian makeover." The interview took place in a loft in downtown Manhattan "scattered with mementos of Ché Guevara." Newman came up with an interesting explanation for his support of the Reform Party: "It's like the left going into unions controlled by gangsters. You have a chance to make a statement to the rank and file, and then maybe you can do something about the gangsters."[69]

This indicates that Newman still thinks like the Leninist operator he was in the days of LaRouche. His cadres, his comment suggests, sustain a long-term "left" goal. The route has turned out to be more circuitous than it had originally appeared to be in his "Marxist-Leninist-Maoist" days. Yet they believe that, someday and somehow, world progress is being served. In the meantime his therapeutically enslaved minions operate within the Reform Party and, in some places, control its apparatus. Political influence and power clearly please Newman and Fulani, while activism keeps the client/organizers busy, their minds empty, and their loyalties guaranteed.

The potential danger in this situation is not to be ignored. After all, Jesse Ventura, a wrestler, ran on the Reform Party ticket in Minnesota in 1998 and won, becoming governor. Considering the public's disgust with the two major parties, it is not to be excluded that the Reform Party can win again. That could place parasitic Newmanites into positions of influence. Once in power, their allegiance would not be to the voters but to their guru Fred Newman. The Newmanites' support for Pat Buchanan has already had the negative and dangerous effect of assisting a right-wing demagogue in channeling legitimate dissatisfaction in a fascistic direction.

Today, in addition to his secretive political activities, Fred Newman considers himself a playwright. He is also the artistic director of the Castillo Theater, an "interactive growth theater," which is a form of therapy directed toward people of color. He is the director of training at the East Side Institute for Short Term Psychotherapy and has written several books that are featured at his Castillo Bookstore. He operates the West Coast Center for Social Therapy in San Francisco and similar centers in Los Angeles, Chicago, and other cities. He describes these centers as "a unique 'laboratory'—the 25–year-old development community of thousands of people who are living more developmental and joyous lives and helping thousands more to do so."[70]

For all the deprivations he has demanded over the years from his followers, he, like other gurus, is not living that badly himself. In the fall of 1993 he purchased, together with longtime member Susan Massad, a large Greenwich Village brownstone at 60 Bank Street for $928,000. Revolution combined with therapy can be profitable.

Conclusion: New Age Leninism

It should come as no surprise that Fred Newman, Lenora Fulani, and other spokespeople for the group do not share our assessment that they run a cult. In fact in 1993 they took legal action against the FBI for characterizing them as a "political/cult organization."[71] Lenora Fulani stated that "the word 'cult' is a weapon, a murderously vicious, anti-democratic weapon used to attack people who are different in any way: religiously, politically, culturally or otherwise. . . . *There is no such thing as a cult* [emphasis in original]."[72] At the time Fulani and Newman's lobbying arm, Ross and Green, was running a campaign in defense of the Branch Davidians after the Waco disaster.

Of course, if cults do not exist, then the Newmanites could not possibly be a cult. The difficulty with this position comes when we confront events like the Jonestown massacre or the more recent Heaven's Gate suicides. Are we dealing in these cases simply with people who are "different," or is there something more sinister involved, which requires serious inquiry?

Fulani and Newman's defense of religious cults like the Branch Davidians,[73] is a recognition of a commonality with them. In other words, if Fulani is wrong and cults do exist, then her statement represents a form of identification with the world of cults. What she is really saying is that these groups are just "different" like *us*.

A study of the Newmanites deepens our understanding of other political cults as well as the cult phenomenon as a whole. This is because Fred Newman's therapeutic approach exposes the essential mechanisms of mind control utilized, though not necessarily admitted to, by all cults. The Newmanites display another interesting feature. Their preservation, though in clandestine fashion, of a Leninist cadre organization, suggests the usefulness of vanguard ideology to political cults. LaRouche, for example, has sustained this side of his thinking during his travel to the extreme right of the political spectrum (see chapter 5).

This outlook has contributed to the manipulative nature of their political activity. Newman, particularly after his LaRouchian period, has been relatively unconcerned with the *content* of politics, while becoming extremely adept at its practice. This has permitted him to support anti-Semitic black leaders, build a vaguely defined left party, run in Democratic Party primaries, support the right centrist Reform Party, and finally assist Pat Buchanan in his presidential bid. Politics is conceived as something to be practiced to achieve influence and power as well as to lead to growth of his core group.

Newman has become a New Age Leninist. While his group has been wildly successful when we look at its meager beginnings in a West Side apartment, it does have its limits. The Newmanites have learned better than most political cults how to successfully manipulate the American political arena and the media. Yet they remain a small group. One estimate does not give them more than a hundred core members today.[74] However, these members are highly skilled political operatives, hard-working and motivated, and they function with lockstep discipline. Newman has done considerable political damage in the past. Given the state of politics in the United States, he may emerge as a serious threat to democratic processes in the future.

Chapter 8

Synanon

Utopia as a Game

It's all done with words.
—Charles Dederich, quoted in Dave Mitchell, Cathy Mitchell,
Richard Ofshe, *The Light on Synanon*

Los Angeles attorney Paul Morantz was worried as he drove to his Pacific Palisades home on the evening of October 10, 1978. He had recently won a $300,000 settlement against the Synanon Foundation. He had heard that Charles Dederich, Synanon's founder, had threatened his life. He took the threat seriously. That afternoon he had met with two agents of the California Attorney General's Organized Crime Bureau. He had examined his car before getting into it.

Arriving at his house, Morantz checked out the bushes. He walked carefully up to his front door. Unlocking it and pushing it wide open, he did not enter immediately. He was relieved to hear the joyful barking of his two collies. He entered the house, went into the kitchen to find the dogs, and let them out the front door for a run. Returning to the car for some groceries, he carried them into the kitchen.

As he passed his mailbox, which was built into the wall beside his door, he noticed something inside. He could not see what it was, as he was not wearing his contacts. Assuming it was a parcel, he opened the mailbox, and reached inside. He grabbed a four-and-a-half-foot rattlesnake and pulled it out. Just as he recognized what it was, the rattler dug its fangs into his left hand. Uncontrollably, his hand swung into the air and the snake landed on the floor.

Morantz had to lean over the coiled snake to close the front door to protect the dogs. Then he dashed out the back door, yelling to his neighbors: "Call an ambulance! I've been bitten by a rattlesnake. . . . It's Synanon!"

His neighbors had him lie down. He grew dizzy and went into shock. The paramedics arrived and rushed him to the USC Medical Center. He almost died.[1]

Origins

> *Our doors are nailed open.*
> —Charles Dederich, quoted in William Olin,
> *Escape from Utopia: My Ten Years in Synanon*

Charles Dederich was born in Toledo, Ohio, in 1913. During the Depression he got a desk job with Gulf Oil in Toledo, married, had one son, and hung out with a group of Communist Party members.[2] In later life he would fuse his Communist experience with what he learned from his capitalist job. In 1944, he suffered from an attack of meningitis that left half his face paralyzed and caused a loss of hearing in one ear. After recovering, he headed for Los Angeles, where he divorced his first wife, remarried, had a second child, and worked a number of different jobs. He had become a confirmed drunk, but unlike most alcoholics, he was also a gluttonous eater. He weighed over three hundred pounds.

In 1956 Dederich's second wife got him to join Alcoholics Anonymous (AA). He went on the wagon and stayed sober until 1978. He took to AA with a vengeance, attending daily meetings, which he dominated, and touring the state for the organization. He was an effective speaker, a born salesman, and an ebullient comic. Dederich left his wife, moved into a small apartment, and lived on a $33 weekly unemployment check. In late 1957 a number of his followers from AA moved into the apartment with him. They spent their days and nights in constant discussion, attracted drunks, and converted them to their version of AA.

In early 1958, Dederich's mob had gotten too large for his apartment. He rented a storefront in Venice, called the place the "Tender Loving Care Club," and broke off relations with AA. A heroin addict stumbled in one day, and Dederich found he was able to break him from drugs. More addicts joined and the alcoholics left or were pushed out by Dederich. In September 1958, he incorporated the group. It had forty members and was already gaining favorable publicity. Synanon had been founded.[3]

Dederich's timing could not have been better. A heroin epidemic was sweeping the country. Psychiatrists believed drug addiction was untreatable. The only treatment available to addicts was to be detoxed in a government hospital. This proved to be a miserable failure, with no better than a 10 percent success rate. Dederich appeared to have stumbled upon a new therapeutic method that succeeded where everyone else had failed.

He took an addict off the street, placed him on a couch in the center of a room, and detoxed him cold turkey, providing nothing more than a bucket to vomit in and the emotional support of a fellow human being. Once their systems were clean of drugs, the addicts were subjected to intense verbal attack as part of a form of group therapy he called the "Game." They were ridiculed if they broke the group's strict rules, and were required to be residents of Synanon. There were only two other rules: no drugs and no violence.

In 1960 Synanon left its Venice storefront and moved into an old armory in Santa Monica. A conflict with the local community, which did not want ex-addicts living near them, only gave Synanon greater publicity. In 1965 a movie, *Synanon*, starring Chuck Connors, Edmond O'Brien, and Richard Conte, added to the group's glamour. Two highly flattering books were published.[4] Thousands entered the program; new residences were established in San Francisco, Oakland, and Tomales Bay; and the money rolled in. Some left Synanon and formed rival drug rehabilitation centers utilizing some of Dederich's techniques: Phoenix House and Day Top Village in New York City, Delancey Street in San Francisco.

Surprisingly no one in the 1960s made a scientific study of the actual effectiveness of Synanon. Dederich built his fame on the testimonials of those he had cured and furnished no statistics on his failures. Sociologist Richard Ofshe conducted such a study in the 1970s and concluded that Synanon's success rate was no better than the 10 percent achieved by hospitals.[5] Synanon was successful as long as the ex-addict remained a resident in one of its facilities, but 90 percent of those who entered Synanon left before being rehabilitated and returned to drugs. This fact, while left out of his public relations releases, was not lost on Dederich. By the late sixties he had given up on returning ex-addicts to society at large in favor of creating a utopian community. Synanon became transformed from a drug therapy program into a communal political cult.

The Game

> *You're working on the ordinary mind, assaulting it, attacking it, rocking it.*
> —Charles Dederich, quoted in David U. Gerstel,
> *Paradise Incorporated: Synanon*

The game was at the very center of Synanon life throughout its entire existence. It was the honey that attracted people to it, the glue that held it together, the weapon that permitted Chuck Dederich to dominate his followers. Its structure was simple enough: a group of a dozen or so people sat on chairs in a circle and talked. Participants were urged to say anything that came into their head, the more emotionally charged and extreme the better. It was a verbal free-for-all, a no-holds-barred oral wrestling match. As Dederich said, "It's all done with words."

"You put the game on a person and the way he sat, the clothes he wore, the expression on his face, the way he talked," the jazz musician Art Pepper, who lived in Synanon for three years, reported. "Those were the things you picked apart. And you got him so angry he lost his inhibitions. You got him so frustrated and humiliated he'd flip out and let his real feelings come forth. The game was a place to cathart. It was a verbal vomiting."[6]

"One player pointed out the defects or mistakes of another, and then other players joined what regularly was an angry attack," William Olin noted. "Unless the accused could quickly talk his way out of the indictment, he faced a snarling pack of game players denouncing him." The victim was confronted with "a tidal wave of hatred. The first time it hits you, it absolutely destroys you."[7]

David Gerstel also discovered the game was not to be played gingerly. "Start yelling, David," he was advised, "a Game isn't an intellectual discussion. You've got to be aggressive in the Game. Fight, attack. Start yelling. Yell anything that comes into your head."[8] As long as they abstained from physical violence, participants were urged to be as aggressive and hostile as they could be *within* the game. However, they were expected to put these sentiments aside once the game was over. The theory was that relieving tensions within the game made it easier for Synanon members to live cooperatively outside the game.

The game was effective on "dope fiends," as they were called in Synanon, by breaking down any rationalizations they may have developed to defend their conduct, and to ensure that they followed the rules of the community related to drug use and stealing. During the early days of an addict's stay at a Synanon facility, the game was supplemented by more drastic means of humiliation. "One Sunday evening, . . ." Olin reported, "I stopped by a room to check on a construction item. I opened the door onto a Kafkaesque scene. Six or eight 'mooks' (big guys) were screaming obscenities at some poor slob with his freshly shaved head sticking out of a cardboard pillory-like contraption. Bright spotlights were aimed right into his blinking eyes. . . . Asking around, I found out that this technique was used, in Chuck's words, 'to get the attention' of character-disorders who commit Synanon felonies."[9]

The Synanon game seemed on the surface to be a free and democratic institution. There was no moderator or leader in the game, and everyone was encouraged to express what he or she really felt. Once participants learned how to play, it could be fun. There were techniques to learn: how to deflect criticism, when and how to shift the game to your attacker ("turn the game back on" someone), how to join in the attack on someone in the hot seat ("rat-packing"), and how to build your attack into "a crashing crescendo of wildly exaggerated criticisms ('engrossments')." There was even a "carom shot," in which a couple of people would be attacked as a way of setting up a major onslaught on a third player. And, of course, a caustic sense of humor could be a potent weapon.[10] "The idea was that ranking you and exposing your bad habits would make you eventually change," Art Pepper summed up, "and it worked, you know, it worked."[11]

The game evolved and took more complex forms as Synanon grew. There was a technique called the "perpetual stew," which started up in the Tomales Bay facility, continued twenty-four hours a day, and went on uninterrupted for years. People would be scheduled for "sixteen-, thirty-, and fourteen-hour segments with two six-hour sleep breaks in between."[12] Sometimes the stew would be moved to another facility, like Santa Monica or San Francisco. The stew members were loaded on a bus, called the Synacruiser. They would "stew" during the drive, and then, upon arriving, would continue at the new facility with new members added.

A technique called the "trip" was a more concentrated and extreme form of the stew. A group would be shipped off to another facility, usually Santa Monica, for seventy-two hours. Instead of their regular clothes, participants wore special robes. The guides for the trip had different-colored robes. Participants were sleep deprived, allowed only one four-hour nap during the treatment. Intense pressure was mounted in the game to force each person to confess to some terrible deed from his or her past. In time each person broke down separately, confessed, and burst into tears. People would rush up and hug them, also crying. Then the participants were hustled back into buses to return, uplifted, hooked on Synanon.[13]

In actual practice, however, the game was far from democratic. From its very origins it became an effective form of thought control. Dederich's will was imposed on his followers through this maddening, exuberant process. To survive at Synanon, one quickly learned to play the game from the "Synanon position."[14] This meant confessing when accused of breaking Synanon rules, and rat-packing against others who purportedly broke rules. If you resisted a Dederich pronouncement or persisted in criticizing Dederich and his chosen representatives, you were subjected to repeated attacks of rising intensity. You were urged to "split." Sooner or later the recalcitrants adapted or left. "Everybody around me was brainwashed into this Synanon system of brotherly love and helping each other," Pepper noted. "If Chuck Dederich . . . were to tell them to jump out of the sixth-story window of the club they'd all jump because they'd think that's the 'Synanon Thing.' . . ."[15]

Drug addicts were cured as long as they remained residents of Synanon. The price they were expected to pay was complete subservience to Dederich. "I made you, buster," he once shouted at his second in command, Jack Hurst, "and by Jesus Christ, I can break you."[16] On another occasion he put it this way: "I made you sane and I can make you insane."[17]

The game represented one of the most effective forms of "groupthink," discussed in chapter 2, that has ever been devised. It resembles closely the criticism/self-criticism sessions of Marxist-Leninist groups, such as Marlene Dixon's Democratic Workers Party (chapter 9). It is quite remarkable that, during the early period of Synanon, its practices caused so little concern among the general public. In fact, Synanon found itself smothered in praise and adulation. We are sure that part of the answer lies with the public's disdain for drug addicts. Finding themselves the victims of drug-related crime, many did not view addicts as people, certainly not people with minds to be protected and rights to be defended. As long as Synanon seemed to "work," few cared what tricks Dederich used to control his dope fiend followers.

The "game" developed at a time when many other new "therapies" were also coming on the scene. It is most closely related to catharsis therapy, sometimes called encounter groups. These therapies include Primal Scream, EST, Lifespring, and Mystic Rose. They are closely related to Harvey Jackins's theory of "discharge" (chapter 6), and they continue to be quite popular. The general idea is to denounce participants, developing group pressure to the point where the client explodes emotionally. This catharsis is supposed to purge the client of bad feelings and hostility, making her or him well. As Singer and Lalich have pointed out, "Catharsis theory in all its forms has been challenged repeatedly over the years. Evidence that expressing angry, violent behavior does not drain it away but increases the chances of its recurrence has been presented in the scientific literature for years."[18] We have already noted that there is no scientific basis to the claim that Synanon's game "worked" as a drug therapy. However, it certainly did work effectively in modifying the behavior of his followers so that Dederich could control them. Catharsis for Chuck was only a preparatory step in a process that subordinated the will of the individual participant to the "Synanon way." Dederich lacked any training in psychology, held no degrees, belonged to no professional associations, and was subject to no form of state regulation.

Thought control in the form of the game was at the heart of the Synanon "cure." Dederich's "gift" to humanity became a curse that created the conditions for Synanon's clash with the rest of society and its final downfall. The one led inevitably to the other as cause leads to effect.

Building Utopia

> *Anything less than changing the world is Mickey*
> *Mouse to me.*
> —Charles Dederich, quoted in Margaret Thaler Singer
> and Janja Lalich, *Crazy Therapies*

Starting in 1968, Synanon underwent a change. Dederich abandoned any effort to rehabilitate drug addicts for reentry into society. "A person with a fatal disease will have to live here all of his life," he proclaimed. "I know damn well if they go out of Synanon, they are dead."[19] His "dope fiend" followers were convinced that their very lives were dependent upon Dederich. They became his most abject followers in a growing utopian community. However, recruitment from this milieu began to taper off as the heroin epidemic crested and Synanon faced competition from other therapy centers, many founded by "splitees."

Dederich responded to this challenge by pitching Synanon to the growing layer of people in the late sixties and early seventies searching for alternative lifestyles. Synanon was being sold as "a better way to live,"[20] an alternative to cravenly materialistic and competitive capitalist society. "Those who know little about Synanon are under the misapprehension that we are in the business of 'curing' dope addiction," Dederich told Guy Endore. "Of course that isn't so. Synanon just happens to be a better way for people to live together. . . ."[21]

Chuck's vision was grandiose. He would build Synanon City on his Tamales Bay property, a city that "can make a demonstration of new ways of doing things, new ways of living that can guide the course of the larger society."[22] John Maher, who left Synanon and went on to found Delancey Street, believed "Dederich concluded that the outside world was crazed beyond redemption," and therefore, "abandoned his early desire to build a revolutionary movement, and steered Synanon into an isolation 'Amish in its totality.'"[23]

He was by no means unsuccessful. By 1972 Synanon boasted 1,700 residents living in facilities in Santa Monica, San Francisco, Oakland, and Tamales Bay; several thousand more part-time participants; tens of millions of dollars in resources; hundreds of talented professionals as members; and a favorable reputation with the public. Synanon was the largest and longest-lasting utopian community constructed in the twentieth century.

The key to this new stage of Synanon growth was the Game Clubs. "Squares," as they were called, attended weekly games at the various Synanon facilities. By 1968 some 3,400 middle-class people were participating on a regular basis. The games would include a sprinkling of older dope fiend Synanon members. Sessions were followed by an informal social gathering. Some music would be played, and soon all would be dancing the "Hoopla," Synanon's form of group rock.

A continuing stream of club members would be convinced to join Synanon full time. This usually took the form of becoming "lifestylers." These were squares who lived in Synanon residences but continued to hold outside jobs. Typically, lifestylers would sell all their possessions and turn over the money, as well as their pay, to Synanon. The most dedicated lifestylers would be encouraged to give up their outside jobs and work full time for Synanon.[24]

Synanon was particularly appealing to single women with children. The woman would find a home and companionship while the children would be taken off her hands and raised by the community. A particularly poignant example of this is described by Deborah Swisher in her one-woman play *Hundreds of Sisters and One Big Brother*. Swisher, who has an African-American father and a white Jewish mother, entered Synanon at the age of seven with her sister and mother. She walked out at age eighteen, but her mother stayed on.[25]

Synanon was a communitarian minisociety. Members had neither personal possessions nor privacy. Most lived in a dormitory setting, men with men and women with women, though some privileged couples lived together. Children were housed separately from adults. Synanon supplied all necessities—clothes, toiletries, bedding—while all meals were eaten in common. Everyone was given a pittance of weekly walking-around money (WAM). Members spent most of their free time in common rooms, playing the game and socializing. All were assigned some form of work in maintaining Synanon, running its money-making enterprises, and constructing its facilities.

Dederich, however, made no pretense at equality. In fact he believed in inequality, rewarding his most loyal supporters with special goods—color televisions, private accommodations, motorcycles—and he lived with his wife, Betty, like a king. However, in a manner reminiscent of Stalinist society, these perks could be, and were from time to time, taken away. Dederich gave and he could take back, for he viewed Synanon as his own possession. "They'd have 'glut' raids," Art Pepper reported, "getting rid of the opulence. Or somebody would attain a high position after years of carrying out his faithful duty to the Synanon doctrines and the word of the great lord and master, Chuck Dederich: He would be rewarded and then all of a sudden the gestapo would come and take away everything he had and make him wash dishes and scrub toilets and make his wife live in a dormitory with the other broads and newcomers."[26]

Gerstel was present when Dederich sent the Synacruiser to Santa Monica, loaded "the dirty double dozen" of dope fiend old-timers on the bus, and brought them up north to the Tomales Bay facility. There he denounced them as "racketeers," took away their possessions, and forced them to take menial positions. This way he kept his underlings in line, and also lessened the influence of the older ex–drug addict element at a time when he was courting the squares.[27]

Synanon was a wealthy community. Its main source of income was Advertising Gifts and Premiums (ADGAP), which sold pens and desk accessories, adorned with company logos, to businesses. ADGAP was the second-largest company in that business, grossing $9.58 million in 1978.[28] The company was staffed entirely by unpaid Synanon members. Another group of members were involved in "hustling," or direct soliciting from companies, foundations, and wealthy individuals. Squares gave Synanon their worldly possessions when they joined. One heiress donated over $1 million. Synanon won a libel judgment against the Hearst Corporation and collected $2.6 million.[29] Synanon also received income from the government for drug addicts and for troubled teenagers sent to it by courts. It received over $1 million in surplus goods from the federal government. Dederich dished out utopia on a silver platter. At least his platter was silver! As Dederich once said, Synanon was sure a "nice little family business."[30]

In 1974 Dederich had Synanon incorporated as a "church." His goal, like that of Scientology, was to take advantage of the tax breaks and lesser degree of government oversight that go with that designation. Was Synanon in reality a religion? It is very difficult to find even the rudiments of what is normally considered a church in Synanon. There were no special religious ceremonies or rituals, and mention of a "higher being" was generally missing from its literature and from game playing. Dederich operated with the minimum of dogma, outside of a fondness for Emerson. For Dederich everything was "process," and scripture was relegated to expletives in game sessions. Synanon was a religion only in the sense that all cults have a religious side to them. It was no more or less a religion than Trotskyism, or Marxist-Leninism, or reevaluation, or radical therapy, in the hands of cultic practitioners.

What makes Synanon interesting is precisely its character as a *political*, as distinct from a religious, utopian community. Efforts in the nineteenth century to establish political utopias were notable failures. Brook Farm, inspired in part by the teachings of Dederich's mentor, Emerson, lasted five years. Robert Owen's New Harmony, remembered mostly for its disharmony and factionalism, also barely survived five years.[31] The Fourierists were even more ephemeral, most phalanxes lucky to make it through a year. Charles Nordhoff's visit to the impoverished Icarians in Iowa, the longest-lasting political utopia, was less than inspiring: "It is the least prosperous of all the communities I have visited; and I could not help feeling pity, if not for the men, yet for the women and children of the settlement."[32] Synanon fared better than any of its nineteenth-century predecessors. It is clear that the reason for its minor success was the cohesiveness Dederich achieved through his group mind-game technique. But Dederich's dominance was also the problem: The longer Synanon lasted, the scarier it got.

Children in Paradise

> *Small children make disgusting noises and smell bad.*
> —Charles Dederich, quoted in David U. Gerstel,
> *Paradise Incorporated: Synanon*

The most striking feature of Synanon's approach to the family was its treatment of children. As soon as a family entered a residential facility, the children were separated from the parents. They lived in dormitories separated by sex and age. Contact between parents and siblings was minimal. Months could go by without a child seeing her or his mother or father.[33] Dederich's aim was to raise a breed of super-Synanon children, loyal only to the community and to him personally. To a great extent he was successful.

One of his failures was Julie Johnson. She joined Synanon with her mother and two siblings in 1971. "We rarely saw our parents. In some cases, parents lived in other facilities over 300 miles away." In the early years the educational approach was very progressive. The teachers were called "demonstrators." "The infants slept on cardboard beds on the floor. They could get in or out at will. They were fed at huge long tables covered with plastic. The demonstrators would dump food out on the table and the children would grab it with their hands." Everyone had a work assignment, with the older children helping with the teaching of the younger ones. "When mail arrived from the outside, the staff would open it up. If there was candy or clothes, they wouldn't give it to us unless it could be shared by the whole school."[34]

At the beginning, the kids were disciplined in a fashion similar to the adults. For punishment they might get their hair shaved off or be given hard work assignments. From the age of four on up, they were expected to play the game. Until 1973, "Synanon was a relatively rational place for the children to live. Sure there were many things happening much different than the outside. We were influenced and constantly told what we were to believe and I think of this as brainwashing. There was none of the craziness, violence, and mixed messages which were about to begin."

In the fall of 1973 Synanon started taking in kids from juvenile courts. Dederich soon found these children could not be handled through Synanon's normal group mind exercises. Synanon assembled these kids in boot camps, made them drill in military style, and physically abused them. At the same time the regular Synanon school came under attack for being run by "a bunch of hip liberal lifestylers." Julie Johnson, who was one of the more rebellious of the children, reported "they threatened to throw me out the window." She was also threatened with spanking with a belt. She witnessed a young girl being beaten with a table tennis paddle.

The violence escalated. "Many kids were brutally hit. Now I don't mean just spanked or slapped across the face. These kids were literally picked up by the collar of their shirt and thrown across the room, punched in the stomach, slammed into bunk beds, all because they had sheets showing underneath their beds or were not standing at perfect attention." Because she did not run well enough, an adult "then proceeded to punch me in the stomach, socked me in the head, and pulled my hair." In one case two boys were beaten "in front of about 500 adults and children."

Julie Johnson ran away from Synanon at the age of fifteen. Her story was confirmed by others. Deborah Swisher, who was seven years old when she entered Synanon along with her mother and sister, had a similar experience. At the beginning, except for missing her mother, it was fun. "Synanon was like summer school. . . . There were bean bags and a pet rat or a snake. We'd study the growth of an embryo. We had a whole science lab." But in time it grew more sinister. She was singled out as "damaged goods," her elders claiming her spirit had been polluted by a negative attitude. She felt herself "mentally brutalized."[35]

A "punk squad" was formed out of the more difficult Synanon children. "For several months they were put through a regimen of marching, calisthenics, running, and hard physical work. They were made to address all adults as 'sir' or 'ma'am.' They stood at rigid attention for inspection by their squad leaders. And they were subjected to physical punishment."[36] Dederich boasted: "After about one week of this treatment, these kids turn into woolly lambs."[37]

The transformation of Dederich's relatively benign (if we leave out the cruelty of separating children and parents) experiment in the progressive rearing of children into a hellish regime far more similar to the Marine Corps' Parris Island than to John Dewey's concepts was, as we will see, reflective of the degeneration that had set into all aspects of Synanon in the middle seventies. However, it was also indicative of the cultic nature of Synanon. Child abuse is fairly common in communal cults.[38] Children are the most vulnerable members in a closed community bent on control and manipulation. Dederich's original idea was to transform the Synanon children into a super race to lead the group into the next century. He turned in the end to a brutality that the greater society, with all its faults, had long since made illegal. The pattern was being established for Synanon as a whole: In the name of the highest ideals, the cruelest treatment and corruption were being practiced. The analogy with state socialism under a Stalin or Pol Pot is hard to resist.

Love and Marriage the Synanon Way

> *Chuck is marvelous. He had this amazing quality of being able to articulate what we want to do before we even know what it is we want.*
> —A Synanon member quoted in Olin,
> *Escape from Utopia*

Many utopians are unable to resist tinkering with the family. There is, of course, a good reason for this. The thought control needed to give a utopian community cohesiveness and to subordinate its members to the community's founder, brooks no competition for the allegiance of the disciples. The family institution competes with the new communal institutional control mechanisms. We have seen the grotesque results in Dederich's child-rearing experiments. Now we turn to his assault upon the emotional bonds between husband and wife.

Synanon's efforts to control sexual relations among its adherents began almost from the origins of the group. After a brief period of somewhat loose and promiscuous relations, sexual conduct was regulated by Dederich's regime. Most residents lived in sexually segregated dormitories. This was true even for married couples during their initial years in residency. There were guest rooms set aside for sexual encounters, and a person was in charge of setting up appointments. You were expected to bring your own sheets and pillowcases. "You get two times a week to start out, just two-hour sessions," Art Pepper was told. "Later you can get four hours and when you have seniority you get overnights."[39]

While it may be difficult to believe, these arrangements did not completely stamp out romance. In fact Art Pepper's account of his pursuit of Laurie, his future wife, is a charming love story, despite the institutional interventions. Pepper first had to request permission from his "tribe" leader (the Santa Monica facility was so big its residents were divided up into tribes) and then meet with Laurie's tribe leader. When both agreed the two were allowed to have a "courtship." This permitted them to spend time together, hold hands, and kiss—nothing more. Art had to repeat the procedure in order to move into a "relationship," with guest room privileges.

"Laurie and I went to the guestroom two or three times a week, and it was great," Art Pepper reported. This went on for two and a half years. After leaving Synanon the two were married. In the end it was Laurie and methadone, not Synanon, that kept Pepper off heroin during his last decade of life.[40]

The high point in the first, manipulative, but relatively benign, stage of Dederich's management of sexual relations came in 1972. Dederich held a mass wedding of 150 couples. By then it was understood that Synanon itself was the "third partner in the first position"[41] in all marriages. Synanon became even more intrusive. Couples were expected to post on the wall a scorecard listing the number of times a week they had sexual relations, with a column so that each partner could grade the performance of the other. The game was used many times for exploring further the sexual conduct of members.

In 1976 Dederich launched a new offensive on the members in a speech entitled "Childbirth Unmasked: Teachings."[42] He claimed that the act of childbirth was overrated, comparing having a baby to "crapping a football." Furthermore, there were too many unwanted babies in the world. Therefore all Synanon men from the age of nineteen on up were to have vasectomies and all pregnant women abortions. One woman, who had never had a child, was forced to abort in her fifth month. Everything was done to make vasectomies, performed by Synanon doctors at the group's facilities, seem a lighthearted matter. "[M]en lay on beds, holding ice packs between their legs. Women bounced around serving cookies and cool drinks and being cheerful. The hard-core porno movie, *Deep Throat*, was playing."[43] Those who resisted Dederich's edict were gamed so severely that they left.

The next year Dederich concluded his flock was ready for "emotional surgery." Chuck's wife Betty had died of cancer. Dederich announced to the community that he was accepting applications from women who wanted to marry him. He tested three out in bed and settled on a new wife. His experiment had worked out so well he decided it was just the thing for all his followers. All married couples were requested to take separation vows. "They told one another how they valued the years they had spent together. They expressed gratitude to Synanon for making those years possible. Moments later, the overhead lights in the theater flickered on. The candles and incense that had been burning were extinguished. Two men rolled in a large blackboard. A . . . manager entered, chalked the names of newly separated men and women on the board, and instructed them to pick new mates."[44] They were to live with their new spouses for three years. Then the process would be initiated all over again. The few Synanon residents who resisted being rematched were pressured to leave the community.

The Squeeze

> *Now I want to move ahead. Do you? . . . I have*
> *to know when to say GO. And then everybody's*
> *got to come along or out. OUT!*
> —Charles Dederich, quoted in Gerstel,
> *Paradise Incorporated*

Dederich, flush with success in the early seventies, had visions of an ever-expanding Synanon City that would attract new recruits because of its superior lifestyle. This was not to come to pass. By 1974 he realized that lifestyle recruiting was tapering off. Fewer people were attending weekly games, and only a trickle of these part-time game players were moving into Synanon residences. He concluded that less was better. He believed that he could sustain the flow of income while having fewer mouths to feed and more loyal subjects. Therefore he forced his members to jump through a series of hoops.

Each member went through something like the hero's journey in classic mythology. The hero, in this case a Synanon member, traveled down a road where he met increasingly difficult trials. View the trials as a series of caves, each more menacing than the last. The hero was tested at the threshold of each one. Finally, he reached the inmost cave. Dederich played all the roles: the threshold guardian placing impediments in the way; the mentor providing the training needed to prevail; the trickster, both entertaining and mystifying. Above all Dederich was a shape-shifting evil shadow. In Dederich's twist on historic mythology, once the hero reached the inmost cave he discovered that there was nothing there— and no way out. [45]

Several of Dederich's directives to his followers originated when Chuck himself needed to make a change because of serious health problems. A communitywide ban on smoking was instituted in 1969. "At first it was a voluntary thing," Pepper reported; but that soon changed: "All the kids in Tomales Bay, the fanatical followers, they got together with Chuck and said, 'To help you stop, we're going to stop smoking.'" [46] Those who couldn't stop smoking, and that included Art Pepper, left. More members were lost through the antismoking squeeze than through subsequent squeezes which seemed, on the surface, more draconian. In part this may have been because it was the first cave for the followers to pass through and thus it sorted out the weakest members. However, the fact that a heroin addict, like Art Pepper, could break from junk but not from cigarettes says something about nicotine's addictive powers.

A series of similar health edicts followed in the mid-seventies. All sugar and refined grains were banned. Then one day in the middle of a game, a "door opened and four men, each grasping the corner of a stretcher upon which was piled a large whitish mass, marched in. . . . Movie cameras tracked the progress. When they reached the stage, they stopped. The mass emitted a groaning sound and slowly heaved itself off the stretcher. It was Charles Dederich, wearing tennis shoes, shorts, and a sweatshirt, with his arm in a sling and his knee in an ace bandage. As the stretcher bearers exited, he limped and staggered onto the stage and gasped into a microphone, 'You're not going to believe this, but I got into marvelous shape after just a month of jogging in place.'"[47]

Soon everyone in Synanon was running in place (RIPing it was called) each day for the prescribed twelve minutes, at the prescribed rate of eighty beats a minute, and lifting their feet the prescribed eight-inch height. Olin, who ran five miles a day, hoped he would be exempt. He was not.[48] Those who would not or could not perform these aerobics left.

Chuck began to worry about his weight. All residents were forced to weigh in each week. The weigh-ins were done in the nude before all residents, and the flabby were mercilessly teased.

Then came the beam incident. One day Dederich was taken on a tour of a newly constructed building on the Tomales Bay property. While checking out the second floor, his head banged into a steel beam that was a little over five feet above the floor. He fell into a rage, demanding to know who among his followers could have been so stupid as to place a steel beam so low. Synanon facilities were covered by a low-wattage FM radio station, called the Wire, that everyone was expected to listen to all day long. It broadcast live all important games as well as pronouncements by Dederich. He proclaimed over the Wire that he blamed himself for placing stupid people in charge of the project and he was going to shave his head, a sign of humiliation.

Within hours all the men in Synanon shaved their heads in support of the Founder. As reports on the haircutting went out over the Wire, a beautiful woman with long black hair that flowed down to her waist, rose from her seat in the game and approached the haircutting area. She demanded the privilege to have her hair cut like the men. As the long strands of hair fell to the floor the scene was reported over the Wire. The women in all facilities "began cutting each other's hair into misshapen pageboys. A young woman with waist-length blonde hair cried as the scissors snapped behind her neck." "Fantastic," shouted Dederich. Within hours almost all women, as well as men, were bald. Those who refused left Synanon.[49]

We have already discussed separately the sexual aspects of the squeeze: vasectomies, abortions, and rematching of couples. All these trials served their purpose in creating a smaller, more docile group of followers. In 1972 there were 1,700 people in Synanon. By 1978 the population had been reduced to 996.[50]

Violence and Paranoia

> *I am quite willing to break some lawyer's legs*
> *and break his wife's legs and threaten to cut*
> *their child's arm off. I really do want an ear*
> *in a glass of alcohol. Yes, indeed.*
> —Charles Dederich, quoted in Olin,
> *Escape from Utopia*

It began with a can of Dad's Old Fashioned Root Beer one afternoon in the summer of 1973. A rather difficult woman was playing the game with Dederich in the circle. She not only showed him no respect but also insisted on interrupting him several times. Dederich grew increasingly agitated. Finally, he got up from his seat, walked over to her, and dumped the contents of his opened and half drunk can of root beer over her head. This seemingly small incident was taken very seriously within Synanon. From its origins in 1958 Synanon had had only two rules: No drugs and no violence. Members were stunned. Some wondered if the "old man" had gone insane. Years later, defectors would refer to the Dad's Root Beer incident as the turning point when Synanon began to unravel.[51]

It was soon after the root beer incident that Synanon began taking in troubled youths from juvenile courts. As we have noted, Dederich made the decision to use corporal punishment on them and then extended its use to Synanon's own children. Dederich encouraged and justified this violence. Members became accustomed to its use and a cult of toughness developed. "Within Synanon there were no controls on him," Gerstel summarized, referring to Dederich, "and he was coming to think of himself as beyond control by outer society."[52]

In 1972 the San Francisco *Examiner* had published a series of articles highly critical of Synanon. Synanon had reacted by suing Hearst. Hearst settled out of court for $2.6 million. Dederich felt emboldened, omnipotent, launching lawsuits for tens of millions of dollars at the drop of a hat.[53]

At the same time the corruption of Dederich and those immediately around him increased at an exponential rate. Synanon bought a beautiful property in Badger, near Sequoia National Park. Dederich moved there, calling it Homeplace. Dederich lived in luxury in a specially built lodge, surrounded by his "toys": luxury cars, motorcycles, airplanes. He was waited on hand and foot, and held sumptuous three-hour dinners, seeking to "squeeze more sensation out of life."[54]

Along with arrogance came paranoia. Dederich became increasingly convinced that the world outside Synanon—a world that had once idealized him—had turned against him. He organized an armed guard, called the "Imperial Marines," to patrol the facilities. Inevitably this led to conflict with his neighbors, particularly in the Tomales Bay region. Yet the major press ignored Synanon, the police trod lightly, and the district attorney took no action. Everyone was afraid of Dederich and his lawsuits.

It is all the more amazing that one small weekly newspaper, with a circulation in the low thousands, the *Pt. Reyes Light*, launched an investigative series on Synanon that eventually won it a Pulitzer Prize. It revealed, among other things, that Dederich had bought 172 weapons—pistols, shotguns, rifles, semiautomatics—and $34,000 worth of ammunition.[55] It also reported that Synanon's income for 1976–1977 was $13,776,108 and that the Dederich family had received $170,000 in salaries (not counting living expenses and other perks provided by Synanon), while Dederich himself had received an additional $500,000 "preretirement" bonus.[56]

In 1978, Charles Dederich made a serious tactical error. Despite his lawsuits, Synanon's reputation was becoming tarnished. He decided to set up a charitable facility in Washington, D.C., to improve his image. Taking over an apartment building in a choice neighborhood, he used intimidation to evict the tenants. The press rallied to the tenants, hounding Dederich as he walked down the street. D.C. was no Pt. Reyes Station. Dederich ran scared, sold his Beltway holdings, switched $2 million to a Swiss bank, and headed for Europe.

George Farnsworth, married at the time to Dorothy Griesbach, a millionaire donor to Synanon and a Board member, traveled first class to Formia, Italy, to stay with Dederich. "Chuck, Jr, his son, told us," he reported, "the old man had fallen off the wagon in his hotel room in London, opening up the mini-bar and seeing all his old elixirs. . . . The story there was that Chuck was 'cured' of his alcoholism and that we were 'all adults' and could drink and eat sugar and skip aerobics (but not smoke). . . . Chuck continued to drink more and more heavily in Formia."[57] Dederich had broken the second cardinal rule of Synanon. He returned to the United States, a sick, demented man; bought a motel in Lake Havasu, Arizona; and moved in.

Next came the incident with Scott Stalling. In 1977 Scott left Synanon after asking the Marin County sheriff to stop the vasectomies. Then he sued for custody of his daughter, who remained in residence. He rose to the top of Dederich's enemy list. The evening of September 21,1978, Stalling stepped out of his car in the driveway of his Bay Area home. He was struck by blows to his head and his knees, and he fell to the ground and blacked out. A neighbor spotted a man who had a crew cut and was carrying a club. The man ran out of the driveway and jumped into a red Toyota. Scott was rushed to intensive care and nearly died.[58] The assault, however, could not be directly linked to Dederich and Synanon.

The next attack would be different. Neighbors of Paul Morantz, the lawyer bitten by a rattlesnake, had spotted a light-green Plymouth that had stopped in front of his home earlier in the day. They saw two men with crew cuts get out, carrying a brown sack. One neighbor wrote down the license number. The car was traced to Synanon. Dederich turned over two young members of the Imperial Marines to the police. One was Lance Kenton—son of the band leader Stan Kenton—who had been raised by the community. The police raided Synanon's Badger facility and carted off crates of tapes. These included Dederich's remarks quoted at the beginning of this section.[59] Dederich, like Nixon, was undone by his own ego.

On December 1, 1978, Dederich was arrested in Lake Havasu. He was so drunk that he had to be carried out of his apartment on a stretcher.[60] In July

1980 he pleaded no contest to conspiracy to commit the murder of Paul Morantz and received probation and a $10,000 fine. He was instructed to sever all ties with the Synanon Foundation.

The rattlesnake incident was the real death of Synanon. It was reviled in the public mind, and contributions ceased to flow in. Above all, Synanon was incurably corrupted within. However, a few hundred followers soldiered on at the Badger facility until declaring bankruptcy in 1991. In one of the most moving scenes in Deborah Swisher's play, her mother is seen, with her worldly possessions in two small bags, leaving her home of twenty-one years. We wonder whether she was able that day to mouth Dederich's most famous saying: "Today is the first day of the rest of my life." In March 1997 Charles Dederich died at the age of eighty-three.[61]

Conclusion

Synanon is particularly interesting as an example of a political cult that grew out of a therapy practice. As in the case of Fred Newman's radical therapy and Harvey Jackins's cocounseling, it illustrates the danger inherent in a therapy process that works because of the powerful influence of the therapist. This is particularly the case when the "therapist" lacks professional training in the field and has no credentials—which was true of Newman, Jackins, and Dederich.

However, Dederich went a step further than Newman and Jackins by attempting to create his own minisociety based on his therapy and his personality. The result proved in the long run to be disastrous. The cohesiveness needed for community coherence was provided by cultic mind control.

As is so typical of cults, it was success that destroyed Synanon. The power Chuck Dederich gained over the minds and lives of over 1,000 followers led to megalomania. This, in turn, produced clashes with civil society, contributing to Dederich's paranoia. Dederich lashed out violently. By breaking with his own principles, he destroyed himself and his creation. Synanon, as Olin put it, died of "arrogance."[62]

Part Four

Cults on the Left

Chapter 9

Marlene Dixon's Little Army

> *We . . .*
> *Could not ourselves be kind.*
> —Bertolt Brecht

Marlene Dixon was at a loss as to what exactly to do with her Democratic Workers Party (DWP) the summer of 1985. The group had been a major factor in San Francisco leftist politics for over a decade, but by that summer its membership was dwindling and, most important, Dixon herself was losing her way. Her drinking was more uncontrolled than usual and her abuse of the members had increased. She gathered together the party leadership and key intellectuals. The purpose of the meeting was to discuss the future policy of the group. However, it was dominated by Dixon's own laments about the quality of her life and her complaints that the group was driving her crazy.

Shortly after that meeting, Dixon left the Bay Area for an extended trip at party expense through Eastern Europe, where she attended international communist conferences dead drunk. In her absence the membership gathered and decided to relieve her of her burdens. They expelled Dixon and dissolved the group.

Origins

In the summer of 1974 thirteen women gathered in an apartment in San Francisco for the purpose of creating a "preparty formation."[1] It was a propitious moment for such activity. The Students for a Democratic Society (SDS) had collapsed and the Vietnam War was no longer an issue. Tens of thousands of former students still sustained a radical vision and had drifted into the cities, taking on menial jobs to support themselves as they searched for ways to continue the "struggle." They formed study groups, feminist centers, living communes, and food buying and health co-ops; they joined unions; and they organized the poor. Thousands of new left radicals came to the conclusion that they needed to be part of a political organization.

Some joined the Communist Party and others joined various Trotskyist groups. However, the bulk of party seekers were influenced by Maoism. This amorphous, diverse, and highly conflictive milieu was known as the "New Communist" movement, and its leading organ was the *Guardian* newspaper.[2] Typically, an affinity group would come together and hold discussions. A dominant personality would emerge and the group would coalesce into a cadre organization.

Twelve of the women were lesbians in their twenties who had met each other through common work in women's groups or knew each other socially. One of these women had been a student of Marlene Dixon and invited her to attend the meeting. Dixon was thirty-nine, had a Ph.D., and was teaching at a Canadian university. She had studied Marxist literature extensively and had an assertive and charismatic personality. She immediately took over the direction of the small group. During its first year of existence, Dixon spent all her vacations in San Francisco. Even while she was in Canada, she guided the group, making almost daily phone calls to the group's leading members.

In its initial period the group had features that set it apart from other preparty formations, giving it an aura of freshness and attractiveness. Most important, it began with an entirely female membership and continued to be led by females. The women's movement was on the rise in this period, while much of the left was dominated by men open to charges of male chauvinism.

The group claimed to be nondogmatic. While most competing groups lined up with the Chinese leadership or supported the "Gang of Four" or Hoxha in Albania, Dixon refused to involve her party in such disputes. She even claimed neutrality in the Sino-Soviet schism.[3] She felt free to attack "Stalinism" as dogmatic, picking and choosing those aspects of Soviet or Chinese theory and practice that appealed to her. This stance made the group quite appealing in sophisticated left intellectual circles.

Dixon had made a more serious study of Maoist practice than most of her *Red Book*–waving competitors. She modeled the internal life of the DWP on the basis of Maoist principles, thereby transforming a group of well-meaning women and men into cult followers. Dixon "became very interested in mass social psychology and group behavior modification. She studied Robert Jay Lifton's (1963) work on thought reform; she studied and admired 'total' communities, such as Synanon, directed methods of change, such as Alcoholics Anonymous."[4] While Lifton saw thought reform, sometimes called "brainwashing," as a great danger, Dixon viewed the process positively, using the Chinese communist word "remolding." The basic texts she used included *Fashen: A Documentary of Revolution in a Chinese Village*, by William Hinton (1966), an account of the "overturning" of the thinking of peasants in a small village; and *Prisoners of Liberation*, by Allyn and Adele Rickett (1973), a defense of the author's own brainwashing in a communist prison.[5]

The DWP was a paradox. It boasted of its feminist leadership, promoted a nondogmatic ideology, and used the word "Democratic" in its name. Yet it was an experiment in Maoist remolding, was extremely rigid in its internal life, and was administered in totalitarian fashion by Marlene Dixon.

The Political Impact of the DWP

The party's strongly feminist, antiracist, and anti-imperialist program attracted supporters from the very beginning. It began to play a role in the International Longshoremen's and Warehousemen's Union (ILWU), as well as in San Francisco city worker unions. In its first year, membership grew to twenty-five. By 1978, the DWP had about a hundred members in the Bay Area, mostly in San Francisco, two-thirds of whom were women. The group prided itself on its intellectual life, producing a theoretical journal, *Synthesis*, which later became *Contemporary Marxism*. It was extremely active and began to play a significant role in San Francisco and California politics.[6]

The DWP created a "mass organization" in San Francisco, the Grass Roots Alliance (GRA). The GRA was modeled after the Communist Party's front organizations. These were conceived of as "nominally noncommunist" but "under party leadership," to use Lenin's words, or as one American communist put it, "transmission belts to the broad masses of non-Party workers."[7] The apparatus of the GRA was completely controlled by the DWP and other left tendencies were excluded, while its members became a prime source of recruitment for the party.

The GRA sponsored three ballot initiatives in 1979 and 1980, seeking to increase the taxes of the major corporations headquartered in San Francisco. The initiative finally passed with 55 percent of the vote in November 1980, though it was never implemented. The GRA, with five hundred members and district committees functioning in all the working-class areas, was a great organizational success for the DWP. By 1980 the DWP had 400 members, including a number of workers.

Between 1981 and 1983 the DWP shifted direction and entered the Peace and Freedom Party. It gained control of the party and ran one of its members for governor in 1982. It was "successful" enough to draw sufficient votes away from the black Democratic candidate, Tom Bradley, to ensure the election of Republican George Deukmejian. In the same period the DWP was active in Oakland, creating another "mass organization," the Peace and Justice Organization.

In 1983 Dixon discovered international solidarity. The DWP took up the defense of Nicaragua and then of the African National Congress (ANC) in South Africa, creating DWP front organizations. Marlene Dixon lost interest in domestic American politics and concomitant work in trade unions and poor communities. She began to spend much of her time traveling abroad in socialist countries. Collecting intellectuals, as well as publishing theoretical journals and books, became a substitute for community organizing. The DWP began to lose members, ending up with no more than 100 at the time of dissolution.

The DWP took advantage of a rather limited window of political opportunity in a very special city with a long liberal tradition. Yet, as its contribution to the election of the Republican Deukmejian in 1982 illustrates, it was confined by the growth of moderate and conservative politics among the population as a whole.

The 1960s produced a massive growth in radical thinking on the university campuses. The campus movement dissipated by the early 1970s, spewing out tens of thousands of graduates who retained their radical outlook even though the events that had originally stimulated that view were now part of the past. Feeding primarily upon itself, though occasionally bringing in new forces, a significant section of this left coalesced into preparty formations of one or another type. It was at this point in the political dynamic that the DWP was formed. For a short period this cannibalization gave the impression of vitality to members of these groups and a sense of optimism persisted. The DWP's GRA campaigns were an example of this process. It soon became clear to objective observers of the left, though not necessarily to the cult members of the DWP entrapped in a closed ideological system, that these vanguards had no significant followers. The political winds shifted dramatically as Reaganism, not radicalism, reshaped America. Conditions were being created for the crisis that would blow apart Dixon's little army.

Criticism/Self-Criticism

The DWP was a tightly run vanguard cadre formation. All members were expected to devote themselves full time to party work. However, Dixon's personal domination of her group, combined with her ability to totally control the members and drive them into frenetic activity, distinguished the DWP as having a cult life from its very origins.

The organization was directed by Marlene Dixon and a small group of close associates. "The discipline demanded of a cadre member included 24-

hour-a-day availability and submission of all aspects of one's life to the needs of the party. . . . She led intense criticism/self-criticism sessions. Anyone who disagreed with her, or poorly carried out an assignment, was subjected to 'class standpoint struggle.' . . . If a dissident's 'class standpoint' did not improve," former members revealed, "demotion, shunning, or a transfer to more menial work followed, all accompanied by relentless criticism, culminating in expulsion if necessary to enforce 'unity.'"[8]

The use of criticism/self-criticism in the DWP was among the most extreme examples of thought reform we have come across in political cults. It was practiced daily, the sessions were extremely intense and vitriolic, and they could go on for seven to ten hours. "I remember so clearly," one former member reported over ten years after the event, "one of the first sessions that targeted me. Sitting in the circle being berated and accused of misdeeds by the group, I felt like my head was literally being yanked from my shoulders, turned around 180 degrees, and set down backwards. I stopped seeing, stopped thinking, stopped speaking my mind." Why did she put up with such extreme mistreatment? "I began to surrender my vision, my mind, my personal experience, and my soul, and to internalize the idea that due to my middle-class background, my own thoughts, ideas, and gut reactions were at best, suspect, and at worst downright evil." [9]

This response was fairly typical of DWP members, and indeed members of other left-wing political cults. An individual with high ideals was recruited to the group. A critical part of the recruitment process was convincing the person that the group was dedicated to the working class and the eventual establishment of an ideal socialist equalitarian society. The person was asked to subordinate individual interests to those of the group and, by extension, the working class. Internal resistance to this transformation process was exposed by the leadership as representing a surviving middle-class (petit bourgeois) side that had to be rooted out through criticism sessions. The new member thus identified her sense of self as representing the evil influence of class society and "group mind" as representing a proletarian outlook. The member was made to feel guilty about her background, whatever minor privileges she had as a child, and the class nature of her parents. Since her background would always be with her, the criticism process never ended.

The legitimacy of the process was reinforced in two ways. One was *international example*: The criticism/self-criticism technique was common in successful revolutionary movements, in particular in China. Members were told that revolutionaries in Vietnam, Cuba, Angola, Algeria, and other Third World countries made even greater sacrifices of self than was being asked of the recruit. The member felt she was part of a worldwide elite conducting its own kind of holy war against world capitalism. The other method of reinforcement was *peer pressure*: Everyone in the group was subjected to similar criticism. It was the normative way of life among the only family the member would soon know. Others accepted it, so why shouldn't she? "I fully internalized the belief that there was no life outside this group and that I might as well be dead as expelled."[10]

Criticism/self-criticism was a two-way street. The member gets to dish out as well as receive punishment. "What horrifies me most when I look back on my time in the party," another ex-member reported, "was the form of human relationship that was promulgated among the membership. Even beyond the endless discipline and criticism, there was the near glee with which each one of us pounded upon the other. . . . Some part of me rather *enjoyed* these [verbal] gang bangs. . . ."[11]

Other Control Mechanisms

DWP members led a frenetic life, with virtually every waking moment, even weekends, taken up with party activity or working. Eighteen-hour meetings were not uncommon. This kept members in a state of exhaustion that discouraged thinking. Members lived in poverty, either receiving a small stipend if they worked for the party or expected to hand over most of their wages if they had an outside job. Most members lived in shared facilities with other cadres. Common quarters increased the members' isolation from the outside world and deepened peer pressure. The cadres were encouraged to break relations with parents, family, and nonparty friends.[12]

The group considered itself an underground organization. Everyone took on a party name and only pay phones were used for party communication, while Dixon "amassed a cache of weapons."[13] "A new member," Lalich reported, "was told (1) to get a post office or rental mail box for receiving all mail; (2) to change the name on household utility bills to an alias; (3) not to subscribe to any publications, particularly leftist publications, in a real name; and (4) to change car registrations and driver's licenses to either a 'safe' address (i.e. the home of an apolitical friend) or the mail box address."[14]

The DWP acted as if it existed within a totalitarian country. While there is ample evidence that during the Cold War the Federal Bureau of Investigation (FBI) and other government agencies carried on unwarranted surveillance of extreme left groups and engaged in disruptive activities,[15] this activity was on the wane in the period under discussion. It was in 1975 that the attorney general ordered the FBI to abandon "preventive law enforcement," that is, to stop infiltrating groups on the grounds that they might, at some future date, carry out illegal activity.[16] Whatever the real or perceived threat, the net effect of the DWP's security efforts was to strengthen the wall between the group and the outside community, an essential step in creating a cult.

Dixon developed a complex top-down leadership structure to ensure total control of the membership. At the top of the pyramid was Marlene Dixon, the supreme and unquestioned leader who made all decisions of any importance. She was assisted by Sandra (a pseudonym), a woman who administered the party in a day-to-day fashion. Next came a layer of middle leadership that ran the branches, conducted classes, and supervised various work stations. At the bottom was the rest of the membership. Dixon rarely had direct contact with ordinary members. Of course, all layers, except Dixon, were subjected to continual criticism/self-criticism. However, the middle-level leaders were permitted to dish out a bit more criticism than they received and were additionally rewarded by being allowed to administer party power.

New members were expected to attend cadre classes and were subject to a system called "One-Help."[17] An older member was assigned to each new member to monitor her development. Reports on the new member were sent up the chain of command. There was even a "Remolding Group"[18] for backsliding members.

The Purges

Dixon conducted periodic purges to secure her total domination of the party. This process began immediately upon Dixon's return from Canada in 1975 to live permanently in San Francisco. There was only one member of the original twelve founders, Helene, with sufficient political knowledge to challenge Dixon. Dixon launched a factional struggle against Helene, attacking her for being "Stalinist and dogmatic." At issue was not her political views but rather the consolidation of Dixon's control over her new followers. Helene was expelled, and a small goon squad of women was sent to her apartment to terrorize her.[19]

Then in 1976 came the "lesbian purge."[20] Dixon feared that there might be rivals to her undisputed power among the original twelve founding members of the group, all lesbians, as well as their lovers and friends. The purge was a preemptive strike. Dixon succeeded in expelling eight of the founders while three others were demoted to low-level positions.[21]

We are reminded of Stalin's "Great Purges" of the 1930s, which were directed primarily against the "Old Bolsheviks" in the party. Of course, Stalin's purges were more deadly; the Old Bolsheviks were murdered. Would Dixon have acted any differently if she had had the power of a state in her hands?

In 1980, after a period of growth that brought party membership to over four hundred, Dixon launched the "right deviationist" purge.[22] New demands were placed on the members, and all those who could not function on a cadre level were expelled. Membership dwindled, but Dixon retained tight control over those who remained.[23] In political cults, growth is universally sacrificed in the interest of control.

The Supreme Leader

As previously mentioned, Marlene Dixon was a well-educated woman with a Ph.D. and considerable teaching experience. She had been brought up in a working-class family and was rightly proud of her academic achievements. She was creative in her intellectual thinking and capable of inspiring others. She was not without charm. As Lalich noted from personal experience, Dixon "was a genius at using a combination of flattery and emotional terrorism."[24] The former trait helped her win over the initial group of twelve. In time, however, the latter predominated. As Dixon herself put it, she used "a little carrot and a lot of stick."[25]

When Dixon arrived from Canada after the end of the first year of the DWP's existence, she insisted upon being put up at party expense in a house in San Francisco. Later the party purchased for her a country home as well. A sports car was added so that she could travel back and forth between the two facilities. Party members were assigned to meet her every need: clean her house, empty ashtrays, open sodas, shop, cook, run errands, and chauffeur her around town. Lalich estimated it cost the group "more than $100,000 a year" to maintain Dixon in the style that she demanded.[26]

Marlene Dixon was an alcoholic. She could remain in an alcoholic stupor for days. She would rant and rave at the members, giving orders that were all but incomprehensible. She combined alcoholism with a delight in belittling and destroying other people. A group of former members reported that those close to her "often endured an almost unbelievable level of personal abuse from her."[27] "A female militant sat for hours," Lalich stated, "while [Dixon], drunk, held a gun to the young woman's head."[28]

A main task of Sandra and other key leaders was to hide Dixon's privileges, drunkenness, and abusive behavior from the membership. Why, we have to ask, did they do so? Dixon had conditioned them to fear her wrath if they did not do so. They believed in her. For years they were convinced that her great strengths outweighed her obvious weaknesses. And they shared in her power. The fact that Dixon was incapacitated by alcohol much of the time gave Sandra the opportunity to run the DWP in her name.

Dixon was a textbook example of the psychopathic cult leader. She was able to attract a following with her charm, charisma, and intelligence. Then she manipulated her disciples to serve her personal needs. These needs included providing her with the lifestyle and support systems she desired. There were even more damaging psychological drives at work. Dixon needed to dominate and humiliate others as a way of trying to build up her own sense of self-worth. As is typical of the psychopath, she could not accept responsibility for her own political and organizational mistakes or her own personal weaknesses, such as her drunkenness. Further, the psychopath lives in constant fear of being exposed for the fraud that she is. The constant harangues and emotional brutalization of those beneath her in the group were to ensure that no one would notice that the empress had no clothes. There is an additional emotional reward for the psychopath: The pain of others can be a source of pleasure. There is every indication that this was the case with Dixon. Better still, the psychopath is completely free from any sense of guilt.

Why the DWP Imploded

It is something of a paradox that a cult as tightly controlled as the DWP should expel its leader and dissolve itself. Former members of the DWP have made an effort to explain this anomaly.[29] We will draw from their efforts, adding insights from a similar implosion, that of Gerry Healy's Workers Revolutionary Party (WRP) (see chapter 10).

It is not purely coincidence that both groups broke up in the same year, 1985. In the United States, President Ronald Reagan had just won reelection and the American left had reached a historic low point. In England, Margaret Thatcher, who modeled herself after Reagan, succeeded that year in decisively defeating the miners, once the most powerful and militant union in the country. The left, both within and outside the Labour Party, was in full retreat.

Political cults, unlike religious ones, are vulnerable to broader movements in politics that can make it harder for leaders to justify to the membership their sacrifices. The fundamental shift in American politics to the right created the objective conditions for a crisis within the DWP. Its membership was reduced to barely a hundred demoralized and overworked members, isolated from mainstream American politics.

Equally important was the reaction of Marlene Dixon to this entropy. The DWP was an orthodox Marxist group in the sense that it believed that the working class had the capacity to carry through a revolution and establish socialism. Its raison d'être was to provide the leadership that the working class needed to achieve this end. Dixon began to obliquely challenge this view, holding that the working class had been corrupted because of the "material advantages it has gained through U.S. imperialism." She turned her focus from the working class to the "progressive petite bourgeoisie."[30] Concretely, this meant a shift away from work in unions and poor communities and toward international support efforts. Resources were placed in theoretical journals, books, and Dixon's tours of socialist countries. The effect was a demoralization, inchoate, suppressed through Dixon's remolding techniques, but nevertheless present in the backs of the minds of many members.

At the same time Dixon became less interested in and less connected with the DWP. Her drinking increased, her personal corruption became more apparent, and she became more abusive.

We have documented a similar trend with the Healy group. Much of the group's working-class membership was expelled in 1976.[31] While making no formal changes in its theory of working-class hegemony—in fact, Healy claimed that England was on the eve of revolution right up to the collapse of the miners strike—there was a critical shift in Healy's political preoccupations. While Dixon scurried around Eastern Europe and Russia, Healy traveled to Libya and curried favor with Arab regimes throughout the region. This debasing of ideology created a gnawing demoralization of WRP members similar to that affecting Dixon's cadre.

He concentrated his energies on Vanessa Redgrave and a milieu of theater and movie people. He spent much of his time at a country estate, provided by the Redgraves and devoted himself to increasingly esoteric discourses on dialectics. Healy also was an alcoholic. His abuse of his supporters increased. Most notable was forced sexual relations with the young daughters of members and his brutalization of his longtime companion.

The third element, critical to the process, was the breakup of the leadership group. Dixon survived as long as she did because her worst features and corruption were hidden from the membership by a tight circle of leaders. Most important was her second in command, Sandra. In 1985 Dixon turned viciously against Sandra. At the same time she expressed her disdain for the group and began to toy with the idea of leaving with a small coterie to set up a think tank in Washington, D.C.

The WRP went through the same process. Healy's longtime companion, whom he had brutalized, exposed his sexual adventures in a letter to the group's leading committee. His closest collaborators in the leadership, with the exception of the Redgraves, turned upon him.

It was the opening provided by divisions in the leadership that permitted an outpouring of the rage of the membership against the guru. The members of the DWP were worn out from working "seven-day weeks and until 1:00 A.M. most nights for years." Many had lived in poverty in collective houses and yearned for a more balanced life with some time for family and career.[32] Children had been neglected.[33] It became harder for members to believe that the very real sacrifices they were making were actually producing results. Once the full extent of Dixon's "alcoholism, abusiveness, irrationality, and privileged lifestyle"[34] was exposed to the membership, there was no putting the pieces of the group back together.

In England revelations about Healy's sexual exploitation of young women led to an irrepressible outpouring from the membership. The organization split apart and largely disintegrated.

Conclusion

We have documented in this book different paths taken by political cults in the face of political adversity. Some groups, like LaRouche's and Newman's, have moved to the right, seeking to keep wind in their sails despite principle. Others, like Perente's National Labor Federation (NATLFED) and Jackins's reevaluation counseling (RC), have found ways to continue to connect with currents of discontent that persist, despite the overall prosperity. The DWP and Healy's WRP did not survive the difficult times for reasons we have explained.

Both groups created internal regimes that were hellish, even by cult standards. The very intensity of cult activity, along with the extreme brutality of the cult leadership and its flagrant disdain for the membership and the purported objectives of the groups, combined together in these groups to create a lethal mixture. The groups were like collapsing stars in which internal pressures had built up to a level that produced spectacular and explosive ends.

Chapter 10

Gerry Healy: Guru to a Star

"Hold your tongue!" said the Queen, turning purple.
"I won't!" said Alice.
"Off with her head!" the Queen shouted at the top of her voice.
—Lewis Carroll, *Alice's Adventures in Wonderland*

A Meeting in Mayfair

They met at Rachel Kempson's flat in Mayfair in London. Kempson was Sir Michael Redgrave's widow and the mother of Corin, Vanessa, and Lynn Redgrave. The room was cluttered with theater memorabilia. In the center of a little group sat Gerry Healy, grim faced, eyes no more than slits, jaw fixed. Healy was a short, barrel-shaped man, built like a bulldog, with an immense almost bald head and no discernible neck. He wore a wrinkled dark suit, with the pants held up by black suspenders; a white shirt; and glasses with black plastic rims. Born to a poor family in Ireland in 1913, once a seaman and later a factory worker, Healy did not fit in with his present surroundings. Yet he was clearly running the show.

Surrounding Healy were Vanessa, Corin, and a handful of factional collaborators. Kempson, not a participant, hovered in the background and supplied the tea. The topic under discussion was the next moves in the factional struggle to control the assets of the Trotskyist Workers Revolutionary Party (WRP), which had just expelled the group and their followers. The year was 1986.[1]

Vanessa Redgrave, daughter of a theater legend, was already established as one of the finest stage and film actresses of her time when she joined Healy's group in 1973 at the age of thirty-six. She was recruited by her brother Corin, also an actor, who had been a party member for several years. Until his death in 1989, Gerry Healy was her political guru and she his ever-faithful sannyasin.*

---

*A disciple in the Indian guru tradition.

156

Origins of a Cult

It was a fateful day in 1943 when Bob Shaw arrived on the London doorstep of Gerry Healy looking for a temporary place to stay. Bob, a product of a deeply religious middle-class family in the Midlands, was married to Mickie, a working-class woman he had met in the Trotskyist group. Bob had been a lay Methodist preacher until the Depression radicalized him.

Bob never lost his religious intensity; he simply transferred his fervor to Trotskyism. Gerry Healy needed allies that year and found in Bob and Mickie loyalists who would stick with him until the 1980s. Soon the couple had a baby girl and named her Aileen. Forty years after that fateful 1943 meeting, Aileen was to become Healy's nemesis.

The year 1943 also proved critical for Gerry Healy's political career. Gerry Healy had migrated to England in 1926, when he was fourteen. He had become a radio operator on ships and joined the Communist Party (CP). In 1937 Healy was recruited to a small Trotskyist group, which became active in the Labour Party. Almost immediately he became part of a split that formed the Workers International League (WIL).[2]

British Trotskyism at the time was split into several groups, and these groups were faction ridden. In many cases personal conflicts and clique formations had more to do with factional conflicts than politics. This atmosphere contributed to the shaping of Healy's political personality. Healy had great energy and drive, excelled in trade union work, and soon became a significant younger leader in the group. However, at the same time, he was hotheaded and had an irascible personality, getting into conflicts with the party leadership. He threatened to resign or actually resigned three times.[3] He had developed the kind of personality that made him an effective builder and attracted people to him. However, he lacked the ability to compromise and work as part of a real leadership team with others.

Healy had gathered together a small group of supporters. The original issues around which the group coalesced have not been remembered by anyone. They didn't matter. What counted was that Healy had loyal followers who supported him against all others in the organization and leadership. He had created a personal clique.

After the group had formed, Healy found allies and a platform by supporting the Fourth International, which was pushing for the unification of the divided Trotskyist groups in England. From this point on Healy either led a faction, which acted as if it were a party within a party, or led a party of his own. He had his loyal followers. Everyone else was his enemy.

This process of clique formation is of considerable importance for our study of political cults. All political cults begin in this fashion as cliques. Not all political cliques end up as political cults. The cult formation process is determined by the degree of control of the clique leader over his followers and the degree of separation of his flock from others.

A Knock on Not Just Any Door

Ken Tarbuck was determined to attend the National Conference of the "Club" that July in 1950. The group had no formal name. The Club was the only Trotskyist group in England, and it functioned underground within the British Labour Party (BLP). Gerry Healy was the group's general secretary, but he could not be certain he would have a majority at the conference. Ken was one reason for Healy's uncertainty. He was part of the opposition.

Ken, a delegate from a branch outside London, headed into the city with only a phone number to call. The day before the conference was to be held, he was informed that its location had changed. Upon arriving at the new location, Ken knocked on an unmarked door, which was then opened only an inch. He gave his party name and the door was closed. It was opened again, minutes later, after his name had been checked on a list. He found a seat in the packed room just in time for Healy's opening remarks. Healy used the opportunity to announce to the assembled delegates that he expected a police raid at any moment.[4]

The Club functioned within the BLP, yet it was organized in a centralist fashion on Leninist principles. Its aim was to eventually build a mass revolutionary party through recruitment from or a split within the host Labour Party. It operated as if it were an illegal organization within a totalitarian state. Everyone had to have a special party name. Documents were distributed to members, to be held for a week only, and then had to be returned to the branch organizer.

Healy faced two serious opposition groups: one led by Ted Grant (see chapter 11) and the other by Tony Cliff (who was later to head the British Socialist Workers Party [SWP]). Tony Cliff was expelled prior to the conference, Ted Grant after the conference. Then all those who did not support the expulsions were expelled. Healy ended up in complete control of the Club, though he paid the price of losing the majority of the membership. However, Healy had achieved his goal. He had his own group and had secured complete personal control.

Healy remained in the BLP until 1964. This "entrist" activity suited him well. It required a secret organization with tight discipline and very limited internal democracy. The group developed a strong sense of cohesion, Healy maintained strict authoritarian control over its apparatus and members, and the rest of the Labour Party was viewed with hostility. A small personal group within the organization followed Healy unquestioningly. The group as a whole had a clique character, while its central core had already become Healy's cult followers.

Peter Fryer's Revelations

On Monday, August 31, 1959, Gerry Healy came to the party headquarters—the organization was now called the Socialist Labour League—at 8 P.M. and discovered that the editor of his paper, Peter Fryer, was missing. Fryer was no ordinary member of Healy's group. He had been a leading member of the British Communist Party and a correspondent for its paper, the *Daily Worker*, during the Hungarian Revolution in 1956. Fryer's truthful accounts of events in Hungary led to the resignations of many CP members. Some of these, including Fryer, then joined Healy.

Healy called a meeting of his Executive Committee at 10 P.M. that night. He announced that Fryer was ill and had left London, and he had the committee appoint him as acting editor. The events over the next few weeks took on a bizarre character. Healy was determined to track down Fryer, while Fryer was equally determined to avoid any meetings with Healy or his deputies.[5]

The American Trotskyist, Art Fox, happened to be in England at the time and Healy enlisted his companionship for a car trip around England. They traveled at top speed in the middle of the night through fog on two-lane highways, checking out different addresses where Fryer might be hiding out. Healy suggested to Fox that Fryer's companion was an agent of the Soviet secret police, the KGB, and that she was seeking to ferret him out of the country. He told Fox he was considering having the ports watched to prevent this. One of Healy's deputies forced his way into the home of two members, looking for Fryer, only to be forcibly removed. Fryer had to get a lawyer to threaten Healy with legal action unless he called off the harassment.

Weeks later, Healy released to the membership an open letter from Peter Fryer which made clear that his break from the Socialist Labour League (SLL) had to do with more than ill health. "The outstanding feature of the present regime in the Socialist Labour League," Fryer stated in his letter, "is that it is the rule of a clique—the general secretary's personal clique. . . ." Fryer then proceeded to give a picture of the inner life at the top of the group: "There is scarcely a single leading member of the League whom the general secretary has not attacked in private conversation with me at some time or other, in such terms as these: 'I have enough on P. to get him sent down for seven years.' 'I don't know what game P. is playing. He could be a police agent.' 'B. is a primitive Irish peasant.' . . . 'G. is a lunatic.' 'A. is quite mad. He beats his wife.'"[6]

The defection of Fryer was part of a crisis in the organization that went on for two years. A group of intellectuals recruited from the Communist Party, including Peter Cadogan, John Daniels, and Ken Coates, left. A faction formed around Brian Behan, another former CP member, whose brother Brendan was a famous poet and writer. Behan's wife, Celia, had tabled a motion in her branch expressing concern over "the concentration of responsibility on the shoulders of comrade Healy who is: General Secretary, Secretary of the International Committee, Editor of the *Newsletter*, and in practice Treasurer and Manager of the print shop. . . ."[7] Alasdair MacIntyre, a prominent British philosopher who supported Behan, had reached the conclusion that "minorities cannot exist in your organization."[8]

We gain a picture of an organization run in a very personal fashion by its leader. Healy made all the key decisions and controlled all party assets. He was highly critical of all other party leaders, even though these leaders completely subordinated themselves to him. He was suspicious of everyone and maintained his power by keeping everyone else on the defensive.

It was an interesting dynamic. Healy was determined to intervene and build his organization, only to discover that growth threatened his control. Then, with just as much determination, Healy would destroy what he had built, reducing his group to his immediate cult followers once again. Soon a new opportunity would arise and the process would begin all over again. The core group, which only slowly changed composition, was a cult around Healy with roots that went back to 1943. Yet his organization was capable of periods in which it broke lose from complete cult control and took on a meaningful political life.

Mary, Queen of Scots, Joins

One day early in 1973 Vanessa Redgrave walked into the offices of the Socialist Labour League in Clapham, accompanied by her brother, Corin. She sat down in Healy's office and Healy launched into a long explanation of his plans to transform the SLL into a new party, the Workers Revolutionary Party (WRP). At the end of the talk Vanessa asked to join the group. Healy turned to Corin and said: "So now Mary, Queen of Scots, has joined us."[9] The meeting would transform both of them, Healy perhaps even more than Vanessa.

The party Vanessa joined in 1973 had changed dramatically since the days of Peter Fryer and Brian Behan. Healy had turned his enormous energy toward the youth within the British Labour Party. He soon captured control of its affiliate, the Young Socialists, and published a widely read paper, *Keep Left*. The key to Healy's success was his hold on a group of middle-class students whom he used to recruit and mobilize working-class youth. These

young people proved more malleable material than the politically sophisticated older Trotskyists of the 1950 period and the former communists of the
1957–1960 period.

In 1964 Healy left the BLP with his youthful cadre and competed as an
open party for the newly radicalized students of the Vietnam War generation.
He denounced the antiwar protests as "middle class," yet recruited primarily
from this milieu. By 1970 he was also able to win over a small, but strategi-
cally placed, group of workers in the Midlands, particularly at British Leyland.
He had also begun to recruit actors, directors, and television people, winning
over Corin Redgrave and, through Corin, eventually Vanessa.

These were prosperous days for Healy. He published a daily paper and
had a sizable full-time staff. His student cadre mobilized working-class youths
for his demonstrations, he had some influence in the trade unions, and he
gained prestige and money from his cultural supporters. Much of this activity was of a "Potemkin Village" character.* That is, it was conducted to
convince the members, as well as potential recruits, that the WRP's dream of
establishing a communist utopia had at least some basis in reality. The daily
paper, which had a minuscule readership and required tremendous human
and financial resources, was produced for such a purpose.

Once a year Healy actually constructed a "village" under a tent at his
summer camp. The last such meeting, held in 1972, had an attendance of
over one thousand. For a week those attending lived and breathed Healy's
politics. Guards patrolled the camp's perimeters twenty-four hours a day.
Healy created a siege mentality within the camps, often waking everyone up in
the middle of the night, assembling them in the big tent, and subjecting them to
fiery lectures on imminent revolution or the dangers of a military coup.

Remarkably, Healy was able to exist from 1960 to 1973 without any splits
or factionalism. He seemed to have overcome the contradiction between his
need to personally dominate his group and his desire to reach out and affect
the external world that had torn him apart in the past.

Healy learned how to turn the selfless idealism of his young middle-class
recruits into a powerful weapon to control them. These recruits accepted the
Marxist belief in the central role of the working class in the revolutionary
process. They were taught to believe that the party they belonged to held the
key to the victory of the working class. Yet Healy continuously stressed the
middle class, and in many cases quite privileged, backgrounds of his followers. The members were trained to feel guilty for having the "wrong" class

---

*The term originates with the effort of Grigori Potemkin in 1787 to impress Empress
Catherine II. According to the story, Potemkin constructed artificial villages—populated
by happy peasants—along the way of Catherine's train trip through the Crimea.

background and to hold themselves, rather than the party's policy and Gerry Healy, responsible for the failings of the party.

One result of such attacks was that members, who in other circumstances might develop doubts about party policy and the internal regime, were forced out of the party before they could find like-minded members and form factions that could challenge the leadership.

Healy combined his own form of "criticism/self-criticism" with crisis mongering. The membership was inspired by predictions of the collapse of the capitalist system that would bring his small party swiftly to power. At the same time Healy sought to frighten them with talk of the imminent threat of dictatorship and fascism. Healy produced a driven membership that worked for the party every waking hour in a frenzied manner. A sense of great urgency prevailed throughout the organization. Every minute counts when revolutionary upheaval is around the corner.

Healy's methods worked. He personally controlled a party of around a thousand members, perhaps 600 of whom were hard-working cadre. He faced no internal opposition. He controlled the thinking, the very lives of his followers. He had succeeded in building a relatively large political cult.

He was left with only one problem: The world around him was not proceeding according to his predictions. Revolution was not on the agenda. On the contrary, the period of worldwide student radicalization had passed. The British labor movement was on the defensive, and the stage was being set for Thatcherism.

Political cults are far more vulnerable to the effects of changes in the political world than are religious cults. Shifts in the political climate demand either a shift in tactics or a willingness to hunker down and be marginalized. In activist cults there comes a moment when many members are no longer able to believe, to carry out one more before-dawn paper distribution, or another ringing of a doorbell, only to be cursed out by the person opening the door. This can lead to individual losses, or can produce explosions that destroy whole organizations.

The forces were building up in the SLL/WRP for such an explosion at the precise time when Vanessa Redgrave joined the group. However, she seemed to be impervious to the tensions within the group she had joined. In fact its most bizarre features appealed to her. For example, in January 1974 there were scare stories in the press about Arab terrorists. One day Tory Prime Minister Heath mobilized some tanks and other equipment around Heathrow Airport as a precautionary step against a possible terrorist missile attack on civilian aircraft. "We increased the print run of *Workers' Press* from fifteen thousand to twenty thousand copies a day," Vanessa reports in her autobiography, "warning of the danger of police-military rule as in Chile."[10]

Vanessa took her role as party member extremely seriously. She described one scene where she was sitting on the side of the bed of her daughter, then a young child and today the actress Natasha Richardson. "Natasha appealed to me to spend more time with her. I tried to explain that our political struggle was for her future, and that of all the children of her generation. She looked at me with a serious, sweet smile. 'But I need you *now*. I won't need you so much then.'"[11]

Terror in the Central Committee

The Central Committee of Healy's party had gathered in a room at the party's printing plant off Old Town Road in Clapham. Gerry Healy sat at a table scowling at the assembled thirty or so committee members. There were no minutes, procedures, or chair. "I wish to make a motion," he began, "to expel Cliff Slaughter from the Central Committee and from the party. He has been acting consciously to destroy our movement and to aid the class enemy at a critical juncture in the crisis of capitalism. Never before have the opportunities for the revolutionary movement been brighter. This only makes Slaughter's treachery all the more intolerable."[12]

Cliff Slaughter was the party's top intellectual. His crime, as Healy then explained, was the failure of the Northwest Region to mobilize a sufficient number of youths for a recent party demonstration. Slaughter was in charge of that area. Each member of the CC in turn took the floor to denounce Slaughter. The level of acrimony and the extremity of the rhetoric increased as the discussion continued.

Cliff Slaughter sat there, his head hanging, staring at the floor. Thinning hair, strong nose, and dark plastic glasses made him look like the professor that he was. It was clear he had not slept in days. He confessed to all the charges. He spoke with a hollow voice, as a shattered man, and without real conviction.

Time was running out on the meeting and steam out of the discussion. Healy finally spoke: "I do not in any way accept Slaughter's empty confessions. I should push my motion to a vote right now. But, for this meeting, I propose to table it. It will be the first point on the agenda of the next meeting."[13]

Kiss Me, Kate

In 1974 a split developed with Alan Thornett and two hundred working-class members from Oxford and the surrounding area. The dispute began rather curiously. The Western Region was led by a very beautiful young woman, Kate Blakeney. She was married and had four children. Yet she threw herself wholly into party work, selling papers, organizing meetings, making collections, distributing leaflets at plant gates.

"We didn't think," she reported later. "We were too busy, always busy, and could hope only to catch a few hours of sleep."

The more money she raised, the more was demanded by Healy. She had signed bank drafts so that funds were directly taken out of her bank account. There was no one left who would lend her money. She was cut off from her parents. She was experiencing difficulty scraping together enough money to feed her children. The more papers she sold, the bigger the bundle the following week. She was charged for papers whether or not they were sold. Bundles of unsold papers began piling up in her closet.

Kate, however, was a believer. She drove herself and those around her to greater and greater sacrifices. She believed, as did the others in the area, that the party would triumph soon. The crisis was getting deeper; a military coup was in the wings. The future of humanity depended upon the party's triumph, and that required her sacrifice.

Then one evening she received a phone call asking her to come to the center and meet with Healy. She readily drove into London, hoping to convince Healy of the need to give her area some respite. Upon reaching the party headquarters, she was directed to rooms across the street where Healy lived. Kate entered Healy's apartment, exhausted, looking for help.

> Healy opened the door for me. He had been drinking. Something was all wrong. I pushed by his large body, sat down in a chair and started to make my report. Healy came towards me, was hovering over me. He was not listening to a word I was saying.
>
> He wanted only one thing from me, my sexual submission. For a moment I just stared at him: fat, ugly, red-faced. Was this the price I was supposed to pay for some respite for my area?
>
> Something snapped in me, I guess it was my faith, my belief. The dream that filled my head and drove me forward now seemed unreal, and reality entered, tawdry, petty, dirty, seamy reality. It wasn't a matter of morality or some special virtue on my part. It was as if everything I believed in was proved, in one revealing second, to be false, lies. I, my husband, my children, my comrades had sacrificed so much, had worked so hard for this . . . animal.[14]

At the next Central Committee meeting, Healy launched a bitter political attack on Kate. She was not about to take it without resistance. She began talking with the trade unionists in her area, particularly Alan Thornett. They were having growing difficulties connecting Healy's unreal perspectives with the day-to-day struggles of their fellow workers. The entire region went into opposition.

Healy's abuse of his members escalated in this period from verbal to physical. Tony Richardson, one of the opposition's leaders, "was called to Clapham for 'discussions.' . . . The interview was . . . in Healy's flat. At his interview considerable physical violence was used on him. . . . These methods were only used on the most loyal members."[15] Two party intellectuals, who had dropped out of the group earlier, reported being beaten by Healy while top party leaders held them.[16]

Healy thoroughly enjoyed these sessions of verbal and physical abuse. During one typical session Healy sat with a smile on his face, licking his lips, rubbing his hands together, and muttering, "It's Christmas."[17] The man had a psychopathic personality. He needed to humiliate others in order to build himself up.

Kidnapped in the "Red House"

"POLICE RAID THE RED HOUSE" screamed the banner headline of the *Observer* on September 26, 1975. Around one hundred policemen with dogs and pocket flares had raided a large brick building in Derbyshire recently purchased by Corin Redgrave for the WRP. The funds for the purchase had been raised primarily by Vanessa Redgrave, who solicited celebrities, including Groucho Marx.[18] The estate was being used by the WRP to house a school on Marxist philosophy.

The story behind the raid throws some light upon the internal life of the WRP in that period. It begins with Irene Gorst, a minor actress who was a girlfriend of Corin's. Gorst was a WRP member and quite active in the group's work among Equity members on the West End. She had not completely severed her relations with friends and former lovers outside the party. She was determined, however, to go to the Red House to attend a two-week class series designed specifically for theater people. For personal reasons, she missed the bus she was supposed to take to the encampment.

The day after Gorst finally arrived, Corin, Vanessa, and two others grilled her from 9:30 A.M. to 5:30 P.M. "They started on me. How long had I been working for Special Branch? Where had I planted bombs and drugs? Why did I miss the coach? Who had told me where the school was? . . . After about an hour I decided to leave. But when I tried to get off my chair I was pushed back by Vanessa who said, 'Sit down.'" They searched her purse and later she found someone going through her luggage.

The interrogators were convinced that she was an agent of the Special Branch. The next day, following the intervention of Gerry Healy, she was allowed to leave the place and she headed back to London. Deeply upset, she went to the *Observer* and told them her story.[19]

Gerry Healy's paranoia spread to encompass most of his Trotskyist competitors. In 1975 he claimed that Joseph Hansen, a key leader of the American Socialist Workers Party (SWP) and former secretary of Leon Trotsky, was an agent of the FBI and of the KGB. As is typical with conspiracy theorists, he made no attempt to explain how Hansen could have simultaneously served rival security apparatuses. When George Novack, an old intellectual who had been instrumental in organizing Trotsky's defense during the Moscow trials, supported Hansen, he, too, was called an agent. He soon expanded this designation to include most of the leaders of the American SWP.

For four years Healy devoted tens of thousands of dollars to his investigation into "Security and the Fourth International."[20] He claimed, without evidence, that Hansen was responsible for Trotsky's murder in 1940 and that Novack shielded the man suspected of setting up the death of Trotsky's son Leon Sedov. On September 14, 1977, over one thousand people gathered in London to hear Ernest Mandel, Tariq Ali, Tamara Deutscher, George Novack, and others repudiate Healy's charges.[21]

The purpose of this campaign, however, was not to win sympathy from other Trotskyists or even within the left as a whole. It was quite the opposite: to build an impenetrable wall around Healy's organization, isolating his supporters from critical left voices. For a period of time this technique worked. It was also a reflection of the mental state of Gerry Healy. Mike Banda, Healy's closest collaborator since the 1950s who had participated in the slander campaign, later characterized Healy's "security" investigation as "paranoid schizophrenia."[22]

The "Red in the Bed" Scandal

Aileen Jennings, the daughter of Bob and Mickie Shaw, Gerry Healy's first recruits, now married to Paul Jennings, wrote a letter on July 1, 1985, to the WRP's Political Committee. Aileen had been born into Healy's group and brought up by two of his most loyal supporters. Healy rewarded his old friends by sleeping with Aileen over a period of twenty years. Describing herself as Gerry Healy's "close personal companion," she alleged that Healy had used party facilities "in a completely opportunist way for sexual liaisons with female members employed by the Party . . . or others." Twenty-six individuals were then listed. This situation "opens the party to police provocation." She concluded: "I cannot sit on this volcano any longer."[23]

That night Aileen met with her husband of twenty years. "Paul Jennings wept as she alleged Healy beat her severely, causing injuries which have led her to become slowly crippled. . . . 'I had suspected nothing until she suddenly told me all one night.'"[24] The next morning Aileen was seen leaving the party flats, a suitcase in either hand.

Her letter touched off a storm that destroyed the WRP. Two key party leaders, Mike Banda and Cliff Slaughter, formed an anti-Healy alliance.

Opposition, led by the group of abused young women, grew within the London District Committee. At the beginning of October, Healy was banned from the party's premises. A Central Committee meeting was held on October 12–13 which voted 25 to 11 to charge Healy over his abuse of women. The minority, including Vanessa Redgrave, walked out. Healy was unanimously expelled on October 19.

The Jennings letter was published, minus the twenty-six names, in the party's paper, *News Line*, and the story was immediately picked up by the tabloid press. Headlines screamed "RED IN THE BED."[25] The *Sunday Mirror* gave the following account, based on an interview with a WRP member, of Healy's "romantic" technique: "He would throw his arms around the women and tell them to submit. If they protested—and some of them did—he would say: 'You are doing this for the Party and I AM the Party.' Each of them was under the impression that she was the only one who had been used by Healy. Most of the women were in their twenties and were selected for their vulnerability."[26]

Stuart Carter gave a harrowing account of life within top circles of the party just prior to Healy's expulsion:

> Healy and Banda wanted to suspend [Sheila] Torrance [a top party leader]. I felt compelled to oppose them. Healy was annoyed because Torrance had, he claimed, been rude to him.
> Healy punched me several times. . . . Later at an aggregate meeting my girlfriend, an area committee member, was picked up by the arms and legs and thrown down the stairs of the YS (Young Socialists) training center. . . . I was given a good kicking by about six comrades including the Bandas who urged them on shouting "Break his legs."[27]

Vanessa Redgrave rallied to Healy's support, holding her own press conference.[28] A court battle raged between contending factions for control of the party's substantial assets. The party owned its headquarters building, flats across from it, a printing plant in the North, the Red House in Derbyshire, six bookstores, and eight youth training centers. It employed ninety-one people, and Healy had a £16,000 BMW sports car at his disposal. However, the party's debt exceeded its assets and within months the entire edifice collapsed. The WRP broke up into competing grouplets. It proved impossible to build a Healyite party of any size without the aging guru—and, in fact, Healy himself also failed at the task.

Three Women

How was it possible that Healy, who had achieved such total control over his members, found himself unceremoniously thrown out by the same members? This process can throw additional light on the dynamics of political cults, particularly of the activist kind.

The collapse of Healy's hold on the WRP can be attributed to the combined effects of three women: Aileen Jennings, Vanessa Redgrave, and Margaret Thatcher. Jennings' account had the effect that it did because Redgrave and Thatcher had prepared the WRP for an explosion. The recruitment of Vanessa gave Healy a powerful resource for advancing his politics and influence. She came along at a critical moment when he was losing his base in the trade union movement and the sixties generation was drifting out of politics. Vanessa provided Healy with a much-needed infusion of funds.

More important than Vanessa's personal assets and her ability to raise money from friends was the political potential of her fame. Healy encouraged Vanessa to go to the Middle East and make a film, *The Palestinians*, supporting the positions of the Palestine Liberation Organization (PLO). With Healy in tow, Vanessa toured the Middle Eastern capitals soliciting funds from the Iraqis, various sheikdoms, including the royal family of Kuwait, Libya,[29] and Iran.[30] Wherever Vanessa went, large sums were raised. "The WRP and its press became largely a service to the Arab bourgeoisie," Cliff Slaughter, the party's top intellectual, reported after the split. "The more it was necessary to 'impress' the bourgeois-nationalist leaders and rulers who bought copies of 'The Palestinian' or 'Occupied Palestine,' or who provided profitable printing contracts (and, in some cases, provided money for 'services rendered'), the more the political line of the WRP and IC was trimmed to suit them. . . ."[31] Another incident is described by Healy's last "close personal companion" and worshipful biographer, Corinna Lotz. "Gerry made several trips to Libya during the 1970s and early 1980s, and held a number of lengthy discussions with Gaddafi in his Bedouin tent. He was proud and amused to have been 'given a lift in the colonel's jet' back to London on one occasion."[32]

This arrangement with Vanessa worked for a decade. Vanessa offered Healy an opportunity to influence world politics, if only on the margin, and to raise funds to keep the party running. The party became more and more a kind of Potemkin Village to impress Vanessa and her newfound Middle Eastern friends so that moneys would keep rolling in. A growing staff of middle-class party members was sustained, though on minimum rations, by the party and was a source of support for Healy. An accommodation was even reached with a left Labour Member of Parliament, Ken Livingstone (currently London's newly elected mayor).[33] However, the more Healy depended on Vanessa, the less important the party's membership became to him. His grip upon them suffered because of his own lack of interest in maintaining it.

At the same time Healy became corrupted by the power he had gained over a rather wealthy little party. He traveled the Middle East with a world-

famous star; visited with heads of states; taught dialectics in a country estate surrounded by admiring acolytes; traveled to and from his assignments in his BMW; and maintained an extremely active sex life for a man in his seventies, sharing with Mao Tse-Tung a special taste for young women. He had traveled very far from his birthplace on a tiny farm in Ireland, his days as a seaman, and his life in faction-ridden small groups during the forties and fifties. His molestations of party members' daughters expressed the disdain he actually felt toward his followers. The followers sensed this, too.

It was a very different Conservative government that came to power in 1979. Margaret Thatcher, who had wide support among the lower middle classes and some sections of the working class, was determined to change the balance of power within England by defeating the trade union movement. The decisive struggle was the year-long miners' strike that ended in a rout of the workers in March 1985. She accomplished this while maintaining an overwhelming majority in Parliament and in the country. The WRP crisis began with Jennings's letter in July of the same year.

The impact upon the WRP was intensified by the extremist interpretation Healy gave to the struggle. On the eve of the miners' strike Healy claimed: "The struggle for power under the leadership of our party is posed under . . . very favorable conditions where the working class [is] in conflict with the capitalist state itself." It was a "pre-revolutionary situation which is rapidly developing into a revolutionary one. . . ."[34] As the miners strike unfolded, Healy characterized the Thatcher government as a Bonapartist dictatorship, predicting that the defeat of the strike would lead to fascism and the illegalization of the party.[35]

It is not hard to imagine the state of the WRP's cadres during the summer and fall of 1985. Dreams of revolution and nightmares of fascism had faded. The response from workers to party propaganda had lessened, yet the pressure on party members for funds and activity increased. The guru seemed preoccupied with his star recruit. The revelations of sexual misconduct had an enormous impact. The emperor had no clothes (as twenty-six young women discovered) and all the rank and file—blinded for so many years—could now see him clearly. There were political issues involved. For example, the close political relations Healy established with Arab governments conflicted with the group's generally hardline orthodox stance on other political matters. Yet most members realized the explosion was over more than politics. *It was a break with cultism itself.*

"We must oppose all attempts to in any way separate the sexual and physical abuse from something called their politics," Slaughter wrote. "The Healy clique . . . are close to every fascist position on the rights of human individuals, rights which for them are reduced to nothing by the requirements of the party."[36] The most perceptive analysis came from two former party members, Robin Blick and David Caldwell. "In many respects," the two com-

mented in the *New Statesman*, "the WRP shouldn't be treated as a secular political movement but as one in the tradition of the millennial movements of the Early Modern Age, along with contemporary religious cults like the Moonies and the 'Peoples Temple' of Jim Jones. . . . "[37]

"Not a Nice Old Man"

On the morning of December 14, 1989, Gerry Healy died in bed in a house provided for him by Vanessa Redgrave. Corinna Lotz, who had served him faithfully since 1985, was at his bedside. He was the head of the Marxist Party at the time of his death. The party was composed of Vanessa, Corin, Corinna, Paul Feldman, and at most a dozen more. All were devoted to him absolutely. Healy had remained politically active to the end. As one associate remarked, "He was not a nice old man sitting in an armchair."[38]

Healy had spent three months in hiding after the split. Vanessa paid for the hiding place and occasionally came by with fish and cooked a meal for him. Lotz took care of his needs the rest of the time, while Corin was his political emissary to the outside world. "We continued our life in hiding," Lotz wrote. "A lot of time was spent collecting people from various places and taking them to see Gerry or driving him to different locations. The meetings were often held in parks."[39] It was all most exciting for the little band of acolytes and their guru. The conspiratorial atmosphere tied them all ever closer to Healy.

Gerry Healy's Seven Seals

"In the distances, the ominous sounds of thunder. Then they come. The four spectral shapes rise out of the night. Four horseman glide across the earth. They have no substance. Nothing can stop them."[40] So begins the first of the Seven Seals from Revelations. David Koresh believed he had discovered the secret meaning of these seals. His followers believed Koresh. He spent his last days in his compound, surrounded by the overwhelmingly superior force of the American state, negotiating in the hopes of going on television and explaining the Seals to the American people. The Seals were Koresh's secret gnosis.[41] Healy had his gnosis as well—his own special knowledge.

Healy had developed a profound interest in Marxist philosophy in the 1960s. He was convinced that dialectics held the key to all revolutionary politics. Failings in the party, weaknesses in party members, as well as the political conduct of opponent left groups were all reduced to philosophical problems. During the 1970s and 1980s, as Healy's politics became more unreal, his emphasis on philosophy became more intense. Dialectics led Healy to claim in 1988 that "Britain was on the eve of a revolutionary change."[42] In

his last years, freed from the day-to-day management of a party and responsible only for a handful of sannyasins in Britain and two small groups abroad, Healy could devote his full energies to his philosophical pursuits.

He took the same text, Lenin's *Philosophical Notebooks*, and worked, reworked, and chewed over again and again the same quotations from Hegel with appended comments by Lenin. "He was now working through his fourth copy of Lenin's *Philosophical Notebooks*," Lotz noted, "having marked up previous copies so heavily they had to be put aside."[43]

Lotz's memoir is filled with abstract philosophical discussion and contains a two-page foldout in two colors with arrows going in all directions. Healy concentrated on "semblance" and other Hegelian categories in his last years. Her description of a discussion at a class held in Spain gives us the flavor of Healy's philosophical efforts:

"One student wanted to know: 'What is the "the-thing-in-itself" in semblance?' This was an important question, since Gerry's presentation shows the objectivity of the moment of semblance. . . . Semblance is a subdivision or moment of essence. . . . Semblance he described as the negative nature of essence."[44] He did not, however, go on to describe what "essence" was or "the-thing-in-itself" for that matter.

Healy's interest in "semblance" could have been related to his creation of the semblance of a party and the semblance of a daily paper, while he preached the semblance of a revolution. Philosophy had become for him a way of avoiding the difficult *facts* of Thatcherite England. He believed that penetrating these abstractions would provide the key to the political universe. With this key in hand, the small band would be able to unlock the chains binding the proletarian giant, and the millennium would be reached. The Hegelian categories became his Seven Seals.

Conclusion

Healy's long history illustrates all the essential features of the political cult. Healy began typically by assembling a group of personal followers. In time he discovered doctrine and politics to justify the separateness of his followers, be they organized as faction or party. He then manipulated these doctrinal positions in order to drive his members to ever-greater exertion. While existing during decades of relative prosperity, Healy was always capable of discerning an underlying crisis that was getting ever deeper. A revolutionary explosion would occur at any moment, which would propel his little band of acolytes into power. Once in power, Healy promised a rather ruthless imposition of a utopian society. Political doctrine functioned for Healy very much as religious belief functions for Jehovah's Witnesses or Seventh Day Adventists.

Healy drove his membership day and night, giving it no time to think critically. An extremely high level of activity is found quite typically in political cults (see chapter 11 for a description of this process in the Militant group). It has a mind-altering effect similar to those induced by religious cults. The member becomes too tired to think critically about the group and its policies. He or she begins to seem to people outside the group like a zombie stumbling through life muttering political dogmas that are incomprehensible to the outside world.

Healy was well aware that members need some kind of external reinforcement for internal dogma. Therefore he created Potemkin Villages in the form of a daily paper, summer camps, demonstrations, and an apparatus out of proportion to the real size of his membership. Membership statistics and circulation figures were exaggerated in order to make this vision seem more realizable and to continue to inspire a wearying membership.[45]

Healy was not totally divorced from the real world. He was a skillful politician and extremely energetic. He searched out and ably exploited political opportunities among dissident communists and Labour Party youths, as well as in the film and theater worlds. However, and this is also typical of other political cults, a period of growth was always followed by crisis and split. He was ever willing to sacrifice members when he felt, justified or not, that his personal grip on his organization was threatened.

Healy pushed the psychotic dimensions of political cultism to their limits. This was most notable in two ways: paranoia and internal terror. He devoted tremendous resources to pursuit of his "Security and the Fourth International" campaign, claiming that his political opponents within the Trotskyist left were agents of the FBI and the GPU (State Political Administration, an early ancestor of the KGB). This allowed Healy to alienate his party's membership from the rest of the left and thus to define the cult boundary. Healy perfected the art of carrying out verbal attacks upon all members, including leaders close to him, in an extremely emotional way. The smallest error was exaggerated beyond all proportion, and the victim, as well as the membership, were made to feel that this error had negatively affected the outcome of the revolutionary process in a fundamental way. Healy went beyond verbal abuse and engaged in physical assaults. Then he transformed his cult into a personal brothel.

In the end the bulk of his membership were able to free their minds of his grip and his organization imploded. They found it a liberating experience, as if a great weight were lifted off them and their minds were freed from the effect of a powerful drug. Most soon dropped out of politics. Cultists like Healy are capable of turning thousands of well-intentioned, idealistic young people, workers, and intellectuals away from politics. For this reason alone they play a destructive role in civil society.

Chapter 11

The Lonely Passion
of Ted Grant

*If you open that Pandora's box you never know
what Trojan 'orses will jump out.*
—Ernest Bevin

Introduction

The year is 1933. Fascism has triumphed in Italy, and Hitler has just come to power in Germany. Tension is rising in Spain and Portugal, where fascist parties have their eyes set on further victories. Already, some voices can be heard predicting that a new world war is inevitable. Millions of German Jews still go about their daily business, unaware of the fate that awaits them. Half a world away, in South Africa, a small group of Trotskyists, including a youthful Ted Grant, has concluded that capitalism cannot hope to survive the combined calamities of depression, fascism, and imminent world war. They fervently believe that, from the flames of conflict, a new world order will be born. But success is only possible, they reason, if a mass revolutionary party based on the teachings of Lenin and Trotsky can be built. Grant and his associates are convinced that they are destined to become such a party. This daunting ambition is summed up in the name they select for themselves—the Workers International League (WIL). All they need is a more receptive climate for their ceaseless work of agitation, propaganda, and organization. Where will they go, and what will they do?[1]

Now, fast-forward to Britain in late 1991. The Workers International League, in its entirety, had emigrated there in the mid-1930s. Ted Grant is in his late seventies, shabbily dressed except when addressing public meetings, and constantly immersed in the latest edition of the *Financial Times*. It has been a lifelong addiction. There is probably no one on the planet who has studied its distinctive pink pages with as much devotion as this man, whose main goal in life is the overthrow of the system the newspaper is pledged to defend.

Grant's faith in "the revolution" is undimmed. For over sixty years he sat in dingy offices in London, and plotted and planned, and hoped and waited. People who encounter him after an interval of many years all come away with the same observation: "He is just the same as always!" If the dialectic is the philosophy of contradiction and change, Ted Grant is to all outward appearances its living refutation. His world outlook is essentially the same today as it was in 1928. He has spent the last seventy years sealed inside the cloistered world of Trotskyist politics. But, as the new year dawns, he faces expulsion from the organization he himself founded so many decades earlier. As his life winds to a close, it will be necessary to start all over again.

For the most part it has been a lonely life. Briefly, in the 1940s, Grant helped lead a unified Trotskyist organization (the Revolutionary Communist Party) which, at its peak, claimed five hundred members. In the 1950s, Grant's coterie shrank to a few dozen people. In the 1980s, the number of his supporters soared, amazingly, to around eight thousand. By this stage the WIL had transmuted into the Militant Tendency—or, in its international variant, the Committee for a Workers International (CWI). Its members joined the Labour Party, hoping to obtain an influence there that they knew they could never achieve under their own banner. In this guise, the CWI had won a majority within the Labour Party's official youth section, the Young Socialists—its major source of recruits in the heady days of the 1970s and 1980s.

Inevitably, as the prospect of revolution receded and fractiousness returned, the CWI was reduced to its original size, a much more humble organization of a few hundred members. Grant had always resembled a down-at-heels teacher in one of the poorer British colleges of further education, rather than a leader of the world revolution. Even his greatest admirers never pretended that he was overly endowed with charisma. How had this most unlikely of gurus managed to build a relatively formidable force, even if only for a short period of time?

This is the story of one man's obsession with the dream of revolution. In the case of Ted Grant there were never any other distractions. Since he was fifteen Trotskyism had been the only passion in a long life dedicated to the overthrow of capitalism. Like their mentor, Grant's supporters lived in an intense and private world where their only intellectual nourishment came from the collected works of Marx, Engels, Lenin, Trotsky—and Ted Grant. The saga of the CWI's rise and fall demonstrates the impasse that awaits high-activity groups that are unable to distinguish between their dreams and reality.

Origins and History

Very little is known about the life of Ted Grant the man, as opposed to Ted Grant the Trotskyist theoretician. Grant would undoubtedly take the suggestion that he had no life outside politics as a compliment. Even his real name is uncertain. Ted Grant is a pseudonym chosen during his fateful trip to Britain in the 1930s, and he has made it a lifelong practice to conceal his original name and date of birth. This concealment is the one fetish to ever rival his obsession with politics. In case this suggests a complete lack of personal sparkle, fairness demands that Grant's enjoyment of cheap sweets and vigorous games of table tennis also be recorded. His only affectation in terms of appearance was embarrassment at losing his hair, an affliction that befell him in late middle age. Ever since, he has worn it brushed vigorously forward, thereby drawing further attention to his shining pate and providing journalists with the only recognizably human trait in otherwise tedious accounts of Grant's career and organization.

From external evidence, it appears that he was born around 1913 in South Africa. In the late 1920s he procured a copy of the American newspaper *Militant*, an organ of what eventually became the Socialist Workers Party (SWP). It was rare for this publication to excite immediate support at this stage, either at home or abroad, but the impact on this unusual adolescent was one of revelation. Revolutionary politics became the abiding passion of his life. Unlike many gurus on the far left or elsewhere, there is no recorded instance of Grant's ever having had amorous attachments to members of either sex. The inordinate urge to displace all his feelings in this way suggests that the motive force behind his obsession with politics is neither entirely normal nor healthy. For Ted Grant, all human interests outside the precepts of scientific socialism are a distraction.

His achievement in constructing an organization that, in the 1980s, briefly attracted the passionate support of thousands of British youth is therefore all the more remarkable. But this development lay far in the future. In the 1930s, isolated and casting around for points of support, Grant's supporters first joined the Independent Labour Party, before entering the Labour Party's youth section, then entitled the Labour League of Youth. Even at this stage their main concern was to build their own organization, rather than become mere members of a larger radical party.

Disappointingly, Britain proved no more receptive to revolutionary ideas than South Africa had been. In the minds of most radical-minded workers and intellectuals the Communist Party still possessed the authority it derived from having led the only successful socialist revolution in the world. Trotskyist critics were denounced as traitors to the proletariat and were inaccurately depicted as working in liaison with Hitler. However, the atmosphere that prevailed inside the Trotskyist groups also helped them to sustain a state of chronic isolation. From their inception, they were beset by an endless series of splits, mergers, and fresh ruptures, on ever more esoteric points of doctrine.[2] Grant and his WIL became one of just several groups, claiming to be the most authentic interpreters of Trotsky's doctrine, and engaged in furious polemics with their immediate rivals on the far left.

From such ashes Grant insistently projected the construction of a world party of socialist revolution. However, the minds of most people remained fixed on the task of defeating Hitler. In this time, the WIL had only one piece of good luck. Grant broke his skull in an accident in 1940 and was declared unfit for military service. This enabled him to spend the war writing lengthy documents predicting the imminent demise of capitalism. Feeble as this activity was, it was just sufficient for the WIL to sustain some hope of recovery and influence in the future.

Official optimism in the face of refutation from the outside world is one of the most recurring traits of the cult groups surveyed in this book. Ted Grant is the virtuoso of optimism. Thus, he produced a document in 1942 entitled "Preparing for Power." In essence, he has been repeating the same themes ever since. Grant suggested that the war had fatally weakened capitalism and imperialism throughout the globe, but especially in Britain. Socialist revolution was a racing certainty, posing before the WIL the most marvelous of prospects:

> Our untrained and untested organization, will, within a few years at most, be hurled into the turmoil of the revolution. The problem of the organization, the problem of building the party, goes hand in hand with the revolutionary mobilization of the masses. Every member must raise himself or herself to the understanding that the key to world history lies in our hands. . . . The organization must consciously pose itself and see itself as the decisive factor in the situation. There will be no lack of possibilities for transforming ourselves from a tiny sect into a mass organization on the wave of the revolution.[3]

As the war drew to a close, Grant's fortunes temporarily improved, before once more being extinguished by chill winds from the outside world. In 1944 the fractious Trotskyist groups united for the first and last time into the Revolutionary Communist Party (RCP). Unfortunately, from the RCP's point of view, Grant's predictions of revolutionary upheaval increasingly clashed with the actual march of events. While RCP members busied themselves preparing capitalism's funeral rites, postwar reconstruction had commenced, and the pulse of economic activity quickened. Although Grant and his cothinkers acknowledged that some growth lay ahead, their basic perspectives remained startlingly unaltered. Catastrophe lurked on the immediate horizon, and state power would be there for the taking. With all the gay abandon of a man dancing on the edge of a volcano, Grant wrote in 1946:

> Events may speed up or slow down the processes but what is certain is the heightening of social tension and class hatreds. *The period of triumphant reaction has drawn to a close, a new revolutionary epoch opens up in Britain. With many ebbs and flows, with a greater or lesser speed, the revolution is beginning.* The Labour government is a Kerensky government . . . the revolution will probably assume a long-drawn out character but it provides the background against which the mass revolutionary party will be built.[4] (Italics in original)

However, in defiance of Grant's prognosis, the 1945 Labour administration proceeded to deliver on its promises of reform. It nationalized the coal and steel industries, and established socialized medicine in the form of the National Health Service. Further compounding the problems facing the entire revolutionary left, and confounding the claims of Marxists to have a special dialectical insight into its dynamics, the capitalist economy did not merely grow, but boomed as never before. Demoralized, faction ridden, and dwindling in numbers, the RCP fused with the Healy organization. In 1950, most of its members were lost through expulsions or demoralization. As we noted in the chapter 10, Grant himself and a handful of supporters were expelled by Healy. It was a bitter period. Nevertheless, Grant remained stubbornly convinced that revolution loomed, and that his primary task was to maintain an organization propagating the need for soviets, workers defense guards, and all the traditional paraphernalia of Bolshevik insurrection.

Entrism and Growth

Ironically, in view of what was to come, the year 1960 saw Grant recruit his own nemesis, Peter Taaffe, in Liverpool. It was to prove a crucial turning point in the organization's fortunes. Seeking shelter from the biting winds outside, Grant's supporters had remained in the Labour Party since their expulsion from Healy's organization—a longstanding Trotskyist tactic of infiltration, which they termed "entrism." The idea was to undermine advocates of reform from within. Trotskyists would become the termites of social democracy, nibbling at its foundations until the whole edifice crashed to the ground.

Feeling more confident, they decided to launch a newspaper to rally their supporters. *Militant* was born in 1964.[5] Henceforth, Grant's organization was known as the Militant Tendency. Publicly, it maintained the fiction that it was only a newspaper, around which readers' meetings were casually organized. Privately, the WIL remained intact, even if it no longer acknowledged the name. It had its own annual conference, employed its own full-time officials, and funneled its money through a labyrinthine web of bank accounts that even most of its leaders later admitted they had never understood.

Grant himself was notoriously inefficient in organizational matters, and increasingly relied on his talented young protégé. Thus, it was Peter Taaffe who on its launch was appointed *Militant*'s editor, and the revamped organization's first full-time organizer. In later years he became the CWI's general secretary. Increasingly, members in the know whispered that he rather than Ted Grant had become the "leading comrade." During the early years, when Taaffe publicly maintained an attitude of deference toward Grant, the founder himself held onto his job as a nighttime telephone switchboard operator. His organization could afford to employ him, even on a paltry salary, only in the late 1960s.

The 1960s was the decade of sexual liberation, the Beatles, swinging London, and student rebellion. The anti-Vietnam War protests intensified the spirit of revolt and provided a vital focus around which the general discontent with society could be rallied. A mood of change was in the air. It was a good time in which to launch a revolutionary newspaper. Anything seemed possible. The notion that there would be a resurgence in support for the ideas of the long-dead Leon Trotsky was not inherently implausible. Nevertheless, throughout the decade, *Militant* largely escaped the contagion of popularity that had unexpectedly descended on many of its rivals.

It was helped in this by the dullness of its pages. While London partied by night and protested by day, *Militant* bored for socialism. Inspired by the personal example of Ted Grant, widely regarded as the dullest writer in the history of the left, the writings of *Militant* leaders were a narcoleptic anthology of clichés. "Dazzling" prospects were always said to exist in the immediate future; "colossal" opportunities to build were identified in every situation; the years ahead were invariably referred to as "the coming period"; and the group's prognoses (always described as "perspectives") were frequently signaled by the tautological expression "we predict in advance." The spectacle was one of thought attempting flight, only to find, in midmotion, that all its moving parts had been superglued together.[6] The masses, for their part, obstinately refused to be electrified.

Linguistic difficulties were compounded by a myopic tendency to characterize every phenomenon as a "class issue," thereby alienating potential supporters. On these grounds, the nascent women's movement was disparaged as a distraction from the real issues facing working-class women. When *Militant* eventually published material on the feminist movement it focused exclusively on low pay, arguing for "campaigns" on the issue by the trade union movement. The Campaign for Nuclear Disarmament, then organizing demonstrations of thousands, was similarly despised. *Militant* theorized that radicalization and hence socialist revolution would not proceed from such issues, dominated by "middle-class trendies," but through a concentration on bread-and-butter issues. Demands for gay liberation were ignored in public, but behind the scenes were treated with contempt. Some CWI leaders argued privately that homosexuality always increased during periods of social disintegration such as occurred during the fall of the Roman Empire. Its emergence as an issue now was simply one more symptom of capitalism's degeneration and impending collapse.

By March 1973 Grant's organization had been active in Britain for forty-odd years: it had accumulated a total of 400 members. However, by the mid-1970s, it gained control of the Labour Party's official youth section, the Labour Party Young Socialists (LPYS). This good fortune was in large measure a parting gift from Gerry Healy (whose activities we discussed in chapter 10). Healy's organization had previously been dominant in the Young Socialists, but successfully contrived to get itself expelled. This removed *Militant*'s main revolutionary competitors inside the Labour Party, which was by then beginning a surge to the left. Once a majority of the LPYS had been acquired (which, given its small size, was a relatively easy matter), *Militant* also automatically secured a place on Labour's governing National Executive Committee (NEC). Trotskyism, for so long stranded on its own remote desert island, had arrived at the very top of Britain's foremost organization of Social Democracy.

Success now bred success. To the consternation of the Labour Party leadership, and the delight of Britain's tabloid press, *Militant* member Andy Bevan ("Red Andy") was appointed Labour's national youth organizer in 1976 and held this position until 1988. The anti-Labour media had a field day, and the unfamiliar attention further reinforced the illusion within *Militant* that, after so many years in the wilderness, its day had come.

Certainly, its situation had improved immeasurably. By the late 1980s it claimed eight thousand members, making it the largest Trotskyist organization in the history of Britain.[7] It also employed two hundred full-time organizers (all of whom earned a pittance and most of whom relied on state handouts), produced a sixteen-page weekly newspaper, maintained an impressive headquarters building in London, and was developing a regional network of offices throughout the country. In addition, three *Militant* members had managed to become Labour Members of Parliament, while others were capturing leading positions within the country's main civil service trade union.

Politically, the organization at this time conveyed the impression of laughing in the face of economic crisis and social breakdown. A typical example of its approach can be seen in a pamphlet produced in the early 1980s by CWI supporters in Ireland. Its central message is summed up in its title: "Socialism or Catastrophe." The pamphlet asserts: "The 1980s will be the most explosive decade in human history, both nationally and internationally. The crisis in the world economic and political systems is developing to new heights and threatens mass unemployment, a return to the conditions of the last century, and in the longer term of 15 to 20 years, the specter of nuclear war and the destruction of the human species."[8]

For reasons that were never adequately explained, it was assumed that economic calamity would produce mass movements anxious to secure the leadership of the CWI. Such fear-arousing tactics provoked a redoubled effort from its already overstretched membership, who were convinced that Armageddon was imminent and that they had no time to waste on the subtleties of introspective analysis.

By this time, *Militant* also had a controlling influence inside the Labour Group of Liverpool City Council. Given the government's policy of cutting back on central government funding for local authorities, this brought *Militant* and the Tory government of Margaret Thatcher into direct conflict. The result was massive demonstration and gridlock in a major metropolitan area of Britain. In addition, the Labour Party was wracked with painful debate on the most appropriate response to the rise of Thatcher and the fundamentalist brand of monetarism which she represented. Should the party swing to the left and articulate a dramatic socialist alternative? Or should it follow the example of European Social Democratic parties by embracing the free market system and proposing whatever reforms the system was judged capable of supporting?

In this debate, what to do with *Militant* became a key issue. Many on the left defended its right to maintain Labour Party membership. Those on the right saw this as infiltration, and demanded its removal as a signal to voters that Labour intended to embrace mainstream politics. The subsequent debate ensured that, for a period in the 1980s, this relatively small Trotskyist organization rarely strayed from the front pages of the national press.[9]

Unknown to the CWI's leader, the high watermark of its influence had already been reached. Within a startlingly short period of time the traditional tension between achieving influence in the real world and exerting control over its own members shipwrecked the entire organization. Scattered groups of survivors, disorientated and frightened by the extent of the catastrophe, wondered how it had it all happened, and stared into a future in which it became increasingly clear that all their best days were now well behind them.

Power Dynamics and Life Within the CWI

Life within the CWI was a constant strain. Members faced ever-greater demands for more activity, more financial sacrifices, and, above all, greater conformity to the ideas of the leadership. An examination of what it was like to be a member sheds much light on why it managed to acquire some influence, but also on why the organization would eventually disintegrate.

Andy Troke joined the CWI as a school student in 1972 and remained involved for five years. Even teenagers were viewed as potential "cadres" and were required to make a commitment that went far beyond anything found in mainstream political parties. Andy had to hand over 10 percent of his pocket money every week. The sum of money involved was small—but this was scarcely the point. It represented a great deal for a new and enthusiastic member. The undoubted sacrifice reinforced his newfound loyalty to revolutionary politics. Years later, Troke reflected on his experience as follows:

> It's like somebody who has been through a religious period. You look to either Trotsky, Marx, Lenin, Engels or Ted Grant or Peter Taaffe and you have got the rationale for why people are reacting this way or that. And obviously, everyone else is illogical, because you have the right view. I believe there was a great deal of that type of thinking: we were the chosen few. We had the right ideology. People like *Tribune*, who were at that time *Militant's* main opponents, didn't know where they were going—nothing. We were the right ones.[10]

Certain questions arise at this point: What did life within the CWI under such a regime feel like to the average member? How typical was the experience of Andy Troke? How were he and so many others recruited? How was their compliance and then conformity to the group's ideology obtained? The following comments on these issues from one interviewee, Ronnie, are typical of the accounts we have heard from many former CWI members. Ronnie spent a number of years working full time for the CWI:

> Six- or seven-day weeks for activists were common, particularly those full time. We nominally had a day off, but I can remember another leader saying to me proudly of another that "he uses his day off to prepare his lead-offs (introductory lectures) for meetings." Full timers were also kept in poverty. Wages were virtually non-existent, and I found out recently that from 1985 to 1991 they got no pay rise at all!
>
> When we worked, the pressure was awful. Key committees often met Saturday and Sunday 9 to 5, on top of your normal week's work. There would be different sessions, with a leader making an hour long introduction which laid out the line. Everyone else then would come in and agree. The more you agreed with the leader the more he or she cited your contribution in a 15–20 minute summing up at the end. If you disagreed, your contribution would be unpicked,

but if it wasn't sufficiently enthusiastic about the line it would—even worse—
be ignored. In this way you soon knew who was in and who was out. There was
a distinct tendency to promote the most conformist comrades to key positions,
even if they were also the most bland.

High dues or subs were extracted from members. A certain minimum sub
per week was set, which at several pounds a week was far in excess of what
normal parties extract. But people were "encouraged" to go beyond this. At big
meetings a speech would be made asking for money. Normally, some comrade
would have been approached beforehand and would have agreed to make a
particularly high donation—say £500. The speaker would then start off asking
for £500, its donation would produce an immense ovation and people would
then be pressurized to follow suit.

Everything was run by committees, and we had plenty of those. Branches
had branch committees which met in advance of branch meetings to allocate all
sorts of work, this went on to districts, areas and nationally and internationally.
Very often it was the same people on these committees wearing different hats!
But nothing moved without the committees' say-so. Also, at national conferences, leaders were elected by a slate system—i.e., the CC proposed a full list
of names for CC membership. If you opposed it you theoretically stood up to
propose a full list of new names, but needless to say no one ever did. New
members were regarded as "contact members" and allocated a more experienced comrade who was supposed to have weekly discussions as part of the
"political education."

I do remember feeling absolutely terrified when I first left—what was there
for me now, what would I do, where did I start? I eventually managed to get my
life together, but it was a hard slog.

Indoctrination began with the recruitment process. Given the CWI's secret
existence within the Labour Party, people who came into contact with it
would not have immediately known that it was an organization, with its own
annual conference, full-time officials, and central committee. Potential sympathizers encountered CWI members in the normal environment of the Labour
Party or trade unions. Once their left-wing credentials were established, they
would be asked to buy *Militant*, make a small donation, and support CWI
motions at other meetings—a process of escalating commitment. Only after
a series of such tests had been passed would the person be initiated into the
secret of the CWI's existence, and provided with internal documents detailing aspects of its program. As many ex-members have testified, the effect of
this was to create a feeling that the potential recruit was gaining privileged
information, and being invited to participate in the transformation of history.
Furthermore, they could only access more of this knowledge by escalating their
involvement with the group. The excitement at this stage was considerable.

In the 1970s, before the CWI grew to any significant size, the mystical
aura around joining was heightened by the formality with which it was concluded. New recruits traveled to London, where they were personally vetted

by the organization's founders. When this became impractical they were formally welcomed "in" by the nearest member of the Central Committee—an exercise close to "the laying on of hands" found in baptism ceremonies. Tremendous feelings of loyalty were engendered by this process, and fused together a group that saw itself as intensely cohesive and blessed with the evangelical mission of leading the world revolution. Research suggests that merely being a member of a group encourages the development of shared norms, beliefs systems, conformity, and compliance.[11] Belonging to a group with such a deep and all-embracing belief system as that offered by the CWI encourages this process all the more.

Once in, however, the picture began to change. More and more demands were placed on members. In particular, they were expected to contribute between 10 and 15 percent of their income to the party, buy the weekly newspaper, contribute to special press fund collections, subscribe to irregular levies (perhaps to the extent of a week's income), recruit new members, and raise money from sympathizers. Tobias and Lalich[12] argue that cults have only two real purposes: recruiting other members, and raising money. These certainly emerge as central preoccupations of the CWI. Crick cites a former member as follows on some of these issues:

> A lot of it boiled down to selling papers. The pace didn't bother me, but one day I suddenly realized that after a year my social circle had totally drifted. I had only political friends left, simply because of the lack of time. There'd be the . . . branch meeting on Monday evening, the Young Socialists meeting another evening, "contact" work on Friday night, selling papers on Sunday afternoon, and on top of that, to prove to the local Labour Party we were good party members, we went canvassing for them every week and worked like hell in the local elections.[13]

Such a level of activity could be physically and emotionally ruinous and required members to redefine their entire existence in terms of their membership of the CWI. Crick cites another interviewee as recalling:

> The most abiding memories of life in *Militant* are filled with the sheer strain of it all. If you were even moderately active, you would be asked to attend up to six or seven boring meetings in one week.
> You built up an alternative set of social contacts as much as political activity. It can easily take over people's lives. It became obsessive. They were almost inventing meetings to attend. There was a ridiculous number of meetings held to discuss such a small amount of work. Even if you didn't have a meeting one evening, you'd end up drinking with them.[14]

What runs through all these accounts is the boredom that accompanied CWI membership, after the thrill of initiation and the feeling of being special had worn off. For example, recruitment itself and much of party life consisted of hearing the same basic ideas endlessly repeated: there might be variations, but they would be variations around a minimalist theme. As Scheflin and Opton point out, paraphrasing no less an expert on mind control than Charles Manson, such repetition, combined with the exclusion of any competing doctrine, is a powerful tool of conversion.[15]

The recruitment process can also be interpreted as a means of indoctrinating new recruits by presenting them with an escalating series of challenges, or ordeals. Wexler and Fraser[15] have argued that this is an important method of establishing the cohesiveness of decision elites within cults, thereby activating the extreme conformity known as groupthink.[16] However, within the CWI, it seems that such methods were used on all new recruits in order to embroil them more deeply in CWI activities. Thus, prospective recruits first expressed private agreement with some CWI ideas. They were then required to advance this agreement publicly at Labour Party or trade union meetings, then to contribute money, to buy literature, and to sell newspapers on the street. This continued until their entire lives revolved around the CWI. The process seems to be one of *extracting commitment and then forcing a decision.*

The evidence therefore suggests that, until the mid-1980s, the CWI was a growing political force, with several thousand predominantly young and enthusiastic members. Prospects seemed limitless. Members were certainly encouraged to believe that the British revolution would develop within a ten-year period, and that their organization would play a decisive role in history's most crucial turning point. It was at this point, with pride at its peak, that disaster struck.

Collapse and Disintegration

The steady growth that the CWI experienced in the late 1970s and the 1980s meant that new members were recruited without the lengthy indoctrination that had previously been a precondition for CWI membership. Consequently, these members' loyalty, conformity, and respect for CWI methods of working were much less pronounced than was the case for their predecessors.

Fundamentally, the CWI was hoping to remain a highly cohesive grouping, but with a mass membership: in essence, it was attempting to design a round square. Given an influx of new members not prepared to devote all their energies to party building, nor to avoid challenging Ted Grant and Peter Taaffe when their predictions failed to materialize, this proved impossible. For many, after a short period of time, applause gave way to a slow handclap. After the CWI split in 1992, the consequences of this situation were frankly

summarized by Grant and the shell-shocked veterans who had gone with
him, as follows:

> 1987 was a watershed. . . . The membership fell each year. . . . Then the sick-
> ness of commandism and substitutionism rose apace. The leadership hid the
> real situation from the ranks. Instead of "success" we were faced with retreat,
> which did not suit the prestige of the leadership. Comrades were telling other
> comrades what they wanted to hear. The Center became more and more out of
> touch with the situation on the ground. The CC generally accepted this state of
> affairs as they were too fearful of raising real criticisms and being labeled "con-
> servative." The situation led to the burning out of a whole layer of comrades
> and Full Timers. Since 1988, the organization halved in size . . . the turnover
> reached 38% in 1990 . . . we have lost 1,000 comrades since Jan. 1991—a turn-
> over of 20% . . . according to the census conducted at the 1990 congress less
> than 1,100 were attending the branches, which includes 200 FTers.[17]

In reality, the first intimations of mortality were felt by the CWI in the early
1980s. Labour leaders devoted more time to combating its influence. The
Labour Party National Executive Committee voted in 1982 to proscribe the
organization. Members would be presented with a choice—renounce their
allegiance to the CWI, or face expulsion from the Labour Party.[18] The process started in February 1983, when the NEC voted to expel the five named
members of the paper's Editorial Board: Ted Grant, Peter Taaffe, Lynn Walsh,
Clare Doyle, and Keith Dickinson.

By and large, what the CWI described as a witch hunt had a limited effect.
Internal CWI documents suggest that by 1991 no more than two hundred
and fifty people had been expelled, at that time a small proportion of the
overall membership. These figures hid the real extent of the crisis that now
gripped the organization. Much CWI activity had been forced underground.
Anyone who continued to identify with the CWI became a target for expulsion, making it difficult to sell *Militant*. The temperature in the womb of the
Labour Party had turned distinctly chilly.

Despite these measures, for a short period, the organization's influence and
fame seemed to grow still further. Liverpool had traditionally been the CWI's
main stronghold. In May 1983, CWI members of the local Labour Party took
effective control of the city council. The deputy leader of the council, who
soon became its public voice, was CWI member Derek Hatton. He was for a
time one of the most pilloried men in Britain, before he scaled down his
political activities and metamorphosed into a well-paid public relations consultant, and subsequently "shock jock" radio host. However, the noose was
tightening. Many CWI Liverpool leaders were expelled from the Labour Party
in 1986, after a prolonged wrangle between the council and the Tory government, which had been attempting to force cuts in council spending.

Predictably, the official position of the CWI leadership remained one of boundless optimism. Ted Grant, still practicing the science of clairvoyance, prophesied in 1986: "*Militant* will become the majority in the Labour Party and the unions and it will transform society during the course of the next decade."¹⁹ Such pronouncements were no more accurate than his funeral orations over the capitalist economy. Within the organization, voices increasingly complained that the "old man" was past it and had become an obstacle to further growth.

The Split with Taaffe

By 1986, Ted Grant realized that he was not being propelled into the limelight through major speaking engagements as much as he had been in previous years. Peter Taaffe's rationale was that Grant's best days were behind him and that perhaps he should think of retirement. Testimony from other members suggests that the truth was more complex and that Taaffe had increasingly tired of his position as second in command. An old-fashioned struggle for power was under way. Gurus generally dislike other gurus, and relations between Grant and Taaffe had been strained for some years. Obstinately, Grant refused either to retire or to die. Time was also taking its toll on the no-longer-youthful Peter Taaffe. If he delayed a move into the top leadership position much longer, perhaps it would be too late and his coronation might never come.

Meanwhile, the pressure outside intensified. In 1990, sixteen Liverpool councilors were suspended from Labour Party membership. The immediate issue was their refusal to set an unpopular local government tax (the poll tax) devised by the Tory government, which meant they were breaking the law in defiance of official Labour policy. The CWI's influence, never quite so great as its media profile had suggested, was very much on the wane. The CWI was now deprived of its representative on Labour's NEC. The mood inside the party had swung against the left in general. The position of those Labour MPs who belonged to the CWI was also under increasing examination, and eventually they too were expelled.

Faced with crisis, the CWI split in two. Taaffe and a majority of the central committee, hand-picked and nurtured by him, concluded that they would enjoy better prospects if they set up their own party. This was a startling revision of its previous position, and one which had after all been its principal distinguishing trait on the revolutionary left. Grant, supported in the main by longstanding member Alan Woods, reached precisely the opposite conclusion: now was not the time to change course, but to reaffirm the traditional tactic of entrism, while waiting patiently for better days.²⁰

The dispute between Grant and Taaffe was resolved in time-honored fashion. Grant and his supporters, by now representing a small minority, were expelled in early 1992. They instantly set up a new Trotskyist international still committed to the traditional policy of entrism. A number of people have testified to us that he immediately recreated the internal regime from which he had suffered under Taaffe, only this time it was aimed against his own dissidents.

Meanwhile, oblivious to the shattered state of his remaining members (and their dwindling numbers), Taaffe launched his new independent party onto the high seas, its banner unfurled. It promptly capsized. None of the expected gains ever materialized, and the comrades increasingly squabbled among themselves. Consequently, the CWI's decline has been precipitous. Initially, in Britain, it called itself "Militant Labour." After an acrimonious dispute in 1996, climaxing in further resignations, it renamed itself the "Socialist Party." Nick Wrack, the editor of the organization's newspaper, was one of the casualties. He had dared to question the new general line and complained bitterly that Taaffe reacted by refusing even to speak to him when they passed in their headquarters building.

By this stage, Taaffe had become even more convinced of his indispensability to the world revolution. Like a punch-drunk boxer planning yet another comeback, he had also grown immune to setbacks. How dare anyone question his genius? Thus, he expelled a substantial section of his few supporters within the United States in 1998 and celebrated 1999 by throwing overboard most of the 1,000 members he had miraculously managed to obtain in Pakistan. Most CWI members in Merseyside, once a major area of influence, were also expelled, while those in Scotland declared independence in all but name.[21] Yet again, control over a dwindling number of true believers took priority over influence in the outside world.

Our sources suggest that Taaffe's organization now has well under 500 members in England, with Grant cheered on by even fewer.

Conclusion

The saga of the CWI is instructive. Rational politics is about building alliances, achieving influence, and making a difference in the real world. In the fantasy universe of Trotskyism, on the other hand, the primary objective is to preserve the purity of the founder's ideals. Unless everyone agrees to play by the leader's rules, *right now*, he will grab his ball and storm off the playing field. Internally, such groups establish punitive regimes, in which anyone who dares to question the leader's genius is driven from the ranks as a heretic. Heretics are forced to create their own organizations, or else to withdraw from politics altogether. In this lies the explanation for the proliferation of warring sects on the outer fringes of left-wing political discourse, each more committed to the annihilation of its rivals than to genuine social change. The desire for purity conflicts at every turn with the desire for influence.

Meanwhile, the catastrophist presumptions of Trotskyist theory drives its adherents into a permanent frenzy of activity, which handicaps their ability to generate creative political insights. Members are too tired, too busy, or too scared to think. What if all this has been a mistake? What if so much sacrifice has been in vain? Better by far to suppress such awful feelings of doubt, and launch a new recruitment campaign, based on the familiar nostrums of the transitional program. Thus, the voluminous writings of Trotsky form an intellectual comfort blanket, warming the group's waning sense of certainty.

For the CWI, as for many others, the result has been oblivion. Its intense devotion to the letter of Trotsky's writings prevents it from developing a theory of its own, while the desire for uniformity repels those genuinely interested in changing society. Its forces, like those of every other Trotskyist group, are reduced to an ever-smaller core of fanatical true believers. In consequence, the leaders of the CWI and Ted Grant's split-off, have "immatured" with age. They have become theoreticians without a theory, and organizers with nothing much left to organize.

The tragedy is immense. With each new setback, Ted Grant has retreated further into the certainties of the world he knows best—the written works of those he regards as his great teachers, which have remained uncontaminated by input from mainstream political parties or anyone else.

Now, in separate buildings, Taaffe and Grant sit in similar offices, producing furious polemics against each other and against their many other rivals on the left. A new millennium beckons, full of terror, uncertainty, and challenge, but the way forward for each of these men is back to the past. Each *knows* that his ideas alone are correct. Anything that suggests the opposite is but a dialectical blip on the radar screen, before the real curve of historical development reasserts itself.

And so, as darkness falls, they both sit, and plot and plan, and hope and wait.

Chapter 12

The Many Faces
of Gino Perente

*The narrative of the guru . . . can be seen as a
version of the myth of the hero. That myth involves
a mysterious birth and early childhood, a call to
greatness, and a series of ordeals and trials culminating in heroic achievement.*
—Robert Jay Lifton, *Destroying the World to Save It*

The Raid

November 11, 1996, was a chilly night in a poor, drab, almost entirely black
section of Brooklyn's Crown Heights. Decaying brownstones lined Carroll
Street. A slight wind blew trash along the sidewalk. The leaves on the few
trees along the block had turned brown. Every now and then a figure scurried up the street and swiftly entered a building. A lone sentry, rifle in hand,
peered down on the scene from the dimly lit fourth-floor window of 1107
Carroll Street.

Then a child's cry rang out from the second floor of the tenement. A neighbor heard the young girl and placed an anonymous phone call to the hot line
of the King's County Society for the Prevention of Cruelty to Children
(SPCC), a voluntary organization.

As George Summerfield and four other members of the SPCC approached
the building, they were spotted by the sentry. It was to be what they called a
"routine door-knock." They would request entrance so that they could observe the condition of any children in the place. Summerfield knocked on
the door of the second-floor apartment and asked to have his group admitted.
They were refused entry. The group went to the local precinct station and
returned with the cops. The patrol officers were turned down, as was a ser-

geant and then a lieutenant. A captain was notified. Worried about a possible hostage situation, the captain called in the emergency service unit, and the building was surrounded by officers in helmets and body armor. Helicopters buzzed overhead and the press arrived. Finally, fifteen cops gained entrance.

The officers soon discovered that they had stumbled upon the national headquarters of one of the most secretive and long-lasting political cults in the United States, the National Labor Federation (NATLFED), front for the Communist Party, U.S.A. (Provisional) (CPUSA [P]). The group's founder, Eugenio Perente-Ramos (aka Gerald William Doeden), had died the previous year. His followers, under new leadership, had soldiered on.

The apartment, known to the cadre as the "Cave," was fitted out as an office. Sitting on the floor in the middle of a large room were thirty-five cult members, arms linked, singing "Amazing Grace." On the wall was a huge organizational chart, scrawled all over in crayon, listing the group's "entities" (front groups) around the country. Files and paperwork were everywhere. Pictures of Ché Guevara and Stalin hung in various rooms. There was sufficient food in freezers and barrels to last for months.

Probing the back wall of a closet, the police discovered a false partition. The Federal Bureau of Investigation (FBI), which had raided the very same building in 1984, had missed it. "New York's finest" did better because they had had considerable recent experience breaking into crack houses and finding hidden stashes. Smashing through the thin wood, they uncovered sixteen pistols, twenty-six rifles, five shotguns, two Thompson submachine guns, five canisters of black gunpowder, and $42,000 in cash. When the cops entered the basement, they found a maze of "dungeons" and tunnels linking three adjoined four-story brownstones, 1107, 1111, and 1115 Carroll Street, all owned by the cult.

After a flurry of news articles,[1] the press lost interest in the group. The police filed no charges. In fact, the group had relatively few children, and former members report that they were treated quite well.[2] The guns were rusty and most members were unaware of their existence. NATLFED's real crime was the destruction of the minds of its recruits, the subjugation of their very beings to a clandestine but internally all-powerful cult.

The Genesis Myth

Early on in his political career Gino Perente fabricated his political history. The high points of this story, referred to by members as "genesis," follow. In 1958 he claimed his "people" were active in the Communist Party. Then they were part of the Progressive Labor Party (PLP). Some of his people went to Cuba as part of a PLP-sponsored delegation.

Then the story turns somewhat bizarre. These same "people," including Perente, went to Guatemala to participate in guerilla warfare. They returned to the United States, traveled to San Francisco, and joined Stanford Professor Bruce Franklin's Venceremos Brigade, which advocated armed struggle. Many former members of Venceremos, the story goes, formed the Communist Party, U.S.A. (Provisional). Then Perente came to New York City and became a close collaborator of Cesar Chavez. A version of this story, based on information supplied by Perente, appeared in the *Nation* in 1980. Perente also claimed that his organization was officially recognized by the Cubans, and was part of an international formation including the FLMN (Farabundo Marti Liberation Front) in El Salvador, the Nicaraguan Sandinistas, and the MIR (Movimento de Izquierda Revolutionaria) in Chile.[3]

The memorial program, distributed at a service on March 23, 1995, on Long Island, claimed that Perente was "of Mexican descent, his family traced its roots back to its arrival in the New World from Spain in 1510. His father was a farmer, a sharecropper, a farm worker and an organizer from the Industrial Workers of the World. Three of his uncles were killed fighting the fascists in the Spanish Civil War."[4]

The truth was far more prosaic. Perente's real name was Gerald William Doeden. He was of Norwegian-American stock and was born in Crookston, Minnesota. His family settled in Marysville, California, a small city in the Central Valley about a hundred and forty miles from San Francisco, where he lived until 1970. He was well known in the area as a hard-drinking, drug-taking, quick-thinking man who was a bit of a con artist. He wrote bad checks in bars and sold fake lottery tickets. He was an amateur actor who could recite from memory long sections of Shakespeare. He injured his leg in an auto accident that forced him to limp or use crutches the rest of his life. In 1960 he married a local woman, Ruth Mikkelsen, who still lives in Marysville and teaches school. The couple had one child, a daughter, and then divorced in 1962. He was a popular disc jockey and sold advertising for a radio station. In 1970 Doeden was arrested and jailed for thirty days for nonpayment of child support.[5]

Doeden left Marysville for San Francisco soon after his incarceration. There he ran the Little Red Bookstore in the Mission District of San Francisco. He gathered a few would-be revolutionaries, who were attracted by his personality. It is quite possible that this initial group included former members of Venceremos and the PLP or that he could have had some minor contact with those groups. Bruce Franklin remembered Doeden as a "peripheral figure" on the radical scene.[6] Venceremos, as well as other Maoist groups, and PLP had an attachment for Stalin. It was in this period that Perente no doubt developed his own lifelong fondness for Uncle Joe.

He called his formation the Liberation Army Revolutionary Group Organization (LARGO). It had no special relationship with Cuba. He issued a bold challenge to the U.S. government. One statement read:

> We do hereby declare, the existence and intent of a National Liberation Front fighting force within the continental confines of the United States of America to be actively engaged in a people's War of Revolution against the aforenamed nation.... We hereby file public notice of our intent to conduct a controlled punitive action against United States Federal Forces and municipal forces on a limited scale, from the city of San Francisco on the south, to the Oregon border on the north, other confines being marked by the State of California boundaries.[7]

LARGO's one known action took place in early 1971:

> On an island in the Feather River, about thirteen people are busy with shovels and picks digging a deep hole. The purpose of the endeavor is to enable them all to have a place to hide in case of a feared upcoming police dragnet. Soon the hole becomes so huge that the diggers need to be pulled up from the bottom before they can climb out. Suddenly a motorboat is heard approaching the island. In the boat are two game wardens. Everyone scrambles and hides in the hole—except one man left standing near the island's shore clutching an M-1 rifle in his hand. Attempting a ruse, he waves to the game wardens and shouts: "Sure hope I get a big buck!"
> "You'd better not, son," yells back one of the game wardens as they putt-putt on down the river. "It isn't deer season yet."[8]

In late 1971 Gerald William Doeden left California and emerged as Eugenio Perente-Ramos in New York City. Perhaps he feared FBI persecution or just wanted to avoid another jail term for failure to pay child support. He went to work in the New York office of Cesar Chavez's United Farm Workers (UFW), which was then conducting a grape boycott. Delores Huerta remembers Perente as a "colorful biker type who played a small role in the boycott for about nine months or a year.... He created a lot of problems for the union, attacking us in the press. Then he went off and formed his own group."[9] The organization Perente created was called the Eastern Farm Workers Association (EFWA). He set up an office in Bellport on the eastern, agricultural end of Long Island.

In December 1972 Perente's group led a strike against a potato processing firm. He claimed to have thirty full-time and seventy part-time "associates." The *New York Times* described Perente as "a flamboyant Mexican-American with flashing eyes and a big mane of black hair."[10] The *East Hampton Star* spoke of Perente's "deep, dark eyes that pierced across the room as he talked about the passion and death of the seasonal farmworker in Long Island."[11]

Perente had failed to register the EFWA as a labor organization and was hit with a cease-and-desist order. This would be his first and last strike. A raid on his Bellport office by the Suffolk police uncovered two illegal handguns. These experiences led him to purchase the Carroll Street brownstone in Brooklyn and move himself, together with key supporters, to the new location. He ran his nationwide operation from the "Cave" over the next twenty years, communicating with members by phone and audio tape, rarely leaving the building even for a breath of fresh air.[12]

Learning from Lyndon

During 1973 and 1974 Perente joined with Lyndon LaRouche's National Caucus of Labor Committees (NCLC) (see chapter 5), which in turn was in alliance with Fred Newman and his supporters (see chapter 7). Whether Perente and his followers actually became members of NCLC is unclear. It is known that Perente was active in LaRouche's National Unemployed and Welfare Rights Organization (NUWRO) in 1973.

In 1974 Perente was elected president of the Nationwide Unemployment League (NUL) while still remaining the leader of the EFWA. The NUL was a front group organized by Fred Newman's International Workers Party (IWP), which had recently split from LaRouche.[13] On May 2, 1975, Perente delivered a speech at the headquarters of Fred Newman's International Workers Party (IWP).[14] Dennis King has suggested that the relationship between Perente and Newman "went on at least through 1977. . . . In 1976 fusion talks were held between NATLFED and IWP."[15]

The most likely scenario is that Perente was attracted to the NCLC in the same time period as Newman. He dropped away from LaRouche when Newman left and continued to collaborate with the IWP. It is not known when or why Perente broke off relations with Newman. Of course, the underlying reason for the various splits was clear enough: The three gurus could not be expected to stay together for long.

There was an important strategic reason as well. The three groups had come together at a time when LaRouche was actively involved, through his NUWRO, in the organization of the poor. By 1974, in his flight to the right, LaRouche had abandoned NUWRO. Newman persisted in local organization, running bucket collections on the West Side in much the same manner that Perente would perfect into a science. We suspect that the remnants of the NUWRO became a basis for the growth of Perente's NATLFED.

Of the three gurus, LaRouche was by far the most theoretically developed. We have documented elsewhere Newman's considerable political and theoretical debt to LaRouche. Perente learned much as well, either directly from LaRouche or indirectly through Newman. This was expressed most clearly in three areas: (1) attitude toward the left, (2) "strata" organizing, and (3) catastrophism.

1. *Attitude toward the left:* Perente joined LaRouche right at the point when he was moving swiftly to the right, breaking all relations with the rest of the left. He had launched his "Operation Mop-Up," which consisted of a series of hooligan attacks on members of the Communist Party and the Socialist Workers Party. Perente, like Newman, shared LaRouche's disdain for the left. He and his group avoided any contact with established leftist groups over the next twenty-five years. This proved to be quite helpful to the preservation of the group as a cult. It isolated NATLFED members from any challenge to their views from other leftists.

2. *"Strata" organizing*: Basing himself on certain themes in the writings of Marx, Lenin, and Trotsky, LaRouche had developed his own conception of "strata" organizing. He denounced existing social service organizations as agents of the ruling "liberal" elite, black nationalists as divisive, and trade unions as expressing a narrow "class-in-itself" ideology. He sought to organize the poor into a classwide formation that he would lead with his "class-for-itself" perspective. It was on this basis that he launched a bitter struggle against the black-led National Welfare Rights Organization (NWRO) in favor of his own front group. The net result was the disintegration of the former and his abandonment of the latter.[16] Perente followed a similar model organizing his "entities" that purportedly represented the poor but were actually controlled by his secret "class-for-itself" elite party.

3. *Catastrophism:* LaRouche perfected a theory of capitalist crisis, borrowed from Marxism, and preached an end-game view whereby civilization would collapse unless he was listened to. This perspective, similar to that developed by Gerry Healy (see chapter 10), was used to drive his followers into frenetic levels of activity. Perente, as we will see, topped both Healy and LaRouche by actually setting the date for the insurrection.

The Politics of Perente

Perente combined what he learned from LaRouche with a study of the Communist Party during its most Stalinist "Third Period" from 1929 to 1933. It was the time of the "united front from below" when other tendencies on the left, particularly the Socialist Party, were denounced as "social fascists," immediate revolution was preached, work in the existing trade unions ignored, and great efforts placed in organizing the unorganized and unemployed into formations controlled directly by the party.[17]

Throughout his career Perente spoke warmly of Stalin. He denounced the rest of the left as "social fascists" and modeled his "entities" on Communist Party unemployment leagues. As we have noted, he had developed these Stalinist views, at least in a nascent form, during his Little Red Bookstore days in San Francisco.

Soon after leaving the UFW Perente rejected working within the traditional trade unions in favor of "loose-knit organizations," essentially groups controlled by his Communist cadre. The manifesto of the National Labor Federation, issued in 1974, proposed to "organize all those who at present time have no independent organization of economic origin."[18] A document entitled *Provisional Thought* declared that "the tendency of political thought characterized by the CPUSA (P) finds itself at theoretical and practical odds with most of the de facto Western European movement." The document endorsed Fidel Castro's *focoismo*, took a neutral stance on the Sino-Soviet dispute, and denounced Maoism and the rest of the left. "The Party recently separated itself theoretically from the entire body of the existential left within the United States of America by announcing its considered position that fascism exists today in the United States of America." It called for a "new leadership and new issues to arise from the masses' struggle: led by the clandestine Formation of the Party."[19]

At one point, early on, the CPUSA (P) had an official membership dues book. This document included the "Mandate," stating that "clearly a Provisional Party is needed to consolidate the gains of the working class of the United States of America." It defined the "Provisional Party" as "a closed, or narrow party as befits the current situation. The actual name of the organization will appear on no documents, no propaganda—the title 'Provisional Party' will act as designate for inner-Party documents and communications. All other organizations attached to the Party will bear their own designation only."[20]

Ideology, however, was never Gino's strong suit. He needed a rationale to exist (the communist goal), a reason for clandestine functioning (the existence of fascism), and a history (largely mythic) to inspire his followers. His main preoccupation was, as we will see, with tactics. He developed a sophisticated and effective system for party building and for extending his political influence in a document called *The Essential Organizer*, sometimes referred to as *Systems '73*.[21]

The Military Fraction

The 1995 raid on NATLFED's Brooklyn headquarters was not the first government action against the group. On February 17, 1984, the Federal Bureau of Investigation (FBI) broke down the door of 1107 Carroll Street, in search of weapons that the government believed were about to be used in an insurrection.[22] The FBI had discovered documents setting the specific date, February 18, 1984, for the uprising. In all probability such documents did exist. For example, the document *Provisional Thought*, previously quoted, stated that "the Party has set a tempio-spacio timetable for revolution, which, for the sake of clarity—and admittedly, controversy—it has set forth clearly as a certain number of months." The problem was that the FBI took Perente at his word, always a mistake. The setting of the date for the revolution proved to be no more than one more trick by Gino to tie his members to him, and to wring more money and work out of them.

On July 26, 1984, Mia J. Prior, a leading party member who had been in the group for almost ten years, decided to leave. "Following customary practice of those who had successfully fled, she sneaked out of the apartment during one of the rare times she had been alone, taking only what she could carry, and leaving behind a letter."[23] Mia Prior, who had come from a wealthy family, received $7,700 quarterly from a trust fund. After she left, members of NATLFED, who functioned as an in-house law firm, took one of her checks, forged her signature, and cashed it. Prior reported the matter to the police. The district attorney filed legal action. The NATLFED lawyers countered with a suit claiming the money was due to them for legal and medical fees. The defendants were convicted, and appeals dragged on for several years. In the end the original charges were partially upheld.

In the course of this process, the FBI report on the February raid and related documents were entered into the court record. These documents claimed that Perente had organized a "Military Fraction." Several of the members of NATLFED's law firm were members of the Military Fraction. The FBI seized floor plans that indicated the location of "16 rifles, two machine guns, two shotguns and eight handguns . . . [and] an extensive stockpile of ammunition, including rifle grenades." A number of specific training orders were also found, including one requiring that a "firing squad ballot be drawn. . . . Our job is to suppress resistance. . . . "[24]

There is evidence that members of the Military Fraction were trained to use weapons and carried on various drills prior to 1984. However, there is no evidence that Perente actually planned any terrorist act. It was more a matter of revolutionary theater to make the internal life of the group a bit more exciting. After 1984 former members report that the Military Fraction was abandoned in practice.[25]

The Perente System

Gino Perente was a man of considerable talent. While he added nothing original to Marxist theory, he developed a complex and successful form of cultic practice. This explains how the group has survived the vicissitudes of very conservative political times. NATLFED can be compared to an onion: You need to peel off a number of layers to get to the core.

Its outer, or fourth, layer is the members of what is known internally as an "entity." The EFWA is one such entity. Others include the Coalition of Concerned Medical Professionals (New York and San Francisco), the Coalition of Concerned Legal Professionals (Bay Area and Philadelphia), the Eastern Service Workers Association (Upstate New York, New Jersey, and Philadelphia), the Western Massachusetts Labor Action (Pittsfield), and the California Homemakers Association (San Francisco and Sacramento).

The typical entity has the appearance of a social work organization. Its announced purpose is to act as a "mutual benefit organization" to aid the poor. The entity is neither registered as a trade union nor as a nonprofit organization. Therefore there is no obligation to make any accounting for its funds. Poor people are signed up as members and asked to pay sixty-two cents a month dues. In return they are promised free food, clothing, medical and legal aid, and other services.

The third layer is made up of the "volunteers" or VOLS. These are the people who sign up members; go out with buckets to raise funds; and staff phone banks to get money, food, clothing, and other items from small businesses, churches, and ordinary citizens. The volunteers are recruited primarily from colleges and are predominantly, but not exclusively, women. In most cases the volunteer has only a hazy understanding of the entity as an organization trying to help poor people.

The volunteers are broken into two groups: those who volunteer to work on a regular basis—such as one or two nights a week—and those who just come in when they feel like it. The regular volunteers are encouraged to quit their schools or jobs, and work full time for the group.

The full-time volunteers make up the "cadres," the second layer. The cadres in turn are differentiated into "tabular" and "viable." The more serious viable cadres are deemed recruitable into the inner party, the Communist Party, U.S.A. (Provisional) (CPUSA [P]), or as it is usually referred to by members, the Formation. This is the inner layer, the core of the onion.

The money raised, as well as food and clothing collected by the volunteers, goes primarily for the sustenance of the full-time cadre and the maintenance of the entity, as well as the maintenance of the national office on Carroll Street. There is some distribution among the poor. It is this activity that acts as a kind of flypaper to attract the volunteers, who in turn are the resource for recruitment and growth of the cult.

The core party has a constitution, a lengthy document members can read but not keep. However, there are no party publications per se and no conventions (though there are occasional aggregate meetings), and therefore there is no leadership accountability. Perente communicated with the members by two means only, orations at the Carroll Street headquarters that went on for many hours, and audio tapes of those speeches that were sent out to members in outlying areas.

Cadres are required to live in communal dwellings where they can be watched over closely by the leadership. They work twelve to fourteen hours a day, eat donated food or just coffee and donuts, and wear ill-fitting donated clothes. They are sleep deprived and protein deprived. The members are cut off from friends and family.

The cadres' sex lives are highly circumscribed. The membership is overwhelmingly female. This, in itself, makes pairing a bit difficult since relationships with nonmembers are not permitted. The members live in dormitories and, unlike Synanon members, have no facilities provided for consensual sex. Their life is essentially monastic with one huge exception: Gino Perente and his closest associates bed whomever they please.[26]

In addition to their recruitment and solicitation work, former members report that they had to process a massive amount of paperwork. NATLFED kept detailed files on all cadres, volunteers, members, and potential supporters, as well as rival political and social work organizations.

Jennifer Kling, a former Williams College student, who was recruited to work in NATLFED's Brooklyn headquarters, reported that she

> found herself trapped in a cramped, tense apartment building, unable to walk outside. Every second was charted. During the day, she filed papers, wrote articles and worked the phone bank, selling advertisements in the organization's publications. In the evenings she was required to attend political lectures that would often go until 4:30 A.M., when she was finally allowed to collapse into a deep slumber in a small room with five other women.
>
> Six hours later, at 10:30 A.M., the wake-up call would come over the loudspeaker, and Ms. Kling and about 50 other members of the group . . . would start the cycle all over again. "They didn't encourage idle chatter," she said. "Time was precious. Every minute was pre-scheduled. They kept you so busy that you didn't have time to think about leaving."[27]

It was an effective system, self-sustaining financially, producing a zombie-like membership unlikely to leave the group, as well as a steady flow of new recruits from the campuses.

The Campus Connection

The entire Perente operation can be viewed as a complex and effective mechanism for the recruitment of young, politically naïve college students to a cult. Every entity had a campus connection.

One of the earliest examples of this parasitic relationship was Antioch College. In 1974 the college offered jobs at the California Homemakers Association (CHA), a Perente entity located in Oakland, California, as part of its off-campus work program. Twenty-three students took part in the program. At least six of these students dropped out of school to work permanently for CHA, several went to work for EFWA on Long Island, and a few returned to organize a Perente entity on campus. Fewer than half of those who participated came back to campus with horror stories. They reported exhausting work, unhealthy food, women staying out in unsafe areas late at night, and lengthy political education classes. In 1978 Antioch removed the group from its approved job list.[28]

Jennifer Kling's recruitment to NATLFED was a recent example of a more than twenty-year relationship between Williams College, a small elite Ivy League school attended primarily by the children of the wealthy, and Perente's Western Massachusetts Labor Action (WMLA), located in nearby Pittsfield. The WMLA had the support of several well-respected college professors, who invited spokespersons for the organization to address their classes and pass around sign-up sheets. In the winter the students would be asked to help cut wood to deliver to poor people who could not afford to pay their utility bills. Volunteers were continually pressed for a regular commitment of time, then more time, and finally asked to become full-time cadre.[29]

The impact that exposure to the real-life conditions of the poor can have on middle-class college students with social consciences is not to be underestimated. An example is the experiences of two reporters from a student newspaper at the State University of New York (SUNY) in Binghamton in upstate New York. They traveled in the middle of winter with a group of EFWA volunteers into an agricultural area in the extreme north of the state.

> It was freezing cold and windy as we made our way through the snow towards the first home. I stood behind Kathy [a team member and friend] as she knocked on the door, which was nothing more than a weather-beaten sheet of plywood hanging by a broken hinge. While it was warm inside, it was extremely small and crowded, with six people living in an old trailer which was their home. . . .
>
> After we left that house, we encountered a pack of cold, starving dogs. We made the next residence just as they began circling us.
>
> Our visit to the next shack was especially disturbing. The shack, which was about fifteen by ten feet, housed thirteen people. Parts of the walls were made of cardboard and a gaping hole in one wall was covered only by a bedsheet which flapped wildly in the wind. The shack was heated by two ancient potbellied stoves which discharged nearly asphyxiating fumes. Everyone wore overcoats to keep warm.
>
> Two older looking men sat in one corner sharing a bottle of whiskey. In another room were eight of the ten children in the family. I noticed that one girl was picking insects out of her brother's hair.[30]

Another major source of support for and recruitment to NATLFED has been the mainstream churches. A group of these churches in the New York area, organized as the Commission on Voluntary Service and Action (CVSA), published an annual guide to volunteer service projects called *Invest Yourself*. It was distributed to churches, schools, and colleges. Counselors and would-be volunteers used the guide to find positions. Most of the listings were for well-established, church-related groups. However, unnoticed by the ministers overseeing the project, in the late 1970s the guide began to list many of Perente's entities as well.

Representatives of various Perente fronts joined the committee, and Diana Ramirez of EFWA became chair. Jeff Whitnack, a former NATLFED member, complained about the situation to church leaders. A struggle broke out for control of the guide. Perente's supporters won, and while the guide lost major church sponsorship, it continues to be published by people affiliated with NATLFED, providing a steady stream of volunteers from church sources as well as campuses.[31] When New York police officers broke into the Carroll Street compound in 1996, one of the women they arrested was Susan Angus, editor of *Invest Yourself*.[32]

The Beat Goes On

Gino Perente was not a man destined to have a long life. He never fully recovered from his auto accident injuries, and he chain-smoked. He lived an unhealthy existence, largely confined to his apartment on Carroll Street, directing his Lilliputian army of would-be revolutionaries.

A college professor, with a close friend in NATLFED, described her visits to the Cave in 1983: "Someone came to the door and asked me what I wanted. Everyone's movements were tightly controlled. . . . Many people were working, talking, holding meetings, swamped under stacks of paper and file cabinets. A woman whose eyes were glazed spoke very intently about the organization. She seemed wired on coffee and cigarettes." The professor said the volunteers appeared to be poorly fed and wore ill-fitting clothes, "like random objects from a Goodwill bag."

On her second visit she met Perente. "It was as if I was being prepared for an audience with the Pope." Perente's apartment, she reported, when contrasted with the Spartan furnishings in the rest of the facility, had the trappings of luxury—a stereo, a bar, a comfortable couch. On a coffee table a pistol lay next to Chairman Mao's *Book of Quotations*.

"Everything seemed calculated. Still, the overall effect was sad and dingy. He had a broken leg. . . . His appearance was striking. He was very thin and had a long, gaunt face, with heavily tobacco stained teeth. His hair, clearly dyed, was jet black and slicked back. He wore a white suit that was filthy. There were clumps of dirt in different places." Three attentive women followed his every move, propping him up with pillows and offering ashtrays while he chain-smoked. Two young people scribbled notes as he spoke.[33]

In January 1994, when his health had deteriorated further, one witness described him "sitting in a wheelchair and alternately breathing oxygen from a machine and chain-smoking Lucky Strikes," as he "gave a lecture to a room packed with devotees. . . . He wore fringed black leather and sunglasses—at two in the morning. Women stood around him, crushing out his cigarette stubs and wiping his brow and chin. Some listeners fell asleep."[34]

Eugenio Perente (aka Gerald William Doeden) died on March 18, 1995. The *New York Times* printed a laudatory obituary on March 20 only to be forced to print a correction on March 21.[35] His organization was taken over by Margaret Ribar, who had headed up its Western office in San Francisco.[36]

The group continues to have between one hundred and three hundred core members. It operates over forty entities scattered around the country, which involve a few thousand volunteers and entity members, while still recruiting fresh forces from the campuses.

Its relative success in conservative times can be attributed to its technique of immersing politically unsophisticated college students in work among a layer of the population, the extreme poor, that has been completely untouched by the general prosperity in the country. Witnessing such conditions, it is not unreasonable for a concerned young person to conclude that fundamental change is needed. It is, of course, quite a leap from recognition of that need to acceptance of the Communist Party U.S.A. (Provisional) as the instrument that could seriously bring about such a change. However, as we have seen, the conversion process takes place under conditions of exhausting work, in isolation from others who might raise critical questions, and in a group environment that encourages agreement.

Not all those who become volunteers succumb and join the inner cult. In fact, only a few do. However, those who do join tend to stay with the group, in many cases for decades. Unlike groups like Marlene Dixon's Democratic Workers Party or Gerry Healy's Workers Revolutionary Party, NATLFED did not resort to criticism/self-criticism in a major way. Arms were used primarily to add revolutionary glamour to the project. What it did do, perhaps better than competing groups, was completely transform the lifestyle of its members through common living arrangements, grueling workloads, full-time employment of cadres, and isolation from the rest of the left, as well as from friends and family. At the same time, there was a bit of a carrot. Its members witnessed the extreme poverty and degradation of America's forgotten and believed they were actually making a difference in these people's lives.

It was all a lie. The net effect of their efforts has only been the self-perpetuation of the cult. But after many years, it can be difficult for a member of such a group to face up to her wasted life.

Conclusion

Politics as Religion

It's déjà vu all over again.
—Yogi Berra

Political and Religious Cults

The political cults discussed in this chapter share basic characteristics with other types of cults as defined by Lifton and discussed by us in chapter 1. All cults insist on "ideological totalism," and practice "milieu control" and the "loading of the language."[1] At the same time, political cults have distinctive features that require separate study. All political cults practice thought reform and are totalistic. Their political world-view separates members from the rest of humanity and justifies their complete dedication to the group. An earthly utopia serves the same essential role in such groups as visions of an afterlife serve in religious groups.

Milieu control features are quite similar. Separation of followers from parents and friends, communal living, and the complete absorption of followers' time are as commonly characteristic of political as religious cults.

Political cults are notorious for their "loaded language." On the left each political cult transforms Marxism-Leninism into a dialect that distinguishes it from other political cults as well as the population at large: "revisionist," "renegade," "Stalinist," "Trotskyite," "petit bourgeois." The right has created its own racist code words: "ZOG," "mud people," "Zionists," "mongrels."

There are important differences in the ways in which religious and political cults achieve thought reform. Religious cults, particularly those based on Eastern religions, utilize various exercises, like sleep deprivation, meditation, the chanting of mantras, spinning, fasting, and sometimes even use of drugs, that are aimed at creating an altered state of mind. These experiences often feel profoundly satisfying, and induce moods of heightened spirituality, commitment, and certainty. Political cults create an altered state of mind only in a far less intense fashion, through sleep deprivation and, sometimes, collective events like rallies, congresses, and demonstrations.

Special mention needs to be made of radical therapy cults in this context. The therapist achieves enormous influence over the patient in the course of therapy. As we explore in chapter 7, a transference often occurs during this process, wherein the patient becomes deeply dependent on the therapist. It is particularly reprehensible when a cult leader takes advantage of this psychological power to control the patient and transform him or her into a political follower.

In Fred Newman's case this process permitted him to assemble a cadre of political automatons capable of supporting a right-wing extremist, like Pat Buchanan, while believing they are advancing a leftist agenda. Chuck Dederich manipulated former drug addicts through group therapy, transforming them into his dependents, rather than curing them of their drug dependency and preparing them for the real world. He then added a goodly dose of idealistic middle-class people and created a utopian commune ruled by his whims. Harvey Jackins, utilizing his own brand of group therapy, built a small international empire ruled in Leninist fashion.

In a religious cult the object of worship shifts from God to God's messenger: the guru or preacher. A similar process has been noted in political cults. A single individual dominates each of the groups studied in this book. Members are encouraged to take a worshipful attitude toward this leader. While the ostensible reason for the existence of a political cult is to destroy existing corrupt society and replace it with a utopia, be it the communist utopia of Marxism or the pure white Christian society of the right, in actual practice the group exists to advance the power and influence of its leader: Gerry Healy, Ted Grant, Peter Taaffe, Marlene Dixon, Chuck Dederich, Harvey Jackins, Fred Newman, Lyndon LaRouche, Bo Gritz, or Gino Perente.

Political cults, like religious cults, combine a self-sacrificing membership with a self-aggrandizing leader. Marlene Dixon lived in an alcoholic stupor in a house provided by the members, drove around in a fancy party car, and was waited on hand and foot. Gerry Healy, Harvey Jackins, and Gino Perente took sexual advantage of their followers on a grand scale. Others, such as Ted Grant, appear to revel simply in being acclaimed as the foremost theoretician of the era, and they combine acceptance of this elevated role with a lifestyle that is quite modest. Few are so abstemious. Chuck Dederich lived like a king, supplied with cars, motorcycles, planes, fine foods, and a majestic home in the Sierras. Lyndon LaRouche enjoys an estate in rural Virginia.

It is plainly difficult for the guru, surrounded by admiring acolytes, to maintain a sense of proportion on any front. An inflated ego convinces itself that it deserves more than its fair share of the world's earthly pleasures. If hard-pressed followers have to work ever harder to provide such opulence, it comes to be seen as part of the natural order of things. Questions that are raised tend to be dismissed as an enemy inspired attack. The members quickly learn to conform or face expulsion—a fate that, to the deeply committed, seems a form of spiritual death, too terrifying to contemplate.

Political cults differ from religious cults in their vulnerability to the political climate of the times. Religious belief is more widely held today in the United States than at any other time in recent history. Religious cults are prospering alongside their established cousins. However, as mainstream politics has drifted toward the middle, left-oriented political cults have been isolated. Conservative times have represented a severe challenge to their belief systems. This contributed to the explosive demise of Marlene Dixon's Democratic Workers Party (DWP) and Gerry Healy's Workers Revolutionary Party (WRP), as well as to the splitting and marginalization of Ted Grant's Committee for a Workers International (CWI). We are aware of one small Marxist-Leninist cult in Minneapolis, known to its members as the "O," which became primarily a vehicle for the building of small businesses for the financial benefit of its leader. Politics was never discussed. Others, like LaRouche's National Caucus of Labor Committees (NCLC), and Fred Newman's New Alliance Party (NAP), have found new political homes on the right. Rightist political cults, on the other hand, have been encouraged by this sea change in politics. Once tiny and almost totally isolated, fascistic groups are recruiting young people and working feverishly in the broader milieus provided by formations like the militias.

Religion as Politics

It can be useful to look briefly at religious cults that have taken up a political practice. We would like to make a general observation: *All cults are political in the sense that they construct miniature totalitarian societies.* The cult, by separating its members from civil society as a whole, cutting them off from friends and family, and constructing an authoritarian internal world, creates the conditions for a collision with state authorities.

Not every cult takes up arms against the state. Many are content to live in obscurity, chanting their mantras and eating brown rice. However, there are many specific reasons why religious cults as diverse as the Rajneesh, the Branch Davidians, the Aum, Scientology, the Unification Church, and People's Temple either have come into conflict with their respective governments or have been prosecuted for violations of the law. Many cults practice child abuse of one sort or another (e.g., Hare Krishna).[2] Cults can develop conflicts with their neighbors (MOVE in Philadelphia,[3] Rajneesh).[4] Cults that build elaborate business empires sometimes violate laws (Unification Church).[5] Most frightening, some cults develop visions of Armageddon, accompanied by a deep paranoia, and seek armed conflict with society (the Aum, Branch Davidians,[6] and People's Temple).[7]

We will look briefly at three highly political religious cults: the Aum, the People's Temple, and the Unification Church.

The Aum: The Aum Shinrikyo cult is headed by Shoko Asahara, a partially blind Japanese mystic. It represents an eclectic combination of Buddhism, Hinduism, Christianity, and various New Age nostrums. Asahara practiced an extreme form of guruism demanding that his disciples seek to "merge" or "fuse" with him to become his clones.[8] The followers were subjected to a number of exercises—meditation, listening to the guru's voice for hours, sleep deprivation, drugs, fasting, even drinking the guru's blood—to produce an altered state of mind. The most devout became *shukke* or renunciants; lived in Aum facilities; were celibate; and devoted themselves to "a perpetual, Sisyphean struggle for purity."[9] They were incapable of any independent thought and became Asahara's shock troops. There were around 1,400 *shukkes* at the height of Aum's strength.[10]

Asahara borrowed the concept of Armageddon, primarily from Christianity. In his view, virtually the entire human population was impure, civilization was sinful, and the "end times" were near. After the destruction of the existing world, Asahara envisioned a new kingdom populated by his adherents and ruled by himself. This vision, shared with many other religious cults including the Branch Davidians, was part of his appeal to new recruits. Many young people in Japan and in other countries feel alienated within the modern materialistic urbanized society. For this reason a religious group like Aum had an essentially *political* appeal.

The vision of Aum took a grotesque turn when Asahara became impatient and decided not to wait for the world's end. Instead, he determined to facilitate it. Having recruited a number of doctors, engineers, and scientists, and accumulated considerable financial resources, he put his followers to work in an effort to build weapons of mass destruction. After botched attempts at germ warfare with botulism and anthrax, he succeeded in making sarin nerve gas and employing it in at least two places, including the Tokyo subway. At the same time he was trying to obtain nuclear weapons. Asahara also carried through assassinations of dissidents and critics. He rationalized his murders by invoking the Buddhist principle of *poa*, claiming that by removing people who lived in a lower state of existence, he was freeing them to return in the next life at a higher state of being.

The experience of the Aum sheds interesting light on the cult phenomenon in general and on political cults specifically. Asahara's ability to rationalize to himself and others such a murderous scheme illustrates the degree to which a cult can control the human mind and force people to carry out inhuman acts. Black means white. Two plus two equals five. In cults, the leader's murderous agenda can readily be depicted as a program of love, their privileged lifestyle as one of penurious self-sacrifice, and their perverted ideology as humanity's last hope for salvation. As we have discussed throughout this book, there is no shortage of techniques to secure the psychological manipulation that allows followers to retain their original, idealized vision of the cult in the face of overwhelming evidence to the contrary from the outside world. By the time reality intrudes into the warped world of cultic living, enormous damage has been inflicted on the member, and frequently by the member on the wider society.

The concept of Armageddon has had wide appeal among those disenchanted with the existing state of society. This end-world scenario is particularly popular as we enter the new millennium. It is part of the basic tenets of established churches, like the Seventh Day Adventists and the Jehovah's Witnesses, as well as small cults like the Branch Davidians.

It also has its parallels among political cults. Left political cults with a Marxist-Leninist ideology have transformed this religious belief into a theory of the collapse of the capitalist system. A world crisis of capitalism is predicted, creating conditions for revolutionary upheavals. The revolutionary party, led by the political guru who heads the political cult, will triumph and a new communist utopia will emerge. The vision of a communal society, based on equality and plenty for all, is similar to religious concepts of a postapocalyptic society. Both respond to the ancient dream of humanity for a world free of hunger and strife.

Gerry Healy's Workers Revolutionary Party (WRP) was particularly fervent in its predictions of capitalist crisis and imminent revolution. As we have seen, however, his enthusiasm for the prospect of impending economic meltdown is widely shared on the far left. Countless Marxist sects insist, despite all evidence to the contrary, that economic earthquakes will facilitate the construction of stable revolutionary parties—with themselves at its core. Economic determinism and an absolute conviction that their own subjective role is of vital importance are stitched seamlessly together.

The political right is even more strident in its predictions of apocalypse followed by renewal. LaRouche has borrowed economic catastrophism from his Marxist past and today preaches that the global economy will collapse unless the world's leaders listen to him. He demands that the political elite abolish democracy and assume fascist-like state power to implement the LaRouchian program. The extreme right, as spelled out in the *Turner Diaries* (see chapter 3) predict race warfare leading to mass destruction of the nonwhite populations and the Jews, to be followed by a new epoch of Christian white race rule.

"The first characteristic of Aum," Lifton comments, "was *totalized guruism*, which became *paranoid guruism* and *megalomaniac guruism.*" He defines megalomaniac guruism as "the claim to possess and control immediate and distant reality."[11] When those who hold such views emerge into the real world, and are confronted by limitations on their vision, the sense of frustration is immense. They are impelled to explain away the various losses of control inherent in cult activity—losses that take place because of defections, child custody battles, conflicts with neighbors, and legal actions taken against the group. Rationalization transforms megalomania into paranoia. This megalomania/paranoia syndrome was particularly pronounced with Healy, Dederich, and LaRouche. All three were prone to exaggerated claims and paranoiac theories. In Dederich's case this led to both the accumulation of arms and physical attacks on critics. Perente invented a personal history to feed his megalomania while accumulating arms to encourage paranoia among his followers. Aum joins an illustrious tradition.

The People's Temple: The Reverend Jim Jones founded his People's Temple in Indiana in 1956 as an ordinary Pentecostal church. From the beginning, however, it began to acquire distinctive features that nudged it in a cultic direction. Members practiced interracialism, preached a social gospel, and were encouraged to worship Jones. "I am the only God you've ever seen," Jones once said.[12] When Jones decided in 1965 to move his flock to Ukiah in northern California, most of his Indiana followers made the trek with him. Jones believed in the imminence of nuclear war and felt that northern California was more likely to survive the coming holocaust.

On the surface Jones's cult was far different from Aum. It functioned like a fundamentalist church, with rocking gospel music, revival meetings, and faith cures. Jones arranged for his assistants to gather animal intestines, added some human blood to the mess, and then convinced parishioners that they were coughing up "cancers" as a result of his laying on of the hands.[13] However, his hold on his members was as intense as that of Asahara and led to even more catastrophic results.

Jim Jones was highly political. As he responded to the left political ferment in the 1960s, his politics became correspondingly more radical. "We believe in reincarnation," one of his followers told Deborah Layton. "Jim was Lenin in his last life. . . . He is trying to teach us that socialism is God. . . . Jim is trying to open the minds of the people. He can only reach them through religion. As he heals and teaches, they will grow to understand that religion is an opiate, used to keep the masses down. Only Jim can bring people into the light. Through him we can make it to the next plane."[14]

It is doubtful whether Jones began his career with such an understanding. He was brought up in a fundamentalist religious environment and began preaching even as a child. However, as time passed, his interests turned to politics and his megalomania produced a highly political religion that acted at times like a Marxist-Leninist cult. He preached socialism with an evangelist's cadences and combined the roles of God and Lenin in his singular, highly unstable, personality. His People's Temple is the best example of a social space where religion and politics have fused.

Jones's politics passed through two phases. Between 1975 and 1977, still using Ukiah as his base, he built the People's Temple in San Francisco. Jones recruited predominantly from the black community. Soon his church had a black majority. He then turned his attention to the city's politics. He was able to mobilize five hundred activists and in that fashion influence local elections. He threw his support behind the liberal George Moscone and contributed to his election as mayor.[15] In return Jones was rewarded by being appointed chairman of the San Francisco Housing Authority. He received the 1977 Martin Luther Humanitarian of the Year award in San Francisco, was feted by Willie Brown (then a power in the California Legislature and more recently mayor of San Francisco), Governor Jerry Brown (more recently mayor of Oakland), and Rosalyn Carter (wife of then President Jimmy Carter).[16]

The publicity thus received further fed Jim Jones's growing megalomania and need for adulation. However, it also brought his group and its cultic ways more into the public spotlight. Adverse publicity resulted, which, in turn, further fueled Jones's paranoia. In 1975 he had launched Jonestown, a utopian communist community to be constructed deep in the jungles of Guyana. He chose Guyana because of its relatively left-leaning government as well as its physical location. No one, he figured, would bother to drop a nuclear bomb on Guyana. A convenient side effect was that it enabled him to isolate his followers from all outside influences. They were increasingly at his mercy, and were convinced that physical destruction awaited them should they step outside the fortified perimeters of Jonestown. During 1977 Jones stepped up his colonization efforts. He himself ran away from the bad press and possible prosecution to Guyana and took almost all his remaining followers in the United States with him. Only a token group was left behind to continue raising funds and spreading the message.

Jonestown, in its early days before the arrival of the guru, was certainly an exciting project. Young people worked hard, trying to transform an unyielding jungle into an agricultural project with much of the zeal of Israel's pioneer kibbutzim. All this changed, once Jones arrived on the scene. He had become increasingly unstable, addicted to painkillers, brutal in his treatment of his followers, and frighteningly paranoiac. The colonizers were forced to work long hours in the hot sun; were fed poorly; and were subjected to continuous, often incoherent, harangues by Jones over a loudspeaker system. Armed guards kept people from leaving, and many were beaten. "White Night" drills were held, in which guards fired into the air in the jungle while Jones pretended the encampment was surrounded by the Central Intelligence Agency (CIA).[17] The deception of the outside world was matched by a deception of the followers within.

Madness grew. All restraints on abnormal behavior were gradually eroded, until only the bizarre remained. Jones himself became obsessed with revolutionary suicide. This was a political concept, not a religious one, and is not to be confused with the outlook of Heaven's Gate[18] or the Order of the Solar Temple.[19] Jones did not promise that his followers would reassemble at the "next level" on a planet or in heaven. He envisioned suicide as the ultimate political statement, an unanswerable act of defiance of his persecutors. He was determined to prove his power over his followers and to make his mark on history at the expense of the lives not only of his followers but his own as well.

In 1979 a U.S. congressman, Leo Ryan, responded to the growing concern of many Jonestown residents' relatives and organized a visit to the Guyanese jungle. Representative Ryan's visit was too much for Jones. It proved to be the final affront from the outside world that severed his tenuous grip on reality. When a small group of followers expressed a wish to return to the United States with Ryan, Jones snapped. In retaliation he arranged for the murder of Ryan and others as they assembled at the local airport, and then carried through the mass murder/suicide of his nine hundred disciples.

After Jonestown, no one can view cultism lightly. The massacre was the result of a political paranoia. It is precisely the *political* aspect of the Jonestown experience that remains only dimly recognized by the public.

Jim Jones was a classic example of the *psychopathic personality*. Robert Hare has defined *psychopaths* as "social predators who charm, manipulate, and ruthlessly plow their way through life, leaving a broad trail of broken hearts, shattered expectations, and empty wallets. Completely lacking in conscience and in feeling for others, they selfishly take what they want and do as they please, violating social norms and expectations without the slightest sense of guilt or regret."[20] As Tobias and Lalich noted, "the combination of charisma and psychopathy is a lethal mixture—perhaps it is the very recipe used at the Cookie-cutter Messiah School!"[21]

We have already noted that Marlene Dixon fitted this profile perfectly. Gerry Healy, Lyndon LaRouche, Chuck Dederich, and Gino Perente, all of whom are discussed in this book, are additional examples. As Jim Jones illustrates, psychopaths are by no means particular to *political* cults. David Koresh comes to mind. However, much too frequently, we find that leaders of all types of cults are psychopaths. Their mutual antipathy masks a commonality of means, ends, and leadership personality traits.

Asahara's Aum and Jones's People's Temple shared a heritage of violence. Dederich's rattlesnake attack, Perente's accumulation of arms, Healy's physical attacks on his members, the Ruby Ridge shootout, and the Oklahoma City bombing suggest that the pervading influence of violence in our culture has affected political cultists as well. This represents a fundamental difference between twentieth-century cultists and those of the nineteenth century. Further, the need to preserve cult boundaries from incursions by the more invasive modern state has led to a paranoia and violence that were absent from the idyllic and pastoral existence of the Oneida Community or the Shakers. This makes it all the more urgent that we understand the cult phenomenon and combat it as best we can.

The Unification Church: Reverend Sun Myung Moon's Unification Church has become the quintessential religious cult in the public's consciousness. Most people have come across Moonies soliciting funds—its members average $100 to $500 a day—or heard of the church's mass marriages. It is well known for its "love bombing" of stray young people. Members, once recruited, are separated from their families and taken to live in church facilities, such as the New Yorker Hotel in midtown Manhattan.[22]

Our interest in the group lies specifically with Reverend Moon's political agenda. A congressional investigation in 1977 found evidence that the Unification Church "had systematically violated US tax, immigration, banking, currency, and Foreign Agents Registration Act laws."[23] Moon served eleven months in federal prison for filing false tax returns.

Moon established close political relations with the right-wing Korean government early on in his career. He was charged in the 1977 hearings with organizing demonstrations of his American followers at the behest of the Korean CIA.

Moon involved himself in U.S. politics almost from the moment he began recruiting followers in this country. His political slant was and is consistently conservative. He organized a media campaign in support of President Richard Nixon during Watergate, claiming that "at this moment in history, God has chosen Richard Nixon to be President of the United States." Nixon, perhaps recognizing an equally corrupt kindred spirit, met with him to thank him for his support.[24]

More recently Moon launched the *Washington Times*, a daily newspaper espousing right-wing causes. The paper has given him a visible presence in the capitol and significant political influence. Former President George Bush "has reportedly received hundreds of thousands of dollars for his appearances at several Moon events." Moon has also arranged speaking engagements for Jack Kemp, Gerald Ford, and Ralph Reed, as well as prominent figures in Britain, including former Tory premier Ted Heath. He has received support from Senator Orin Hatch who "extolled the long suffering and personal sacrifice of Mrs. Moon and her husband." Trent Lott introduced a resolution on the Senate floor supporting Moon's "True Parents Day" campaign.[25]

Moon's approach to American politics, particularly after his jail term, has proved to be more effective and longer lasting than the apocalyptic rantings and terrorist tactics of the Aum. It could prove, in the long run, more damaging to the body politic. Moon exercises an intense control over the minds of his followers. He utilizes the funds they raise as well as their numbers to advance the conservative causes he believes in. As a result, his mind-warping cult has gained considerable respectability and has come to exercise undue influence over American political life.

Moon has become disappointed, however, with his American operation. Membership has reportedly dwindled from an inflated 30,000 to around 3,000. His holdings in South Korea, estimated to be worth billions, have suffered from the economic turmoil that gripped Asia in the late 1990s. He is preparing a move into the greener pastures of Catholic South America, investing some $30 million and buying up 220 square miles of farmland in the underpopulated Brazilian State of Mato Gross do Sul. One cannot but think of Jones in Guyana. There is considerable unease over the potential influence of this cult in the area, as well as throughout Brazil. Conflict with neighboring communities and the state could be brewing.[26]

Scientology has followed a similar trajectory in recent years. It has pulled back from a confrontational approach to the federal government and won, with the help of its movie star recruits Tom Cruise and John Travolta, official status as a church with the Internal Revenue Service (IRS). This saves the group millions of dollars. However, problems persist. It has faced an investigation by the Florida state attorney over the death of a member, Lisa McPherson, at its headquarters in Clearwater.[27] Relations with governments abroad are strained, particularly in Germany[28] and Russia.[29]

Marxism-Leninism: Seedbed for Cults

Many of the groups surveyed in this book trace their origins to Marxism-Leninism. These include the Maoist/Stalinist Democratic Workers Party and the Communist Party (Provisional), the Trotskyist Workers Revolutionary Party and Militant Tendency, the Radical Therapy Newman/Fulani group, and the rightist National Caucus of Labor Committees. Harvey Jackins and Charles Dederich were both influenced by Marxism-Leninism, while Jim Jones considered himself a reincarnation of Lenin. Given the enormous influence of this ideology on the left, it is appropriate to consider whether it has become inherently cultic in its political practice. The groups discussed here could be exceptions, with other currents in the same tradition updating their ideas, maintaining a healthy internal regime, and achieving wider influence.

Our study of left-wing political cults, including many that are not discussed in this book, leads us to the conclusion that the ideology in question has become cultic. Each and every Marxist-Leninist (or Trotskyist) grouping that we have examined has exhibited the same cultic symptoms— authoritarianism, conformity, ideological rigidity, and a fetishistic dwelling on apocalyptic fantasies. These characteristics vary from group to group in degree but not in kind. Not all Leninist groups are full-blown cults. However, we have yet to discover a single one lacking at least some cultic features.

For example, Tony Cliff's Socialist Workers Party, the largest Trotskyist group in Great Britain, and its American affiliate, the International Socialist Organization, has an internal dynamic that is similar to the Grant group at its height.[30] In France, Lutte Ouvrière has been relatively successful. Its annual fete attracts around 30,000 people and it presently has representation in the European Parliament. However, as reported in the French press, it operates in a clandestine fashion, and forbids marriage and having babies.[31] Both the American Socialist Workers Party and the Communist Party display a rigid internal life and cultic adulation of their leaders. The Spartacist League has made a specialty out of disrupting other organizations and has become increasingly bizarre.[32] The Maoist Revolutionary Communist Party's members wave red flags at street corners and hawk their paper, *Revolution*, which sings the praises of the brutal Marxist-Leninist Shining Path of Peru. The list goes on and on. It is difficult to avoid the conclusion that the "source code" for cultic practice must lie within Leninism itself.

There are many causal factors for this. Here, we will highlight but a few. Marxism-Leninism insists on the necessity of building "mass revolutionary parties" around the principles of "democratic centralism." Without this, its adherents believe that humanity is doomed. It is this perspective and this method of organizing that lies at the root of the movement's degeneration into myriad cultic sects.

The notion of a vanguard revolutionary party inherently predisposes its adherents to view themselves as the pivot on which world history is destined to turn. Revolution is seen as the only route by which humanity can avoid annihilation, but revolution is only possible if a mass party is built around a group of "cadres": that is, devotees of the party with a particularly deep insight into its ideology. Members become possessed by a tremendous sense of urgency and a powerful conviction of their group's unique role in bringing about the transformation of the world. They develop delusions of historical grandeur. Religious zealotry soon follows.

As Lenin spelled out in *What Is to Be Done?*, socialist ideas were to be introduced into the working class from the "outside" by professionals, drawn largely from the middle classes. This essentially elitist view leads members of Leninist groups to view themselves as a kind of chosen people, the possessors of a gnosis beyond the grasp of ordinary folk. Therefore, *separate organization* is in order, *tight discipline* is required, and *superhuman sacrifice* is demanded from members. A *centralized party structure* transforms the cadres into the willing tool of the self-appointed disciple of Lenin.[33] All the elements of cultic organization and conduct thus flow quite naturally out of Leninist tenets.

It is beyond the scope of this book to explore the extent to which the Leninist *tradition*, as practiced by contemporary Leninist groups, accurately expresses the views and practices of Lenin. Nor do we intend to discuss the cultic aspect of the former Soviet Union (what Khrushchev called the "cult of the personality") and other states based on the same model. Our concern is with the actual practice of self-described Leninists.

In the 1930s, Keith Woods joined the Communist Party after attending a congress in Paris. He wrote a letter to his wife, attempting to convert her to the cause. The letter perfectly captures the messianic mood we are describing here, and flags the presence of a cultic belief system. His words also convey the internal atmosphere we have found in all the leftist groups discussed in this book:

> I am fired with a new zeal and I am going to pass it on to you or die in the attempt. . . . Just think what a difference it would make to have something in life to strive for that was bigger than you, bigger than me, bigger than both of us, something that burns down deep in your bones, that gives you strength and imagination and the courage of which you never thought you were capable, which gives a meaning to life where before there was nothing but a selfish search for pleasure, that helps you to feel in true relationship not only to present history but to all history. Can't you feel it pulsating within me, the hope and the certainty that if the millions of ordinary people like you and me would only take fate by the throat and strangle it, we can literally change the world?[34]

How could intelligent people think like this, then and now? To understand this complex issue requires an attempt to penetrate the mind-sets of true believers, so that we can grasp why they believe the fanciful, suppress any knowledge of the grisly reality behind their political practice, and lure others into the same web of deceit in which they themselves have been caught.

The writer Arthur Koestler also belonged to the Communist Party in the

1930s. The accounts of many writers who shared the same experience are revealing on this point. Koestler characterized his state of mind while he was a Communist Party member in the following terms:

> Gradually I learnt to distrust my mechanistic preoccupation with facts and to regard the world around me in the light of dialectic interpretation. It was a satisfactory and indeed blissful state; once you had assimilated the technique you were no longer disturbed by facts; they automatically took on the proper color and fell into their proper place. Both morally and logically, the Party was infallible: morally, because its aims were right, that is, in accord with the Dialectic of History, and these aims justified all means; logically, because the Party was the vanguard of the proletariat, and the proletariat the embodiment of the active principle in History.[35]

In addition to foregrounding the need for a revolutionary party, Marxist-Leninist groups insist that such a party must be governed by the principles of what Lenin termed democratic centralism. For those on the far left, Lenin is regarded as a demigod, beyond criticism. The hope is that imitating his practice and rote-learning his writings will, by alchemy, transform groups from small sects into mass organizations.

Democratic centralism sees the "party" as a tightly integrated fighting force with a powerful central committee and a rule that all members publicly defend the agreed positions of the party, whatever opinions they might hold to the contrary in private. The goal of the members is to become professional revolutionaries, preferably on a full-time basis. Between conferences the party's leading bodies have complete authority to manage its affairs, arbitrate in internal disputes, update doctrine, and decide the party's response to fresh political events. As Lenin expressed it: "The principle of democratic centralism and autonomy for local party organizations implies universal and full freedom to criticize, so long as this does not disturb the unity of a defined action; it rules out all criticism which disrupts or makes difficult unity of action decided upon by the party."[36]

Given what is now known of social influence, this approach is intrinsically destined to prevent genuine internal discussion. First, it is not at all clear when "full freedom to criticize" can be said to disturb the unity of a defined action. The norms of democratic centralism confer all power between conferences onto a central committee, allowing it to decide when a dissident viewpoint is in danger of creating such a disturbance, normally presumed to be lethal. The evidence suggests that they are strongly minded to view *any* dissent as precisely such a disruption, and to respond by demanding that the dissidents cease their action on pain of expulsion from the party. It should be borne in mind that the leaders of these groupings view themselves as the infallible interpreters of sacred texts which are seen as essential for the success of the world revolution. This "all-or-nothing" approach to political analysis reinforces the tendency to view dissent as something that automatically imperils the future of the planet, and a justification (perhaps unconscious) of whatever measures are required to restore the illusion of unanimity. All organizations on the Marxist-Leninist left claim to permit open democratic debate among their members. We know of none that do.

Second, Bob Cialdini has reviewed a variety of studies that show that, when people take a public position in defense of a proposition, there is then a strong tendency for their private attitudes to shift so that they harmonize with their public behaviors.[37] In short, if people tell others that they support X (for whatever reason) their belief system will begin to agree that indeed they do support X. The more public such declarations have been, the more likely it is that such a shift will take place. This will then contribute to future public activities in line with a now firmly held belief. Such findings suggest that if, in the name of democratic centralism, party members publicly uphold the party line, it becomes increasingly difficult to hold a private belief at variance with attitudes publicly expressed. Conformity in public tends to equal conformity in private.

Tightly disciplined and driven cadres are capable, in some periods, of having a significant impact on broader political processes. Perhaps the most impressive example of this was Ted Grant's Militant Group in England. It controlled the city government in Liverpool and had members in Parliament. Marlene Dixon gained influence in San Francisco as well as control of the Peace and Freedom Party through her disciplined cadres. LaRouche's right-wing cult captured significant positions within the Illinois Democratic Party. Fred Newman played a role in black politics through support of Jesse Jackson, Louis Farrakhan, and the Reverend Al Sharpton, ran an effective progressive third party; and has influence today within Perot's Reform Party and the Buchanan campaign. NATLFED functions exclusively through "entities," its name for front groups. The Communist front form of organization is particularly suited to political cult manipulation. It permits the cult leader to control the environment within which his or her followers operate, to exclude competing political tendencies that could "corrupt" cult members, and to recruit from the front group's membership.

The far left is organized, or disorganized, around these guiding principles. In consequence, it has become a warring assortment of tyrannical fiefdoms, locked into a spiral of irrelevance, fragmentation, and ideological petrifaction. Their internal regimes emulate that of Stalin. Had they state power, they would also emulate his blood lust. Accordingly, they display an intense veneration for "October," as a distraction from their present-day impotence. Activists become archives of useless trivia from the history of Bolshevism. This prevents them from updating their analysis of the 1917 Revolution and its aftermath.

Many on the left have begun to revise their earlier reliance on Leninist orthodoxies. They have concluded that the October Revolution was by no means above criticism.[38] In addition to such a political reappraisal, left-wing activists need to temper enthusiasm for change with a stronger awareness of the techniques of social influence, and a greater skepticism toward totalistic philosophies of change. Without such an approach, individuals face lifelong disillusionment with any form of political action. In learning from organizations such as those discussed in this book it will be more possible to engage in political action which genuinely liberates our thinking, and thereby influence the political process.

Cultic Belief Systems and the Standard of Falsification

Political cults are built around complex and self-contained belief systems. These provide the impetus for frenetic levels of activity and the creation of high-control environments, in which the authority of the leader expands in all possible directions. Cults promote a doctrine of *exceptionalism* toward their own belief system, in which nothing can be criticized, combined with incessant attacks on other ideologies, organizations, and leaders. Such exceptionalism gains a hold over the minds of many precisely because our thinking tends to be distorted by a number of logical fallacies.[39] These include the following:

• *Theory often influences observation, rather than the other way round.* As discussed in chapter 1, the *expectations* we have of our environment affect how we perceive it. In right-wing politics, a theory that suggests that some group is the source of all society's problems encourages its adherents to perceive only instances of alleged misbehavior by members of the stigmatized group and to ignore the more numerous occasions when they behave quite normally. The gurus who lead Marxist sects typically scan the press for the gloomiest facts and figures available on the state of the economy. This is depicted as reflecting the views of "the serious strategists of capital." Any analysis that suggests further growth is likely to occur will be ignored. It connotes "bourgeois propaganda." The heavily filtered economic data are then presented to the panic-stricken members as a "scientific" analysis that supports the group's Armageddon perspective. Thus, facts are twisted into whatever shape is suggested by the ideology of the group.

- *Anecdotes are regarded as a good basis on which to declare a new "science."* Researchers have found that most of us tend to place too much reliance on stories and to distrust more rigorous forms of data. ("There are lies, damned lies, and statistics.") This allows what may be nothing more than unrepresentative scare stories to gain a grip on our overheated imaginations. For example, two researchers looked at how teachers and administrators in schools responded to recommendations contained in reports.[40] They found that the teachers were quite supportive of particular recommendations when the report contained no statistics, were slightly supportive if frequency data and percentages were included, but tended to reject the same set of recommendations if the report contained notations for type of statistical analysis and significance. We have repeatedly documented instances of bogus belief systems that attempt to claim the sanctity of science. In general, however, they rest only on a small number of cases (as with reevaluation counseling; see chapter 6) or even on outright guesswork. A genuinely scientific approach, on the other hand, requires us to quantify a large number of examples, in order to prove clear causal trends.

- *Scientific language is assumed to denote a science.* Recognizing this, many defective belief systems camouflage their prejudices in the jargon of science. This is especially true of many adherents of Marxism and its innumerable warring fragments. Since the days of Marx and Engels, its adherents have described their belief system as "scientific socialism." The nomenclature sounds objective, truthful, accurate, and irrefutable. Who wouldn't be in favor of that? In reality, we need to ascertain the extent to which the belief system is based on real evidence, rather than wind and hyperbole. It should produce testable theories and display an openness to self-criticism before it can be regarded as truly scientific. None of the cultic belief systems explored in this book meet these criteria.

- *Bold statements carry more conviction than admissions of uncertainty.* Each of the cults discussed in this book claims to have discovered the "Truth." Moreover, they generally assume that their version of the truth is at the cutting edge of knowledge or is at least indispensable for salvation. Were any of this true, then the extraordinary efforts demanded of cult members might indeed be justified. However, such claims are not made because they are accurate. Rather, they reflect the cult leadership's understanding that most of us are impressed by dramatic claims, since these create a messianic aura around the ideology and leaders concerned, while appearing to offer a range of sensational benefits. Cult leaders seek to terrify people with the specter of imminent catastrophe, while simultaneously offering the only sure-fire means of averting it—for the small outlay of your mind.

- *Heresy is often confused with correctness.* The apparent failure of many established ideologies encourages us to believe that only something completely new offers a way forward. Ergo, in periods of disillusionment, a novel theory has a head start over its weary rivals. For this reason, many people suffering from severe illnesses embrace the ministrations of uncredentialed alternative practitioners. We often fail to appreciate that novelty does not equal creativity, or even common sense. Our only protection is to insist that innovative ideas be subject to the same standards of evidence and proof as more established ideologies.

• *Failures are rationalized.* Cults do not frame their theories in the form of predictions that can be falsified, and that might call their underlying propositions into question. A genuinely scientific theory asserts a general law, which in turn suggests a series of testable propositions. Cults, on the other hand, propose general theories, but any fact that contradicts the theory is rationalized as an exception that leaves the underlying rule intact. Thus, many right-wing cults maintain that the U.S. government was itself responsible for the 1995 Oklahoma bombing. Evidence to the contrary is interpreted as an indication of the devious nature of the Zionist conspiracy against the right. No amount of evidence can be imagined that would cause such groups to revise their initial interpretation.

For the left, the failure of the capitalist system to collapse in the manner predicted by many Marxist gurus poses a conundrum. Rather than review the original prediction, stabilization and growth are dismissed as components of a freakish aberration, like a heat wave in winter. Again, there is no conceivable turn of events that could be interpreted as evidence that the organization's most fundamental assumptions are mistaken. Even if capitalism now embarked on a hundred-year boom, of a magnitude unprecedented in human history, it would be viewed as a temporary detour, before Marx's predictions will with certainty be borne out.

• *Hasty generalizations are the norm.* One piece of evidence is used to prematurely create a theory. When the ancient Greeks first witnessed mounted horse riders, known as Scythians, they concluded that the horse and rider were one, and went on to invent the legend of the centaur. In politics, likewise, cults often leap to conclusions based on isolated events. Despite their exceptional character, and despite the possibility of other interpretations, such events are viewed as confirmation of the group's most important ideological assumptions. In a major overgeneralization, left-wing cults tend to assume that a single event (the 1917 October Revolution) offers the only viable model of social reconstruction for all countries on the planet. The need for new Octobers becomes a mantra, chanted in the loneliness of the night. On the right, it is often assumed that relatively minor gains for minority groups (e.g., positive action to produce more minority students on university campuses) represent conclusive proof of systematic discrimination, and even genocide, against whites.

Like Arthur Koestler, the poet Stephen Spender belonged to the Communist Party during the 1930s. Years later, he reflected sadly on his experience, and observed that "nearly all human beings have an extremely intermittent grasp on reality."[41] We see what we want to see. We see what our theory tells us to see. We see what we think ought to be there, rather than what is. Cults specialize in the ruthless exploitation of precisely these gaps in human perception.

Millennial Madness

We have explored political cults on both the left and the right. Our conclusion is that the major threat of terrorist acts and armed confrontations today comes primarily from the extreme right. Deeply disappointed by the swing within the conservative camp in a more moderate direction, attracting followers from individuals whose social roots have been uprooted by globalization and the development of new technologies, rightist cults are arming themselves to the teeth. Many are convinced that the end times are here and now. We live, or so they maintain, in the twilight of human civilization. A long, cold night lies ahead. As Aum illustrates, it is not a big leap from predicting race war and apocalyptic confrontations with the state to provoking such outcomes.

The threat of right-wing terrorism takes two forms. Most common is the deranged individual, drawing his ideology from a cross section of groups, who transforms himself into a one-person cult, picks up the gun, and goes on a rampage, shooting up abortion clinics, killing blacks or Jews, or blowing up government buildings. The right wing is particularly receptive to this individualistic activity. Such Rambo types, while not part of a group environment centering on an individual leader, as in a typical political or religious cult, are nonetheless cultic. They share a worldview in common with organized groups, are driven by a mind-set created in the cultic environment of rightist political circles, and view their actions as part of a war of survival against an evil society.

A number of cultic groups have also been spawned, that have separated themselves from society at large and have accumulated great stores of arms. Limited gun controls in the United States make their task all the easier. Millennial events can lead some of these groups to feel themselves under siege and instigate armed conflicts, as in Ruby Ridge and Waco. As Robert Jay Lifton[42] and Walter Laqueur[43] warn, and Aum illustrates, it is not to be excluded that political cults could in the near future get their hands on relatively compact and cheap weapons of mass destruction. If they do, the consequences may be catastrophic.

Left cults represent a different kind of danger. Terrorist activity has fallen out of favor. Old guerilla groups in Germany, Italy, Japan, Guatemala, El Salvador, Uruguay, Chile, and elsewhere, have either dissolved or given up arms and entered the democratic political arena. Uruguay's Tupamaros were once among the most secretive and feared terrorist groups in South America. Their kidnapping and execution of Daniel A. Mitrione, a CIA agent, was the basis for the Costa-Gavras film *State of Siege*. They are now a legal party, are part of the broad leftist Frente Amplio, and hold two seats in the senate and four more in the chamber of deputies.[44]

However, the left cults that survive continue to have a pernicious influence. Organizations like the National Labor Federation (NATLFED) still recruit, though in relatively small numbers. However, each recruit is a young life wasted, and a family disrupted. Others, like the Fred Newman–Lenora Fulani cabal in the Reform Party, illustrate that a relatively small group of talented individuals, organized to operate in lockstep under the direction of the political guru, can do significant political harm.

We have made no attempt in this book to be encyclopedic. Instead, we have chosen to discuss specific political cults that are illustrative of the phenomena. There remain hundreds of political groups in different countries that share some, if not all, cultic characteristics with the groups we have studied. In each case, they have become miniature totalitarian societies. Only their small size prevents them from wreaking much greater social havoc. Whatever ends they proclaim in public, their real goal is to perpetuate their own existence. Genuine relevance to real social problems is not on the agenda. In understanding this dynamic, we are reminded of George Orwell's novel *Nineteen Eighty-Four*, which stands as an unsurpassed account of totalitarianism. Here, O'Brien is explaining to Winston Smith the raison d'être for the existence of the party:

> The Party seeks power entirely for its own sake. We are not interested in the good of others; we are interested solely in power. Not wealth or luxury or long life or happiness: only power, pure power. . . . Power is not a means, it is an end. One does not establish a dictatorship in order to safeguard a revolution; one makes the revolution in order to establish the dictatorship. The object of persecution is persecution. The object of torture is torture. The object of power is power. Now do you begin to understand me?[45]

Conclusion

Our study of political cults has convinced us that the human mind is vulnerable to control and manipulation by others. We are social beings. This makes us extremely sensitive to the moods, feelings, and views of others. Our sense of self is always, in part, a social product. And so it should be. The success of the human race is derived from a combination of individual intelligence and social existence. However, what makes us capable of living in peace and harmony can also be manipulated to subordinate us to the whims and evil purposes of strong individuals. Sometimes, this happens to whole countries. The cases of Hitler's Germany, Stalin's USSR, and Pol Pot's Cambodia illustrate the point.

Cults, however, cannot be suppressed. To suppress them would be to surrender to the mentality of cult leaders. Further, the effect would be to drive such groups underground where they would function better. Strange as it may seem, while those who perform surgery on our brains require lengthy training and are subject to state and professional licensing boards, there is little regulation of those who perform "psychic surgery" on our minds, the product of our brain. One is tempted to demand new laws and better regulation, at least of phony therapy cults. However, in a free society, such cures generally prove to be worse than the disease.

Freedom can never be protected by legislating that it must always be used wisely. The only effective weapon against cults is to expose them in the course of a democratic dialogue as part of developing an educated civil society. The stronger the fabric of such a society, the less vulnerable we will all be to cultic manipulation and abuse.

The influence of cults grows when people believe that the existing system is the preserve only of the rich and powerful, and offers no way forward. Elizabeth Dole is by no means an underprivileged victim of society. However, when someone in her position bows out of a presidential race, admitting that she can never raise the funds needed to challenge a well-connected rival, ordinary people are even more likely to draw back in disgust from the political process.

The challenge facing politics throughout the world is the same. It is to ensure its continued relevance to the lives of ordinary people. Radical politics, in particular, faces the need to break from the remnants of its vanguardist past, and to fashion a new ideological support structure that takes account of events after 1917.

Our study of political cults illustrates all too clearly the alternatives that lie ahead. For many people, the political system is now at the edge of its relevance to their lives and problems. Change has become a torrent, sweeping away the certainties of the past. Buffeted by events, cut adrift from the past, many of us can dimly apprehend the alluring figures of cultism, and can hear seductive voices promising good times ahead.

If the present system offers only anguish, the songs of the sirens may yet become irresistible.

Notes

Introduction

1. G. Esler, *The United States of Anger* (London: Michael Joseph, 1997).
2. The Gallup Organization, *State of Disunion Survey* (University of Virginia, 1996).
3. Esler, *Anger*, p. 32.
3. *The Observer Business Supplement*, July 26, 1998, pp. 1–2.
4. *Sydney Morning Herald*, October 21, 1997.
5. Ibid., August 14, 1998.
6. Esler, *The United States of Anger*, p. 28.

Chapter 1

1. J. Hochman, "Iatrogenic Symptoms Associated with a Therapy Cult: Examination of an Extinct 'New Psychotherapy' with Respect to Psychiatric Deterioration and 'Brainwashing,'" *Psychiatry* 47 (1984): 366–377.
2. S. Hassan, *Combating Cult Mind Control* (Rochester, NY: Park Street Press, 1988).
3. M. Langone, "Helping Cult Victims," in *Recovery from Cults*, ed. M. Langone (New York: Norton, 1993), p. 29.
4. I. Haworth, "Myths and Realities," *Counseling News* (June 1993): 14.
5. M. Singer, with J. Lalich, *Cults in Our Midst: The Hidden Menace in Our Everyday Lives* (San Francisco: Jossey-Bass, 1995.)
6. American Family Foundation, "Cultism: A Conference for Scholars and Policy Makers," *Cultic Studies Journal* 3, no. 1 (1986): 119–120.
7. R. Lifton, *Thought Reform and the Psychology of Totalism: A Study of "Brainwashing" in China* (New York: Norton, 1961). Most quotations from Lifton in this section come from this book.
8. Ibid., p. 435.
9. A. Pratkanis and E. Aronson, *Age of Propaganda: The Everyday Use and Abuse of Persuasion* (New York: Freeman, 1991).
10. H. Tajifel, *Human Groups and Social Categories* (Cambridge: Cambridge University Press, 1981).
11. L. Festinger, *A Theory of Cognitive Dissonance* (Evanston, IL: Row and Peterson, 1957).
12. R. Cialdini, *Influence: Science and Practice*, 3d ed. (New York: HarperCollins, 1993).

13. M. Wexler and S. Fraser, "Expanding the Groupthink Explanation to the Study of Contemporary Cults," *Cultic Studies Journal* 12, no. 1 (1995): 49–71.

14. N. Morrow and O. Hargie, "Influencing and Persuading Skills at the Interprofessional Interface: Training for Action," *Journal of Continuing Education in the Health Professions* 16 (1996): 94–102.

15. T. Wohlforth, *The Prophet's Children: Travels on the American Left* (Atlantic Highlands, NJ: Humanities Press, 1994).

16. D. Tourish, "Ideological Intransigence, Democratic Centralism and Cultism: A Case Study from the Political Left," *Cultic Studies Journal* 15 (1998): 33–67.

17. R. Ezekiel, *The Racist Mind: Portraits of American Neo-Nazis and Klansmen* (London: Penguin, 1995).

18. L. West and M. Singer, "Cults, Quacks and Nonprofessional Therapies," in *Comprehensive Textbook of Psychiatry III*, ed. H. Kaplan, A. Freedman, and B. Sadock (Baltimore: Williams and Wilkins, 1980).

19. R. Lifton, *The Nazi Doctors* (London: Macmillan, 1986).

20. M. Tobias and J. Lalich, *Captive Hearts, Captive Minds: Freedom and Recovery from Cults and Abusive Relationships* (Alameda, CA: Hunter House, 1994).

21. Lifton, *Thought Reform*, p. 419.

22. Ibid.

23. Ibid., p. 421.

24. Ibid., p. 422.

25. Ibid., p. 423.

26. Ibid., p. 428.

27. Ibid., p. 429.

28. Ibid., p. 430.

29. Ibid., p. 431.

30. C. Hargie and D. Tourish, "Relational Communication," in *The Handbook of Communication Skills*, 2d edition, O. Hargie, ed. (London: Routledge, 1997).

31. B. Crick, *In Defence of Politics*, 4th ed. (London: Weidenfeld and Nicolson, 1992).

Chapter 2

1. M. Langone, ed., *Recovery from Cults* (New York: Norton, 1993), pp. 40–44.

2. R. Enroth, *Youth, Brainwashing, and the Extremist Cults* (Grand Rapids, MI: Zondervan, 1977); W. Wallace, "Cult Following: Evangelical Groups are Recruiting Hard on Britain's Campuses," the *Guardian Higher Education*, June 20, 2000.

3. C. Serino, "The Personal-Social Interplay: Social-Cognitive Prospects on Identity and Self–Others Comparison," in *Social Identity: International Perspectives*, ed. S. Worchel, J. Morales, D. Paez, and J. Deschamps (London: Sage, 1998).

4. C. Nemeth, "Minority Dissent as a Stimulant to Group Performance," in *Group Process and Productivity*, ed. S. Worchel, W. Wood, and J. Simpson (London: Sage, 1992).

5. I. Janis, *Victims of Groupthink: A Psychological Study of Foreign Policy Decisions and Fiascos*, 2d ed. (Boston: Houghton Mifflin, 1982).

6. J. Codol, "On the So-Called 'Superior' Conformity of the Self Behavior: Twenty Experimental Investigations," *European Journal of Social Psychology* 18 (1975): 457–501.

7. J. Stoner, "Risky and Cautious Shifts in Group Decisions: The Influence of Widely Held Values," *Journal of Experimental Social Psychology* 4 (1968): 442–459.

8. P. Cushman, "Why the Self Is Empty—Toward a Historically Situated Psychology," *American Psychologist* 45, no. 5 (1990): 599–611.

9. E. Torrance, "Some Consequences of Power Differences on Decision Making in Permanent and Temporary Three-Man Groups," (research paper, State College of Washington, 1995), pp. 22, 130–140.

10. R. Brown, *Group Processes*, 2d ed. (Oxford: Blackwell, 2000).

11. S. Sutherland, *Irrationality* (London: Constable, 1992).

12. L. Ross, D. Greene, and P. House, "The 'False Consensus Effect': An Egocentric Bias in Social Perception and Attributional Processes," *Journal of Experimental Social Psychology* 13 (1977): 279–301.

13. H. Zinn, *Declarations of Independence: Cross-Examining American Ideology* (New York: HarperCollins, 1990), p. 265.

14. S. Milgram, *Obedience and Authority* (London: Tavistock, 1974).

15. R. Baron, N. Kerr, and N. Miller, *Group Process, Group Decision, Group Action* (Buckingham, UK: Open University, 1990), p. 125.

16. An excellent summary of these experiments can be found in Brown, *Group Processes*, pp. 246–248.

17. J. Goldhammer, *Under the Influence: The Destructive Effects of Group Dynamics* (Amherst, NY: Prometheus, 1996), p. 16.

18. S. Hassan, *Combating Cult Mind Control* (Rochester, NY: Park Street Press, 1988). This phenomenon is also well documented in several of the chapters in Langone: *Recovery*.

19. E. Jones, *Ingratiation* (New York: Appleton-Century-Crofts, 1964).

20. E. Jones, *Interpersonal Perception* (New York: W.H. Freeman, 1990).

21. D. Byrne, *The Attraction Paradigm* (New York: Academic, 1971).

22. P. Rosenfeld, R. Giacalione, and C. Riordan, *Impression Management in Organizations* (London: Routledge, 1995).

23. R. Robins and J. Post, *Political Paranoia: The Psychopolitics of Hatred* (New Haven: Yale University Press, 1997).

24. Ibid., p. 37.

25. P. Zimbardo and S. Anderson, "Understanding Mind Control: Exotic and Mundane Mental Manipulations," in Langone, *Recovery*.

26. J. Turner, *Social Influence* (Milton Keynes, UK: Open University, 1991).

27. R. Rorty, *Achieving Our Country: Leftist Thought in Twentieth Century America* (Cambridge: Harvard University Press, 1997), p. 115.

28. Zimbardo and Anderson, "Understanding," pp. 120–122.

Chapter 3

1. M. Barkun, *Religion and the Racist Right: The Origins of the Christian Identity Movement* (Chapel Hill: University of North Carolina Press, 1994). The story of Gordon Kahl is told on p. 206.

2. J. Dyer, *Harvest of Rage: Why Oklahoma City Is Only the Beginning* (Boulder, CO: Westview, 1998), p. 94.

3. Barkun, *Religion*, p. 189.

4. R. Abanes, *American Militias: Rebellion, Racism and Religion* (Downers Grove, IL: Intervarsity, 1996), p. 145.

5. Ibid.

6. E. Henderson-King and R. Nisbett, "Anti-Black Prejudice as a Function of Exposure to the Negative Behaviour of a Single Black Person," *Journal of Personality and Social Psychology* 71 (1996): 654–664.

7. Barkun, *Religion*, p. 110.

8. Ibid., p. 112.

9. L. Bobo, and J. Kluegel, "Modern American Prejudice: Stereotypes, Social Distance, and Perceptions of Discrimination Towards Blacks, Hispanics and Asians" (paper presented at the American Sociological Association Meeting, Cincinnati, Ohio, 1991).

10. R. Ezekiel, *The Racist Mind: Portraits of American Neo-Nazis and Klansmen* (London: Penguin, 1995), p. 75.

11. Barkun, *Religion*, p. 110.

12. Dyer, *Harvest*, p. 107.

13. This and the following quotation are both taken from Barkun, *Religion*, p. 213.

14. W. Pierce, *The Turner Diaries* (Hillsboro, WV: National Vanguard Books, 1978).

15. Barkun, *Religion*, p. 229.

16. Ibid., p. 107.

17. P. Adams, "Running on Empty," *Weekend Australian,* October 23, 1999, p. 32.

18. G. Moorhead and R. Griffin, *Organizational Behavior* (London: Houghton Mifflin, 1988).

19. G. Allport, *The Nature of Prejudice* (New York: Addison-Wesley, 1954), p. 29.

20. C. Berger, "Communicating Under Uncertainity," in *Interpersonal Processes: New Directions in Communication Research*, ed. M. Roloff and G. Miller (London: Sage, 1987).

21. J. Leyens, V. Yzerbyt, and G. Schadron, *Stereotypes and Social Cognition* (London: Sage, 1994).

22. M. Rothbart and M. Taylor, "Category Labels and Social Reality: Do We Know Social Categories as Natural Kinds?" in *Language, Interaction and Social Cognition*, ed. G. Semin and K. Fiedler (London: Sage, 1992).

23. Andrew Duncan interview with Jeremy Clarkson, *Radio Times*, August 15, 1998, p. 24.

24. M. Hewstone, *Causal Attribution: From Cognitive Processes to Collective Beliefs* (Oxford: Blackwell, 1991).

25. R. Dawes, *House of Cards: Psychology and Psychotherapy Built on Myth* (New York: Free Press, 1994).

26. E. Jones, *Interpersonal Perception* (New York: W.H. Freeman, 1990).

27. O. Hargie, D. Dickson, and D. Tourish, *Communication in Management* (Aldershot: Gower, 1999), p. 259.

28. S. Duncan, "Differential Social Perception and Attribution of Intergroup Violence: Testing the Lower Levels of Stereotyping about Blacks," *Journal of Personality and Social Psychology* 34 (1976): 590–598.

29. T. Adorno, E. Frenkel-Brunswick, D. Levinson, and R. Sanford, *The Authoritarian Personality* (New York: Harper, 1950).

30. E. Young-Bruehl, *The Anatomy of Prejudices* (Cambridge, MA: Harvard University Press, 1996), p. 32.

31. R. Lifton, *The Protean Self: Human Resilience in an Age of Fragmentation* (New York: Basic Books, 1993).

32. These studies are discussed in detail by Young-Bruehl in *Anatomy*, p. 53.

Chapter 4

1. N. Hunt, "Hate Groups Seek to Recruit Through Internet," *Reuters Report,* July 5, 1999.

2. "Hatred in High Places," *MSNBC News Release,* August 16, 1999.

3. Cited in B. Knickerbocker, *When the Hate Comes from "Churches"* (Boston: The Christian Science Publishing society, July 30, 1999).

4. J. Preston, "US Group Reports Sharp Rise in Web Hate Sites," Reuters, February 24, 1999.

5. K. Stern, *A Force upon the Plain: The American Militia Movement and the Politics of Hate* (New York: Simon and Schuster, 1996).

6. Stern, *Force*, p. 15.

7. R. Ezekiel, *The Racist Mind: Portraits of American Neo-Nazis and Klansmen* (New York: Penguin, 1995), p. 93.

8. G. Barret, "FBI Hate Crime Data Is Spotty," *Gannett News Service*, July 16, 1999.

9. Ibid.

10. Stern, *Force*, p. 244.

11. Preston, "Web Hate Sites."

12. M. Wolk, "Aryan Leader Says L.A. Shootings Part of Race War," *Reuters News Report*, August 20, 1999.

13. Many detailed accounts of the events at Ruby Ridge have been published. They often conflict on points of detail. Some, sympathetic to the Weaver family, relegate the death of William Degan to a footnote, but stress that the Weaver's family dog was killed. We have mostly relied on the comprehensive and admirably balanced work of Stern, *Force*.

14. Stern, *Force*, p. 64.

15. J. Dyer, *Harvest of Rage: Why Oklahoma City Is Only the Beginning* (Boulder, CO: Westview), p. 82.

16. P. Lewis, "Preventable Agricultural Deaths in Oklahoma 1983–1988: Self Inflicted or Suicides" (Agriculture Engineering Department, Oklahoma State University, unpublished paper, 1989).

17. Dyer, *Harvest*, pp. 40–44.

18. Ibid., p. 62.

19. The rise of the Klan is discussed in detail by Stern, *Force*, at various points in his book.

20. This and the following two quotations are cited in Stern, *Force*, p. 50.

21. Wickstrom's colorful career is described in some detail at the following Website: http://www.hatewatch.org.

22. Dyer, *Harvest*, p. 98.

23. Stern, *Force*, p. 136.

24. Wolk, "Aryan Leader."

25. Ezekiel, *Racist*, p. 138.

26. Dyer, *Harvest*, p. 250.

27. Ezekiel, *Racist*, p. 42.

28. G. Barrett, "FBI Hate Crime."

29. "Hatred In High Places," *MSNBC News Release*, August 16, 1999.

30. Dyer, *Harvest*, p. 88.

31. A. Jacob, "Murder Exposes the Rise of Sweden's Far Right," *Guardian Weekly*, October 28, 1999, p. 29.

32. As quoted in Knickerbocker, *When Hate*, p. 2.

Chapter 5

1. Letter dated November 24, 1994, from Don Morrill to Alan Wald. Copy in Tim Wohlforth's possession.

2. This was when one of the authors, Tim Wohlforth, met him.

3. A. Gramsci, *The Modern Prince and Other Writings* (New York: International, 1972), pp. 118–125; A. Sassoon, *Approaches to Gramsci* (London: Writers and Readers, 1982), pp. 116–126.

4. G. Lukács, *History and Class Consciousness* (Cambridge, MA: MIT Press, 1968), pp, 204–205; M. Lowy, *Georg Lukács—From Romanticism to Bolshevism* (London: New Left Books, 1979).

5. T. Wohlforth, *The Prophet's Children* (Atlantic Highlands, NJ: Humanities, 1994), pp. 130–135.

6. This group later became known as the Workers League.

7. Wohlforth, *Prophet's Children*, pp. 132–133.

8. *Campaigner* 3, no. 1 (New York).

9. *Campaigner* 2, no. 2 (New York).

10. Wohlforth, *Prophet's Children*, p. 134.

11. D. King, *Lyndon LaRouche and the New American Fascism* (New York: Doubleday, 1989), pp. 19–24.

12. C. Berlet and J. Bellman, *Lyndon LaRouche: Fascism Wrapped in an American Flag* (Cambridge, MA: Political Research Associates, 1989), p. 4.

13. *NCLC: Brownshirts of the Seventies* (Arlington, VA: Terrorist Information Project), p. 15. The editor of this pamphlet, though unidentified, was Chip Berlet.

14. Ibid., p. 19.

15. King, *LaRouche*, p. 26.

16. Ibid.

17. C. Berlet, "Bringing a Cult and Its Kingpin into Focus," *In These Times* (October 28–November 4, 1986).

18. Berlet and Bellman, *LaRouche*, p. 4.

19. King, *LaRouche*, pp. 25–31.

20. "Breaking the Silence: An Ex-LaRouche Follower Tells Her Story," *In These Times* (October 29–November 4, 1986).

21. Ibid.

22. Ibid.

23. King, *LaRouche*, pp. 75–76.

24. Berlet and Bellman, *LaRouche*, p. 9.

25. S. McLemee, "Spotlight on the Liberty Lobby," *CovertAction* (Fall 1994): p. 29.

26. King, *LaRouche*, pp. 280–285.

27. Berlet, and Bellman, *LaRouche*, pp. 9, 14.

28. King, *LaRouche*, p. 373.

29. J. Mintz, "Critics of LaRouche Group Hassled, Ex-Associates Say," *Washington Post,* January 14, 1985.

30. J. Mintz, "Some Officials Find Intelligence Network 'Useful,'" *Washington Post,* January 15, 1985.

31. C. Berlet, "Tracking Down LaRouche," *In These Times* (April 2–8, 1986).

32. Berlet and Bellman, *LaRouche*, p. 11.

33. L. Wald, "DuPont Heir's Gifts to LaRouche Spark a Battle," *New York Times*, January 29, 1990.

34. D. King and P. Lynch, "The Empire of Lyndon LaRouche," *New York Times*, May 27, 1986.

35. "Small Town in Virginia Tense Host to LaRouche," *New York Times*, April 11, 1986.

36. Berlet and Bellman, *LaRouche*, p. 2.

37. P. Pae and L. Smith, "LaRouche Back in Loudoun After 5 Years in Prison," *Washington Post,* January 27, 1994.

38. L.H. LaRouche, *In Defense of Common Sense* (Washington, DC: Schiller Institute, 1989).

39. C. Berlet, *Right Woos Left* (http://www.publiceye.org). See also chapter 7 for a discussion of Fred Newman and Lenora Fulani's bloc with Buchanan.

40. "To Win the World War, We Must Transform the Soul of President Clinton," *Executive Intelligence Review,* September 18, 1998.

41. "What Each Among All Nations Must Do Now," *Executive Intelligence Review,* October 9, 1998.

42. "Appeal to President Clinton," *Executive Intelligence Review,* October 9, 1998.

43. "To Win the World War."

44. Ibid.

45. "An 'American Century' Seen as a Modular Mathematical Orbit," *Executive Intelligence Review,* July 24, 1998.

46. Ibid.

47. "What Each Among All."

48. "To Win the World War."

49. "What Each Among All."

50. Berlet and Bellman, *LaRouche,* p. 1.

51. "LaRouche Seeks Matching Funds," Web-posted *CNN News*, August 18, 1999.

Chapter 6

1. These, and many other bizarre therapies, are discussed in M. Singer and J. Lalich, *"Crazy" Therapies: What Are They? Do They Work?* (San Francisco: Jossey-Bass, 1996).

2. M. Lyons, "Sex, Lies and Co-Counseling," *Activist Men's Journal* (August 1994): 1–11.

3. The Study Group on Psychotherapy Cults has produced two informative documents detailing the career of Harvey Jackins and the evolution of RC. These are *A Documentary History of the Career of Harvey Jackins and Re-Evaluation Counseling* Belgium: Study Group, 1992) and *A Documentary History of the Career of Harvey Jackins and Re-evaluation Counseling: Final Supplement* (Belgium: Study Group, 1997). Unless otherwise indicated, quotations and facts pertaining to RC in this chapter can be found in one of these two books.

4. H. Jackins, *Logical Thinking About a Future Society* (Seattle: Rational Island, 1990), p. 78.

5. This version is reported at length in one of the earliest publications to pay attention to RC: R. Rosen, *Psychobabble* (New York: Athenaeum, 1978), p. 78. A slightly different version is repeated by Harvey Jackins at length in what proved to be his last book: *The List,* 2d ed. (Seattle: Rational Island, 1997), pp. 1–5. In this, "Charlie" has become "Merle," and the nature of his difficulties has changed somewhat.

6. A simple exposition of basic RC theory, along these lines, is reproduced on the back page of each edition of the organization's quarterly journal, *Present Time.*

7. See note 3.

8. See note 3.

9. R. Evison, and R. Horobin, "Co-Counseling," in *Innovative Therapy in Britain,* ed. J. Rowan and W. Dryden (Milton Keynes, UK: Open University).

10. An excellent discussion of how such memories are often created, and then believed in, can be found in M. Pendergrast, *Victims of Memory: Incest Accusations and Shattered Lives* (London: Harper-Collins, 1995). This book includes stome case-study material from a participant in RC.

11. These difficulties are discussed in more detail in D. Tourish and P. Irving, "Group Influence and the Psychology of Cultism Within Re-Evaluation Counseling: A Critique," *Counseling Psychology Quarterly* 8, no. 1 (1995): 15–30.

12. P. Cushman, "The Self Besieged: Recruitment-Indoctrination Processes in Restrictive Groups," *Journal for the Theory of Social Behavior* 16, no.1 (1986) pp. 1–32.

13. E. Aronson, and J. Mills, "The Effects of Severity of Initiation on Liking for a Group," *Journal of Abnormal and Social Psychology* 59 (1959): 177–181.

14. Jackins, *Logical Thinking*, p. 11.

15. H. Jackins, *The Upward Trend* (Seattle: Rational Island, 1978), p. 411.

16. Jackins, *The List*, p. 117.

17. F. Conway, and J. Siegelman, "Information Disease: Have Cults Created a New Mental Illness?" *Science Digest* (January 1982): 86–92.

18. Lyons, "Sex, Lies," p. 2.

19. The Study Group, *A Documentary History* (1992).

20. S. Sutherland, *Breakdown: A Personal Crisis and a Medical Dilemma,* 2d ed.(London: Oxford University Press, 1998).

21. Jackins, *Upward Trend*, p. 337.

22. The Study Group, *A Documentary History* (1992).

23. Jackins, *The Human Situation*, (Seattle: Rational Island, 1973) p. 168.

24. Jackins, *The List*, pp. 117–118.

25. M. Temerlin and J. Temerlin "Psychotherapy Cults: An Iatrogenic Perversion," *Psychotherapy* 19, no. 2 (1982): 131–141.

26. G. Brown, "Do You Want to Get Out of Your Distress?" *Present Time* 79, no. 2 (1990): 5–8.

27. J. Holroyd, and A. Brodsky "Psychologists' Attitudes and Practices Regarding Erotic and Nonerotic Physical Contact with Patients," *American Psychologist 32* (1977): 843–849.

28. Sutherland, *Breakdown*, p. 269.

29. H. Jackins, *Fundamentals of Co-Counseling Manual*, 3d ed. (Seattle: Rational Island, 1982), p. 29.

30. The transcript of these interviews is available on the Liberate RC Web site: http://home.stlnet.com/~rcinfo/.

31. The Study Group, *A Documentary History* (1997).

32. Much of this evidence is reviewed in chapter 1 of *Making Monsters: False Memories*, *Psychotherapy and Sexual Hysteria,* R. Ofshe and E. Watters (London: Andre Deutsch, 1995).

33. See *Present Time*, 21, no. 1 (1990): 29, for the full text and an accompanying discussion. This issue is also discussed—again—in Jackins, *The List*, p. 134.

34. D. Dixon, "Attacks, Criticism and Gossip Undermine Leadership and Closeness," *Present Time* (October 1996): 29–30.

35. Ibid., p. 30.

36. H. Eysenck, "The Outcome Problem in Psychotherapy" in *Psychotherapy and Its Discontents*, ed. W. Dryden and C. Feltham (Buckingham, UK: Open University Press, 1992).

Chapter 7

1. B. Shapiro, "Buchanan-Fulani: New Team?" *Nation,* November 1, 1999, p. 21.

2. D. King, "West Side 'Therapy Cult' Conceals Its True Aims," *Heights and Valley News*, November 1977, p. 14.

3. C. Berlet, *Clouds Blue the Rainbow: The Other Side of the New Alliance Party* (Cambridge, MA: Political Research Associates, December 1987).

4. F. Newman, *Power and Authority: The Inside View of Class Struggle* (New York: Centers for Change, 1974), p. 1.

5. Berlet, *Clouds*, p. 3.

6. Newman, *Power*, p. vi.

7. Berlet, *Clouds*, p. 3.

8. Newman, *Power*, p. xvi.

9. Ibid., p. xii.

10. Ibid., p. xii–xiii.

11. *Right on Time*, May 11, 1974. This was the publication of Newman's Center for Change.

12. *Right on Time*, March 7, 1974.

13. Newman, *Power*, p. 113.

14. Ibid., p. 3.

15. Ibid., before p. 1.

16. Ibid., p. 113

17. Ibid., p. 112.

18. Ibid.

19. Ibid., p. 74.

20. Ibid., p. 112.

21. Ibid., p. 123.

22. *Z Magazine,* May 1989.

23. W.C. Sheasby, *A Brief History of Coalition: Third Parties and the Rocky Road to the White House* (Sierra Madre, CA, 1996). Sheasby was a Green Party congressional candidate in California's twenty-seventh district.

24. Press release issued by Workers and Oppressed Unite, dated May 2, 1976.

25. "IWP Admits Snitching To FBI!" undated statement issued by the above group sometime shortly after May 5, 1976.

26. King, "West Side 'Therapy Cult,'" p. 16.

27. D. King, *Lyndon LaRouche and the New American Fascism* (New York: Doubleday, 1989).

28. King, "West Side 'Therapy Cult,'" p. 14.

29. Ibid.

30. Ibid., pp. 14–15.

31. J. Finn, "Proof: Therapy Cultists Lied to Community," *Heights and Valley News* (New York), holiday season, 1977, p. 18.

32. B. Shapiro, "Dr. Fulani's Snake-Oil Show," *Nation,* May 4, 1992, p. 586.

33. Ibid., 587.

34. Berlet, *Clouds*, p. 1.

35. L. Fulani, *Lenora's Political History*, http://www.fulani.org.

36. Sheasby, *Brief*, p. 4.

37. B. Wittes, "Lenora and the Money-Go-Round," *Washington City Paper* (Washington, DC), July 8, 1994.

38. *Coming Up!* (San Francisco), January 1989.

39. Berlet, *Clouds*, p. 7.

40. "Statement Issued by Marina Ortiz" (Cult Awareness Network Meeting, New York, June 16, 1993).

41. Shapiro, "Snake Oil," p. 592.

42. A. Gramsci, *The Modern Prince and Other Writings* (New York: International, 1957), pp. 118–125; G. Vacca, "Intellectuals and the Marxist State," in *Approaches to Gramsci*, ed. Anne Showstack Sassoon (London: Writers and Readers, 1982) pp. 63–67.

43. Berlet, *Clouds*, p. 7.

44. Ibid., p. 9.

45. J. and T. R. Goldman Cohen, "Controversial Lobbyists Stirring Up Waco Fight," *Legal Times* (Washington, DC), May 2, 1994.

46. "Never Again!" *Village Voice* (New York): November 5, 1995, p. 5.

47. Shapiro, "Snake Oil," p. 587.

48. D. King, letter to the editor, *New York Times,* August 13, 1992.

49. Shapiro, "Snake Oil," p. 587.

50. Sheasby, *Brief History*, p. 2.

51. F. Bruni, "Perot and Populist Group See Benefits in an Alliance," *New York Times,* August 21, 1996.

52. Fulani, *History*, p. 2.

53. Bruni, "Perot.*"

54. Ibid.

55. R. Worthington, "Ex-Perot Stalwarts Establish New Party," *Chicago Tribune,* October 6, 1997.

56. L. Fulani, *The Democracy Slate*, http://www.fulani.org.

57. *The Platform of the Independence Party of New York,* http://www.fulani.org.

58. Bruni, "Perot.*"

59. Originally posted online circa February 1996 by the Committee for a Unified Independent Party. See http://www.publiceye.org.

60. *Buchanan, Fulani, Perot and the Reform Party,* http://www.publiceye.org.

61. Shapiro, "Buchanan."

62. S. McCaffrey, "Lenora Fulani Endorses Buchanan," *Associated Press,* November 12, 1999.

63. Ibid.

64. "Reform Party Warming to Buchanan," *Washington Post,* September 20, 1999.

65. J. Bennet, "The Cable Guys," *New York Times Magazine,* October 24, 1999, p. 79.

66. T. Kingston, "The Seedy Side of the Rainbow," in *Coming Up!* (San Francisco), November 1988.

67. See note 40.

68. Wittes, "Money Go Round."

69. Bruni, "Perot."

70. Posted on the Internet at http://webpsych and at http://www.pond.com.

71. Ross and Green, *What Is the Cult Awareness Network and What Role Did It Play in Waco?* (Washington, DC: WRS, 1993), p. 10.

72. L. Fulani, *We Must Stand Up for Democracy!* (New York: Castillo Communications, May 23, 1993).

73. M. Breault, and M. King, *Inside the Cult* (New York: Signet, 1993); B. Bailey and B. Darden, *Mad Man in Waco* (Waco, TX: WRS, 1993).

74. Shapiro, "Buchanan,*" p. 22.

Chapter 8

1. D. Mitchell, C. Mitchell, and R. Ofshe, *The Light on Synanon* (New York: Seaview, 1980), pp. 193–194; David U. Gerstel, *Paradise Incorporated: Synanon* (Novato, CA: Presidio, 1982), pp. ix–x.

2. Gerstel, *Paradise*, p. 34.

3. Ibid., pp. 33–37; Mitchell et al., *Light*, pp. 141–144.

4. L. Yablonski, *Synanon: The Tunnel Back* (New York: Macmillan, 1965); G. Endore, *Synanon* (Garden City: Doubleday, 1967).

5. Mitchell et al., *Light*, p. 44.

6. A. and L. Pepper, *Straight Life* (New York: DeCapo, 1994), p. 431.

7. W. Olin, *Escape from Utopia: My Ten Years in Synanon* (Santa Cruz, CA: Unity, 1980), p. 12.

8. Gerstel, *Paradise*, p. 28.

9. Olin, *Escape*, pp. 61–62.

10. Ibid., pp. 39–40.

11. Pepper, *Straight*, p. 405.

12. Ibid., p. 69.

13. Ibid., pp. 444–450. Olin, *Escape*, pp. 50–58.

14. Olin, *Escape*, p. 58.

15. Pepper, *Straight*, p. 406.
16. Olin, *Escape*, p. 75.
17. Gerstel, *Paradise*, p. 278.
18. M.T. Singer and J. Lalich, *Crazy Therapies* (San Francisco: Jossey-Bass, 1996), p. 128.
19. Mitchell et al., *Light*, p. 147.
20. Ibid.
21. Endore, *Synanon*, p. 10.
22. Gerstel, *Paradise*, p. 32.
23. Ibid., p. 138.
24. Olin, *Escape*, pp. 51–66.
25. F. Morgan, "One Big Dysfunctional Family," *Salon Magazine,* March 29, 1999.
26. Pepper, *Straight*, pp. 407–408.
27. Gerstel, *Paradise*, pp. 99–111.
28. Mitchell et al., *Light*, p. 149.
29. Ibid., p. 167.
30. Gerstel, *Paradise*, p 162.
31. A. Bestor, *Backwoods Utopias* (Philadelphia: University of Pennsylvania Press, 1950), pp. 160–201.
32. C. Nordhoff, *The Communistic Societies of the United States* (New York: Dover, 1966), p. 339. See also R.P. Sutton, *Les Icariens* (Urbana: University of Illinois Press, 1994).
33. Deborah Swisher's play provides a wrenching personal account of this separation.
34. J. Johnson, *Synanon Story*, http://www.nicom.com/~georgef/zine/synanon/jj.
35. Morgan, "Dysfunctional."
36. Gerstel, *Paradise*, p. 160.
37. Olin, *Escape*, p. 242.
38. M.T. Singer with J. Lalich, *Cults in Our Midst* (San Francisco: Jossey-Bass, 1995), pp. 87–88.
39. Pepper, *Straight*, p. 429.
40. Ibid., pp. 425–430.
41. Morgan, "Dysfunctional."
42. Gerstel, *Paradise*, pp. 208–210.
43. Ibid., pp. 223–224.
44. Ibid., p. 244.
45. C. Volger, *The Writer's Journey* (Studio City: Michael Wiese, 1992).
46. Pepper, *Straight*, p. 451.
47. Gerstel, *Paradise*, p. 163.
48. Olin, *Escape*, p. 195.
49. Gerstel, *Paradise*, p. 71.
50. Mitchell et al., *Light*, p. 151.
51. Gerstel, *Paradise*, p. 151.
52. Ibid., p. 154.
53. Mitchell et al., *Light*.
54. Olin, *Escape*, p. 248.
55. Mitchell et al., *Light*, p. 26.
56. Ibid., p. 73.
57. "George Farnsworth—My Dirty Rotten Story," http://www.gfonline.org/Synanon/my_story.htm.
58. Gerstel, *Paradise*, p. 263.
59. Mitchell et al., *Light*, pp. 224–225.

60. Ibid., pp. 266–268.

61. M. Yee, "Charles Dederich, Founder of the Cult-Like Religious Group Synanon, Dies at 83," Associated Press, March 5, 1997.

62. Olin, *Escape*, p. 249.

Chapter 9

1. J. Lalich, "The Cadre Ideal: Origins and Development of a Political Cult," *Cultic Studies Journal* 9, no. 1 (1992): 9–14. The "Workers Democratic Union" referred to in this study is a pseudonym for the Democratic Workers Party, and "Doreen Baxter" is Marlene Dixon.

2. A. Belden Fields, *Trotskyism and Maoism: Theory and Practice in France and the United States* (Brooklyn, NY: Autonomedia, 1988), pp. 197–212.

3. P. Siegel, N. Strohl, L. Ingram, D. Roche, and J. Taylor, "Leninism as Cult: The Democratic Workers Party" *Socialist Review* no. 96 (November–December 1987): 62.

4. Lalich, "Cadre," p. 13.

5. Ibid., pp. 41–42.

6. The material on the political activity of the DWP comes from Seigel et al., "Leninism."

7. H. Klehr, *The Heyday of American Communism* (New York: Basic Books, 1984), p. 104.

8. Seigel et al., "Leninism," p. 65.

9. M. Landau Tobias and J. Lalich, *Captive Hearts, Captive Minds* (Alameda, CA: Hunter House, 1994), p. 216.

10. Ibid., p. 217.

11. Lalich, "Cadre," p. 66.

12. Ibid., pp. 53–62; Seigel et al., "Leninism," pp. 67–68.

13. Lalich, p. 15.

14. Ibid., pp. 44–45.

15. N. Blackstock, *Cointelpro* (New York: Pathfinder, 1988).

16. F.J. Donner, *The Age of Surveillance* (New York: Vintage, 1981), p. 73.

17. Lalich, "Cadre," p. 45.

18. Ibid., p. 43.

19. Ibid., pp. 26–29.

20. Ibid., pp. 49–50.

21. Ibid., p. 27.

22. Seigel et al., "Leninism," p. 71.

23. There is a parallel here with the history of Gerry Healy in Great Britain. Healy would go through a period of significant membership growth, inevitably followed by a factional struggle leading to a split that reduced the membership to a core of personal followers. This would be followed in time by a new spurt of growth leading to a new split. See chapter 10.

24. Lalich, "Cadre," p. 26.

25. Ibid., p. 40.

26. Ibid., p. 54.

27. Seigel et al., "Leninism," p. 65.

28. Lalich, "Cadre," p. 29.

29. Lalich, "Cadre," pp. 71–76; Seigel et al., "Leninism," pp. 75–85.

30. Seigel et al., "Leninism," p. 76.

31. We are referring to the Thornett group. See chapter 10.

32. Siegel et al., "Leninism," p. 74.

33. See M.O. Maguire (pseudonym), "Returning to Humanity" in *Captive Hearts,* ed. Tobias and Lalich, pp. 216–221.

34. Seigel et al., "Leninism,*"* p. 81.

Chapter 10

1. C. Lotz, and P. Feldman, *Gerry Healy: A Revolutionary Life* (London: Lupus, 1994), p. 21.

2. S. Bornstein, and A. Richardson, *Against the Stream: A History of the Trotskyist Movement in Britain 1924–38* (London: Socialist Platform, 1986), p. 275.

3. S. Bornstein, and A. Richardson, *War and the International: A History of the Trotskyist Movement in Britain 1937–1949* (London: Socialist Platform, 1986), p. 101. For Healy's early history see also Lotz and Feldman, *Gerry Healy*, pp. 194–211.

4. This account was supplied to Tim Wohlforth by Ken Tarbuck, a delegate (tape in possession of authors). For events leading up to this conference, see Bornstein and Richardson, *War*, pp. 209–234.

5. "Resolution by Brian Behan on Peter Fryer 5.12.59," "A Statement by the National Committee 16/17.1.60," *Internal Bulletin,* no. 2 (Socialist Labour League, June 1960).

6. P. Fryer, "An Open Letter To Members of the Socialist Labour League and Other Marxists" (undated document issued in late 1959).

7. *Internal Bulletin,* no. 3 (Socialist Labour League, June 1960), p. 4.

8. A. MacIntyre, "A Letter to G. Healy 10.5.60," *Internal Bulletin,* no. 4 (Socialist Labour League, June 1960), a mimeographed document.

9. V. Redgrave, *Vanessa Redgrave, An Autobiography* (New York: Random House, 1994), p. 191.

10. Ibid., p. 203.

11. Ibid.

12. T. Wohlforth, *The Prophet's Children: Travels on the American Left* (Atlantic Highlands, NJ: Humanities Press, 1994), pp. 228–229.

13. Ibid.

14. Ibid., pp. 264–266.

15. Ibid., p. 229.

16. Ibid., pp. 229–230.

17. Ibid., p. 242.

18. Redgrave, *Vanessa*, pp. 207, 211.

19. *Observer* (London), September 28, 1975; Redgrave, *Vanessa*, pp. 243–248; "Beauty and the Beast," *Esquire* (London), November 1993, pp. 78–79.

20. For Healy's "case," see *Security and the Fourth International: An Inquiry into the Assassination of Leon Trotsky* (New York: Labor Publications, 1976). For the SWP's answer, see *Healy's Big Lie—The Slander Campaign against Joseph Hansen, George Novack and the Fourth International* (New York: Education Department, SWP, 1977).

21. *Intercontinental Press* (New York), February 7, 1977.

22. "Michael Banda's '27 reasons,'" *Intercontinental Press* (New York), March 24, 1986, p. 193.

23. *The Star* (London), November 8, 1985.

24. Ibid.

25. *The Mirror* (London), October 31, 1985.

26. "Secrets of Randy Comrade Casanova," *Sunday Mirror* (London), November 3, 1985, p. 1.

27. *WRP Internal Bulletin*, no. 7 (London: Workers Revolutionary Party, March 14, 1986), pp. 33–34.

28. *Standard* (London), November 11, 1985, p. 1.

29. Redgrave, *Vanessa*, pp. 248–261.

30. It appears that printing work for the Iranians was going on at the time of the split in the WRP. "Letter to CC from Peter Rickard, 23 February 1986," *WRP Internal Bulletin*, no. 8 (London: 1986), p. 1.

31. "Notes from C. Slaughter for the 8th Congress," *WRP Internal Bulletin*, no. 7 (London: 1986), p. 50.

32. Lotz and Feldman, *Gerry Healy*, p. 47.

33. Livingstone spoke at Healy's funeral and provided an introduction for Lotz and Feldman, *Gerry Healy*.

34. Lotz and Feldman, *Gerry Healy*, pp. 290–291.

35. "Letter of Political Committee of the Workers League," *WRP Internal Bulletin*, no. 4 (London: Workers Revolutionary Party, 1986), p. 64.

36. "Letter of Cliff Slaughter to Dave North, Tuesday 26 November 1985," *WRP Internal Bulletin* (London: Workers Revolutionary Party, 1986, not numbered), pp. 23, 31.

37. "The Life and Times of Comrade H," *New Statesman* (London), December 6, 1985.

38. Lotz, and Feldman, *Gerry Healy*, p. 140.

39. Ibid., p. 22.

40. M. Breault, and M. King, *Inside the Cult* (New York: Signet, 1993), p. 16.

41. Pagels, E., *The Gnostic Gospels* (New York: Vintage, 1981).

42. Lotz, and Feldman, *Gerry Healy*, p. 149.

43. Ibid., p. 44.

44. Ibid., pp. 84–85.

45. For an early study of this process, see Tony Whelan, *The Credibility Gap—The Politics of the SLL* (London: International Marxist Group, 1970).

Chapter 11

1. The limited information available on Grant's early years is well summarized in chapter 2 ("The Long Trudge of Ted Grant") of *Faces of Labour,* by A. McSmith (London: Verso, 1996).

2. For those interested in more information about Trotskyism's early years in Britain, a huge amount of detail can be found in P. Shipley, *Revolutionaries in Modern Britain* (London: Bodley Head, 1976).

3. Grant's selected writings were published in T. Grant, *The Unbroken Thread* (London: Fortress, 1989); "Preparing for Power" is reproduced as pp. 35–56. The extract quoted here appears on p. 55.

4. McSmith, *Faces*, p. 97.

5. M. Crick, *The March of Militant* (London: Faber and Faber, 1986).

6. These issues are discussed further in D. Tourish, "Ideological Intransigence, Democratic Centralism and Cultism: A Case Study from the Political Left," *Cultic Studies Journal*, 15 (1998): 33–67.

7. P. Taaffe, *The Rise of Militant* (London: Militant, 1995). This is obviously a highly tendentious account of the organization's origins, but nevertheless provides worthwhile detail on its chronology and political evolution over the years.

8. Like most Trotskyist publications, the pamphlet contains no publishing details (e.g., year published, where, publisher).

9. The CWI's impact in the Labour Party is well summarized in *Discipline and Discord in the Labour Party,* by E. Shaw (Manchester: Manchester University Press, 1988).

10. McSmith, *Faces*, p. 104.

11. J. Turner, *Social Influence* (Milton Keynes, UK: Open University, 1991).

12. M. Tobias, and J. Lalich, *Captive Hearts, Captive Minds* (Alameda, CA: Hunter House, 1994.)

13. Crick, *March*, p. 178.

14. Ibid., p. 182.

15. A. Scheflin, and E. Opton, *The Mind Manipulators* (New York: Paddington, 1978).

16. M. Wexler, and S. Fraser, "Expanding the Groupthink Explanation to the Study of Contemporary Cults," *Cultic Studies Journal* 12, no. 1 (1995): 49–71.

17. See T. Grant and unnamed others, "The Case Against Bureaucratic Centralism: In Defense of Internal Democracy," *Essex* (no date). A copy is in the authors' possession.

18. Chapter 12 in Shaw's *Discipline and Discord*, gives a particularly detailed account of Labour's efforts to rid itself of Militant's influence.

19. McSmith, *Faces*, p. 113.

20. See "For the Scottish Turn," 1991 (CWI document); and "The New Turn," 1991 (opposition document). Both are in the authors' possession.

21. Many documents chronicling these developments can be found at the following website: http://www.cpgb.org.uk/theory/index.html#spincrisis.

Chapter 12

1. J. Kifner, "Child's Cries Lead Police to Arsenal in Brooklyn," *New York Times,* November 12, 1996; S. Forrest, T. George, and G. Mustain, " 'Grace' Under Pressure: Group Sang Hymn During Cop Gun Raid,"*New York Daily News,* November 13, 1996; J. Lambiet, J. Harney, T. Raftery, and S. Mcfarland, "Weapons Haul in Brooklyn," *New York Daily News,* November 12, 1996; Laura Italiano,"Fears of Two Little Girls' Safety Led to Chilling Find," *New York Post,* November 13, 1996; C. Jones,"Grand Jury Seeks Reason Behind a Group's Arsenal," *New York Times*, November 14, 1996.

2. As reported to Tim Wohlforth by Irene Davidson, the mother of a former member.

3. J. Whitnack, "Gino Perente, NATLFED and The Provisional Party," *Public Eye* (Summer 1984): 23–24.

4. "Organizer Par Excellence." Document in authors' possession.

5. D. Weidner, "Man's Death Rekindles Memories of Colorful Life," *Appeal-Democrat* (Marysville-Yuba City, CA), April 11, 1995.

6. C. Nickerson, "Boston Antipoverty Group Linked to a Radical Wing of Communists," *Boston Globe,* March 1, 1984.

7. Ibid., p. 18.

8. Ibid., p. 17.

9. J. Russakoff, "Doorway to a Cult?" *City Paper* (Philadelphia), June 26–July 3, 1987.

10. D.A. Andelman, "L.I. Migrant Farm Workers, Backed by Union, Fighting Eviction," *New York Times,* December 19, 1972.

11. U. Berliner, "Labor Group: Saga of a Cult," *East Hampton Star,* September 18, 1986.

12. R.E. Kessler, "Shadowy Past: Gun Arrests Latest Event in Group's Secretive History," *Newsday*, November 11, 1996.

13. "NCLC and Its Extended Political 'Community,'" *Public Eye* (fall 1977): 23–24; Chip Berlet, *Clouds Blur the Rainbow* (Cambridge, MA: Political Research Associates, December 1987).

14. Eugenio Parente, "The Unemployed: If We Don't Organize Them, the Opposition Will," (Printed in a publication of Fred Newman's International Workers Party, New York, May 28, 1975), p. 2.

15. Whitnack, "Gino Perente," p. 34.

16. "NCLC," *Public Eye* (fall 1977).

17. H. Klehr, *The Heyday of American Communism* (New York: Basic Books, 1984), pp. 3–68.

18. "Manifesto of the Committee for a National Labor Federation."

19. Mimeographed unsigned document in the authors' possession.

20. Issued by the authority of the Central Committee of the CPUSA(P), *Communist Party USA Provisional Official Membership Book.* Undated document in the authors' possession.

21. M. Seeber and P. Gardner, eds. *The Essential Organizer: A Training Manual for Eastern Farm Workers Association.* Mimeographed and issued around 1973, though updated from time to time.

22. Berliner, "Labor Group."

23. Court of Appeals, State of New York, The People of the State of New York Against Daniel P. Foster and Kathleen Paolo, p. 7 (court documents in the authors' possession).

24. Defendant's Background; FBI Report on Provisional Party of Communists (PPC), Floor Plan Location. All documents attached to "People of the State of New York," (see note 23).

25. See note 2.

26. See note 2.

27. J. Rabinowitz, "College Idealism Was Fertile Soil for Fringe Group," *New York Times,* November 15, 1996.

28. "Co-ops Pulled in Questionable 'Left' Sect" *Record* (Antioch, Ohio), June 9, 1978.

29. L. de Bourbon, "Western Mass. Labor Action: Its Hidden Veneer of Good Masks a Hidden Agenda," *Williams Record* (Williamstown), October 3, 1995; J. Resnick, "Service Group Linked to 'Cultic' Organization," *Williams Record* (Williamstown), October 3, 1995.

30. P. Burke, and S. Solow, "Two Days with the EFWA in Northern New York State," *Pipe Dream* (State University of New York– Binghamton, NY), February 27, 1977.

31. C. Fager, "Conning the Churches: The Edge of Right," *Public Eye* (1984): 27.

32. J. Kifner, "Its Leader Dead, Fringe Group Lives on for Its Own Sake," *New York Times,* November 11, 1996.

33. Berliner, "Labor Group."

34. Kifner, "Leader."

35. R.D. McFadden, "Eugenio Perente-Ramos Is Dead: Farm Labor Organizer Was 59," *New York Times,* March 20, 1995; "Correction: Obituary Omitted Key Facts on Labor Organizer," *New York Times,* March 21, 1995.

36. Kifner, "Leader."

Conclusion

1. R. Lifton, *Thought Reform and the Psychology of Totalism: A Study of 'Brainwashing' in China* (New York: Norton, 1961), pp. 25-26.

2. L. Goodstein, "Hare Krishna Movement Details Past Abuse at Its Boarding Schools," *New York Times.* October 9, 1998.

3. M. Galanter, *Cults: Faith Healing and Coercion*, 2d ed. (New York: Oxford University Press, 1999), p. 118–121

4. F. Fitzgerald, *Cities on a Hill* (New York: Simon and Schuster, 1986), pp. 247–381.

5. Galanter, *Cults*, pp.122–126.

6. M. Breault and M. King, *Inside the Cult* (New York: Signet, 1993).

7. D. Layton, *Seductive Poison* (New York: Doubleday, 1998).

8. R. Lifton, *Destroying the World to Save It* (New York: Henry Holt, 1999), p. 23.

9. Ibid., p. 25.

10. Ibid., p. 35.

11. Ibid., p. 203.

12. J. Reston Jr., *Our Father Who Art in Hell* (New York: Times Books, 1981), p. 56.

13. T. Reiterman, *Raven: The Untold Story of the Rev. Jim Jones and His People* (New York: Dutton, 1982), pp. 16–17.

14. Layton, *Seductive*, pp. 45–46.

15. Shortly after winning the election, George Moscone and gay supervisor Harvey Milk were murdered by a deranged right-wing supervisor, Dan White.

16. J. Mills, *Six Years with God* (New York: A and W, 1979), p. 46.

17. Layton, *Seductive*, pp. 119 ff.

18. G. Niebuhr, "On the Furthest Fringes of Millenialism," *New York Times,* March 28, 1997.

19. C. Nullis, "Leader's Paranoia Led to Swiss Cult Deaths, Invesigators Say," *Associated Press,* November 20, 1994.

20. R. D. Hare, *Without Conscience: The Disturbing Wolf of the Psychopaths Among Us* (New York: Pocket Books, 1993), p. xi.

21. M. Tobias and J. Lalich, *Captive Hearts, Captive Minds* (Alameda, CA: Hunter House, 1994), p. 68. See chapter 5: "Characteristics of a Cult Leader," for an excellent description of the cult leader as a psychopath.

22. D. Durham, *Life Among the Moonies* (Plainfield, NJ: Logos, 1981).

23. K. St. Clair, "Rev. Moon Has a Vision for America's Youth," *East Bay Express* (Berkeley), November 5, 1999, p 11.

24. Galanter, *Cults*, p.124.

25. St. Clair, "Rev. Moon," p. 11.

26. L. Rohter, "Suspicion Following Sun Myung Moon to Brazil," *New York Times,* November 28, 1999.

27. D. Frantz, "Death of a Scientologist Heightens Suspicions in a Florida Town," *New York Times,* December 1, 1997.

28. C. R. Whitney, "Scientology and Its German Foes: A Bitter Conflict," *New York Times,* December 2, 1997.

29. A. Dolgov, "Moscow Scientology Center Raided," *Associated Press,* February 26, 1999.

30. J. Higgins, *More Years for the Locust: The Origins of the SWP* (London: International Socialist Group, 1997).

31. T. Crawford, *Amended Report on the LO Fete of 30, 31 May & June 1, 1998* (in the authors' possession).

32. "The Road to Jimstown," *Bulletin of the External Tendency of the IST,* no. 4 (Oakland, CA, May 1985).

33. R. Blick, *The Seeds of Evil: Lenin and the Origins of Bolshevik Elitism* (London: Steyne, 1995).

34. P. Cohen, *Children of the Revolution: Communist Childhood in Cold War Britain* (London: Lawrence and Wishart, 1997), p. 152.

35. A. Koestler, in *The God That Failed*, ed. Richard Crossman (London: Right Book Club, 1949), p. 43.

36. V. Lenin, *Collected Works,* vol. 5 (Moscow: Progress, 1977), p. 433.

37. R. Cialdini, *Influence: Science and Practice*, 3d ed. (New York: Addison Wesley and Longman, 1993).

38. See, for example, Blick, *Seeds.*

39. These fallacies are discussed in detail by Michael Shermer, *Why People Believe Weird Things: Pseudoscience, Superstition and Other Confusions of Our Time* (New York: W.H. Freeman, 1997).

40. R. Brown and D. Newman, "An Investigation of the Effects of Different Data Presentation Formats and Order of Arguments in a Simulated Adversary Evaluation," *Educational Evaluation and Policy Analysis*, 4 (1982): 197–203.

41. S. Spender, in Crossman, *God*, p. 254.

42. Lifton, *Destroying*.

43. W. Laqueur, *The New Terrorism* (New York: Oxford, 1999).

44. C. Krauss, "Ex-Guerrilla Takes Struggle to the Campaign Trail," *New York Times*, November 27, 1999.

45. G. Orwell, *Nineteen Eighty-Four* (London: Penguin Books, 1977; first published, 1949), p. 212.

Index

About the Authors

Dennis Tourish is Reader in Communication Management at the University of Aberdeen, Scotland. He has published and lectured widely on the issue of cults and has published articles in *Cultic Studies Journal*. He has also addressed the annual conference of the American Family Foundation, which pioneers education and research on cults in the United States. This is his third book.

Tim Wohlforth is a journalist and a writer of fiction and nonfiction books. His most recent book is *The Prophet's Children: Travels on the American Left* (1994). He has written articles for the *New Left Review*, *In These Times*, and *Against the Current*. He wrote the section on Trotskyism in the *Encyclopedia of the Left*. Presently he is a member of the Democratic Socialists of America.